Patrick Bond

Elite Transition

From Apartheid to Neoliberalism
in South Africa

Pluto Press
LONDON • STERLING, VIRGINIA

University of Natal Press
Pietermaritzburg
South Africa

First published 2000 by Pluto Press
345 Archway Road, London N6 5AA
and 22883 Quicksilver Drive, Sterling, VA 20166–2012, USA
Published in South Africa 2000 by
University of Natal Press
Private Bag X01. Scottsville 3209, South Africa

Copyright © Patrick Bond 2000

The right of Patrick Bond to be identified as the author of
this work has been asserted by him in accordance with
the Copyright, Design and Patents Act 1988

British Library Cataloguing-in-Publication Data
A catalogue record for this book is available from
the British Library

ISBN 0 7453 1024 9 hbk Pluto edition
ISBN 0 7453 1023 0 pbk Pluto edition
ISBN 0 86980 971 7 South African edition

Library of Congress Cataloging in Publication Data
Bond, Patrick.
    Elite transition : from apartheid to neoliberalism in South Africa/
Patrick Bond.
        p. cm.
    Includes bibliographical references.
    ISBN 0–7453–1024–9
        1. Elite (Social sciences)—South Africa. 2. South Africa—Economic
conditions—1991– 3. South Africa—Politics and government—1994–
I. Title.

HN801.Z9 E427 2000
305.5'2'0968—dc21
                                                    99–048854

Designed and produced for the publisher by
Chase Production Services, Chadlington, OX7 3LN
Typeset from disk by Stanford DTP Services, Northampton
Printed in the EU by TJ International, Padstow

Elit **Aldham Robarts LRC**
Liverpool John Moores University

WITHDRAWN

Books are to be

Contents

List of Acronyms and Abbreviations

ABSA	Amalgamated Banks of South Africa
AC	*African Communist*
ANC	African National Congress
BEE	Black Economic Empowerment
Cansa	Campaign Against Neoliberalism in South Africa
CBM	Consultative Business Movement
CBO	Community-Based Organisation
CIA	Central Intelligence Agency
CoNGO	Co-opted Non-Governmental Organisation
Cosatu	Congress of South African Trade Unions
DBSA	Development Bank of Southern Africa
DDA	Department of Development Aid
DEP	Department of Economic Planning (ANC)
Fabcos	Foundation for African Business and Consumer Services
FM	*Financial Mail*
Frelimo	Front for the Liberation of Mozambique
GATT	General Agreement on Tariffs and Trade
GDP	Gross Domestic Product
Gear	*Growth, Employment and Redistribution*
HIPC	Highly-Indebted Poor Countries
HSRC	Human Sciences Research Council
HWP	*Housing White Paper*
IDT	Independent Development Trust
IFC	International Finance Corporation
IFP	Inkatha Freedom Party

IMF	International Monetary Fund
Iscor	Iron and Steel Corporation
ISP	Industrial Strategy Project
JCI	Johannesburg Consolidated Investments
JSE	Johannesburg Stock Exchange
KP	Conservative Party
LAPC	Land and Agricultural Policy Centre
LGTA	Local Government Transition Act
LTCM	Long-Term Capital Management
MDC	Movement for Democratic Change
MDM	Mass Democratic Movement
Merg	MacroEconomic Research Group
Nail	New African Investments Ltd
NEM	*Normative Economic Model*
NGDS	*National Growth and Development Strategy*
NGO	Non-Governmental Organisation
NHF	National Housing Forum
NIS	National Intelligence Service
NP	National Party
Numsa	National Union of Metalworkers (South Africa)
OECD	Organisation for Economic Cooperation and Development
PEP	Professional Economists Panel
PPT	Presidential Project Team (Umtata)
PR	Public Relations
R&D	Research and Development
RDP	*Reconstruction and Development Programme*
RDS	*Rural Development Strategy*
SAB	South African Breweries
SACP	South African Communist Party
SADC	Southern African Development Community
SAHT	South African Housing Trust
Sanco	South African National Civic Organisation
SANDF	South African National Defence Force
Sangoco	South African Non-Governmental Organisation Coalition
TAU	Transvaal Agricultural Union
TEC	Transitional Executive Committee
THEMBA	'There Must Be an Alternative'
TINA	'There Is No Alternative'

UDI	Unilateral Declaration of Independence (Rhodesia)
UDS	*Urban Development Strategy*
UF	Urban Foundation
UNCTAD	United Nations Conference on Trade and Development
UNDP	United Nations Development Programme
WTO	World Trade Organisation

Introduction

Dissecting South Africa's Transition

This book aims to fill some gaps in the literature about South Africa's late twentieth-century democratisation. There is already an abundance of commentary on the years of liberation struggle and particularly on the period 1990–94 – empiricist accounts, academic tomes, self-serving biographies – and many more narratives have been and are being drafted about the power-sharing arrangements that followed the April 1994 election, as well as the record of the ANC in its first term.

Some of these have been penned by progressives and are generally critical of the course the transition has taken thus far. In the development of an extremely rich heritage of thinking and writing about change in South Africa, have the dozen or more serious commentaries from the Left missed or skimmed or perhaps de-emphasised anything that this work can augment?

I believe so, namely a radical *analytic-theoretic framework* and some of the most telling *details* that help explain the transition from a popular-nationalist anti-apartheid project to official neoliberalism – by which is meant adherence to free market economic principles, bolstered by the narrowest practical definition of democracy (not the radical participatory project many ANC cadre had expected) – over an extremely short period of time. It is sometimes remarked that the inexorable journey from a self-reliant, anti-imperialist political-economic philosophy to allegedly 'home-grown' structural adjustment that took Zambian, Mozambican/Angolan and Zimbabwean nationalists 25, 15 and 10 years, respectively, was in South Africa achieved in less than five (indeed, two years, if one takes the *Growth, Employment and Redistribution* document as a marker).

Inexorable? It is important now, while memories are fresh, to begin to describe with as much candour as possible – even at the risk of unabashed polemic – the forces of both structure and agency that were central to this process. Historians with better documentation (and, as in other settings, retroactive kiss-and-tell accounts by spurned ministers and bureaucrats, perhaps) will have to fill in, more comprehensively and objectively, once a fully representative and verifiable sample of evidence is in the public domain. In the meantime, a key motivation is that the near-term future for South African progressive politics relies upon identifying what was actually feasible, which initiatives derailed, when and how alliances were made, which social forces (and individuals on occasion) hijacked the liberation vehicle, where change happened and where it didn't, and what kind of lessons might be learned for the next stage of struggle.

These questions are only part of the unfinished discussion of South Africa's transition, of course. But they allow us to contemplate arguments that I think have already stood the test of time, and indeed this is where my emphasis in telling this story departs from others of the Left who have written about the end of apartheid. For tracing how capitalist crisis coincided with the emergence of neoliberal ideas, and in turn exacerbated 'uneven development', has helped me, personally, to come to grips with political processes in the United States, Zimbabwe, Haiti and various parts of South Africa. Many leading intellectuals from whom I take inspiration – the names Samir Amin, Robert Brenner, Simon Clarke, Diane Elson, Ben Fine, David Harvey, Dani Nabudere, Neil Smith and Ellen Meiksins Wood stand out today, but of course Marx, Engels, Hilferding, Lenin, Trotsky, Grossmann, Luxemburg, Mattick, de Brunhoff and Mandel among others set the stage over the past century and a half for Marxist political economists who followed – have mapped out this path of analysis, highlighting the link between core processes of capital accumulation, uneven development, crisis tendencies and the temporary ascendancy of a financial fraction of capital (see below). Just as importantly, an increasing number of activists across the globe seem to be independently confirming the arguments through their own practices.

The South African case is still hotly contested, though, and there can be no conclusive statement about what is happening and how we should confront it until more arguments are tested against time and opposing viewpoints. However, what is increasingly universal in the progressive literature on South Africa (not just books but the many discussion documents, academic papers and popular articles) is concern about the new government's deviation from the liberation movement mandate. Sometimes this deviation is related directly to political and economic pressures, sometimes to the whims of individuals. Sometimes the implications for the oppressed have been asserted, often not. Sometimes, such as in the ANC's 1999 campaign literature, it is argued that the process has been slow, but that there is progress nevertheless – yet as I argue below, the steps backward taken by neoliberalism in development policy and economic management throw this assertion into question.

To begin systematically to tackle neoliberalism requires moving through and beyond rhetoric about the nationalist 'sell-out', to documenting what precisely is wrong (defined as unjust, inappropriate, unworkable or untenable) with the ANC's rightward trajectory. The subjects I have chosen to explore include ineffectual economic crisis management (and crisis-induced policies) just prior to and during the political transition (Chapter 1); the all-pervasive but ill-fated social contract philosophy, which glued together elites from various camps (Chapter 2); post-election conservatism in social and developmental policy-making in relation to an (often radical) electoral mandate (Chapter 3); incompetent, market-oriented delivery of housing and urban services (Chapter 4); the pernicious influence of World Bank and International Monetary Fund advisory missions (Chapter 5); and the implications of the late 1990s world financial crisis for geopolitics and South Africa's positionality (Chapter 6). At a time when global economic turbulence has left orthodoxy in intellectual and practical tatters, these areas of discussion – by no means comprehensive – are at least sites of *some* of the most important recent and future contradictions.

I have tried, in the process, to pass rapidly over general information that has been covered in more detail elsewhere, or that is common knowledge, and instead to jump into the specific kinds of argument that progressives deployed during the 1990s in a few key socio-economic policy debates – and which, I am convinced, will still be extremely pertinent to struggles early in the twenty-first century. Thus, the book assumes both South African and international readers are familiar to some extent with apartheid, the South African liberation struggle and the political-ideological role of the African

National Congress, and are interested in locating these politics within broader global processes also unfolding during the 1990s.

But even if my analysis of the apparently universal neoliberal trajectory is accurate and the critique is sound, readers should ultimately trust their own sources for the *micro-level experiences of daily life* – in all their fragmented, richly textured, contradictory and symbolic forms – around these core areas of post-apartheid social and economic policy. The gut feeling of joy (even if temporary) when acquiring a new collective water tap in a desperately poor rural area, or conversely the fury and indignity of a water cut-off due to inability to pay, are, frankly, beyond the comprehension of any white, petit-bourgeois male academic. And although I try regularly to point out strategic implications of the analysis for the democratic social movements, also by way of caveat, I leave immediate, practical political conclusions to others with better connections to mass movements and with more experience in popular mobilisation.

At the political and moral levels, I do, however, rely unashamedly upon the integrity of decades worth of South African social struggles, even if these came to be understood in very different ways – and in many cases negated – by conservative-nationalist politicians and their neoliberal policy advisers during and immediately after the allegedly democratic transition. For if this is in part a book that argues for the need for greater political accountability than many ANC leaders (and virtually all bureaucrats) are willing to acknowledge, it is also an assertion that the radical mandate they were given – from the 1955 Freedom Charter to the 1994 *Reconstruction and Development Programme*, via any number of hard-fought social struggles – was not a bad one. In particular, the *RDP* was not unrealistic or infeasible, either, given the balance of forces in the contemporary world.

What does South Africa have to teach other societies? The manner in which neoliberal forces have come to dominate the globe since the 1970s – initially emblematised by Milton Friedman's role in post-coup Chile, the 1976 International Monetary Fund loan to Britain and then, more decisively, the reign of Paul Volcker at the US Federal Reserve beginning in 1979, followed by Thatcher, Reagan, Kohl, the 1980s handling of the Third World debt crisis and 1990s liberalised trade, investment and capital flows – can probably only be understood through detailed country case-studies. International comparisons are certainly relevant, and I try to draw out some of the more obvious ones in the conclusion. For it is now broadly accepted that a general force pushing globalisation (especially the dominance of the neoliberal ideology) has been *international financial power*, hastening simultaneously with slowing world economic growth.

It is, thus, the particular transition in the 'form' of capital that this book highlights in naming its subject 'neoliberalism': away from a white, sub-imperial 'settler capital' whose accumulation the past century and a quarter was based on the (often artificial) availability of cheap black labour, the extraction of minerals and generation of cheap electricity, and the production of protected luxury goods. Some have termed this form of capital 'racial Fordism', to summarise South Africa's racially inscribed failure to link mass production and mass consumption (in the manner Henry Ford accomplished at his Dearborn auto plant in 1913, and that advanced capitalist countries practised for a quarter-century following the Second World War). I wouldn't endorse this particular heuristic device, for it distracts us from more durable aspects of capital accumulation and crisis formation; however, as we see below, it is certainly an influential way of understanding South Africa's inheritance.

What form of capital accumulation lies ahead? More of the same? 'Post-Fordism', as the leading state strategists (especially in the Departments of Labour and of Trade and Industry) and some trendy Cape Town and Sussex University intellectuals hope? Or just deeper accumulation crises born of the neoliberal orientation to financial speculation rather than productive profit-making?

My bet is on continuing crisis – even if it is often stalled, shifted and displaced (to South Africa amongst other sites of economic volatility) and blunted in the North by bank bail-outs and occasional 'Keynesian' stimulants (as appear, finally, to apply in Japan). And here is where, instead, the overarching theory of uneven development comes in. Karl Marx regarded uneven development as a necessary process under capitalism by arguing that 'in the same relations in which wealth is produced, poverty is produced also'.[1] This 'absolute general law of capitalist accumulation', as he termed it, means that some economic sectors and geographical areas rise and others decline, but in a manner that does not achieve equilibrium, as free market economists would assume, but instead continually *polarises*. Such is the case on the world scale, but also in South Africa.

Leon Trotsky later made explicitly political arguments about combined and uneven development in his 1905 book *Results and Prospects*, which served as an analytical foundation for the idea of 'permanent revolution'. The theory suggests that in the twentieth century there would be scope for telescoping the bourgeois (read in Southern Africa as nationalist or anti-colonial) revolutions and proletarian revolutions into a seamless process, led by the working class. In reality, however, the century has provided combinations of political demobilisation and repression sufficient to overwhelm the subjective conditions necessary for socialist mobilisation, no matter how strong, objectively, the case for socialism remains. Sadly, this will remain the situation for some time to come, one fears, even in industrial Johannesburg, given how forcefully African nationalism triumphed as the philosophy of South Africa's new petit-bourgeois political elite. There is, hence, very little in respect of the Trotskyist party-building project to which I can contribute in this study.

Instead, it is to a broader debate about uneven development – revived when Marxist social science, especially geographical studies, regenerated during the 1970s – that we can turn for supportive analytical traditions.[2] The phenomenon of uneven and combined development in specific settings has been explained as a process of 'articulations of modes of production'. In these formulations, the capitalist mode of production depends upon earlier modes of production for an additional 'super-exploitative' subsidy by virtue of reducing the costs of labour-power reproduction. South Africa and its bantustan labour reserves are illustrative, given the super-exploited role of rural women in nurturing workers during their youth, and caring for them in their retirement and during illness (hence allowing urban capitalists a lower wage floor, relatively devoid of educational, medical and pension expenditure).[3]

Neil Smith insists, however, that 'it is the logic of uneven development which structures the context for this articulation', rather than the reverse.[4] That logic entails not only differential – sometimes termed 'disarticulated' – production and consumption of durable goods along class lines (as is attributed to racial Fordism).[5] It also embraces 'disproportionalities' that emerge between departments of production – especially between capital goods and consumer goods, and between circuits and fractions of capital.[6] For example, the rise of financial markets during periods of capitalist overproduction – or 'overaccumulation' crisis – amplifies unevenness, as South Africa demonstrates clearly.[7] Indeed if there is a thread that ties the chapters together, it is this latter sentence (see below).

The confidence to make the bold assertion that through classical Marxian approaches to political economy we can best understand the elite character of South Africa's 1990s political transition, stems in large part from my own good fortune to have been in the right place at the right time on occasion. Furtermore, I have had the encouragement of comrades and enemies alike to document continually what I saw around me, and some journalistic opportunities to do so in the region's lively periodicals. If I had any sort of privileged access – first to Marxist theory (1985–87, studying with David Harvey in Baltimore), then to mass struggle and later, briefly, close to the ANC inner sanctum – this in turn reflected such an extraordinary open-mindedness on the part of so many South Africans that it is hard to know where and how to make acknowledgements. Too many individuals have helped to shape the arguments to list, but my gratitude to them all is enormous.

There were, however, institutions which facilitated matters, and they require specific acknowledgement. From 1990 to 1994 I was based at Planact, a then radical urban technical NGO closely aligned to the Johannesburg township civic movements and to the ANC. In 1995 I taught at the Johns Hopkins University School of Public Health. From 1996 to mid-1997 I was a researcher at the National Institute for Economic Policy in Johannesburg and have, since then, taught political economy at the University of the Witwatersrand's Graduate School of Public and Development Management. I also want to thank publishers of articles and chapters that contributed to the arguments presented here, and the odd funder that provided resources for me to engage in non-commodifiable work.[8]

My family and friends gave me the space and were sufficiently tolerant to allow this work to come, gradually, to the stage of publication; thanks are also due the patient Pluto editor, Roger van Zwanenberg and his team as well as Glenn Cowley and the University of Natal Press. But my greatest gratitude is for the maturing of political consciousness in South Africa's radical labour and social movements, to the point that the Left critique is acceptable as constructive public discourse, not dismissed as unpatriotic, ultra-left diatribe.

If polemic regularly emerges in this book, nevertheless, it reflects the fact that by no means was South Africa's neoliberal status pre-determined, nor is it permanent. (Nor is it meant to be 'personal': as Marx remarked in *Capital*, 'Individuals are dealt with here only in so far as they are the personifications of economic categories, the bearers of particular class-relations and interest.'[9]) Being quite close to key decision-makers, both political and bureaucratic, has given me the conviction that a thorough-going democratic transition beyond what elite South Africa offers is not only a matter of understanding the objective structural preconditions – which now, at the moment of neoliberalism's global gaffes, are ripe indeed – but subjectively a matter of political will. Rebuilding the mass democratic movements to articulate a programme for a society and economy beyond what decaying world capitalism has on offer, is thus now more urgent than ever.

Johannesburg, July 1999

Overaccumulation, uneven development and the rise of finance

How do we understand the tendency of capital to 'overaccumulate'? A quick terminological review is in order so as to locate this theoretical tradition more precisely.

To go back to basics, capital accumulation refers to the generation of wealth in the form of 'capital'. It is capital because it is employed by capitalists not to produce with specific social *uses* in mind, but instead to produce *commodities* for the purpose of *exchange*, for profit, and hence for the self-expansion of capital. Such an emphasis by individual capitalists on continually expanding the 'exchange-value' of output, with secondary concern for the social and physical limits of expansion (size of the market, environmental, political and labour problems, etc.), gives rise to enormous contradictions. These are built into the very laws of motion of the system.

Perhaps the most serious of capitalist self-contradictions, most thoroughly embedded within the capital accumulation process, is the general tendency towards an increased capital–labour ratio in production – more machines in relation to workers – which is fuelled by the combination of technological change and intercapitalist competition, and made possible by the concentration and centralisation of capital. Individual capitalists cannot afford to fall behind the industry norm, technologically, without risking their price or quality competitiveness such that their products are not sold. This situation creates a continual drive in capitalist firms towards the introduction of state-of-the-art production processes, especially labour-saving machinery. With intensified automation, the rate of profit tends to fall, and the reasons for this are worth reviewing. Profit correlates to 'surplus value', which is only actually generated through the exploitation of labour in production.

Why is labour paid only a certain proportion of the value produced, with a surplus going to capital? Since capitalists cannot 'cheat in exchange' – buy other inputs, especially machines that make other machines, from each other at a cost less than their value – the increases in value that are the prerequisite for production and exchange of commodities must emanate from workers. This simply means, in class terms, that capitalists do not and cannot systematically exploit other capitalists, but they can systematically exploit workers. Here arises the central contradiction: with automation, the labour input becomes an ever-smaller component of the total inputs into production. And as the labour content diminishes, so too do the opportunities for exploitation, for surplus value extraction and for profits.

This situation exacerbates what becomes a self-perpetuating vicious spiral. Inter-capitalist competition intensifies within increasingly tight markets, as fewer workers can buy the results of their increased production. In turn, this results in a still greater need for individual capitalists to cut costs. A given firm's excess profits are but only temporarily achieved through the productivity gains which automation typically provides, since every capitalist in a particular industry or branch of production is compelled to adopt state-of-the-art technologies just to maintain competitiveness. This leads to growth in productive capacity far beyond an expansion in what consumer markets can bear. (It is true that there are countervailing tendencies to this process, such as an increase in the turnover time of capital, automation and work speed-up, as well as expansion of the credit system. But these rarely overwhelm the underlying dynamic for long.) The relentless consequence, a continuously worsening problem under capitalism, is termed the *overaccumulation* of capital.

Overaccumulation refers, simply, to a situation in which excessive investment has occurred and hence goods cannot be brought to market profitably, leaving capital to pile up in sectoral bottlenecks or speculative outlets without being put back into new productive investment. Other symptoms include unused plant and equipment; huge gluts of unsold commodities; an unusually large number of unemployed workers; and, as discussed below, the inordinate rise of financial markets. When an economy reaches a decisive stage of overaccumulation, then it becomes difficult to bring together all these resources in a profitable way to meet social needs.

How does the system respond? *There are many ways to move an overaccumulation crisis around through time and space* (including what we later describe as 'stalling and shifting' tactics). But the only real 'solution' to overaccumulation – the only response to the crisis capable of re-establishing the conditions for a new round of accumulation – is widespread *devaluation*. Devaluation entails the scrapping of the economic dead wood, which takes forms as diverse as depressions, banking crashes, inflation, plant shutdowns and, as Schumpeter called it, the sometimes 'creative destruction' of physical and human capital (though sometimes the uncreative solution of war). The process of devaluation happens continuously, as outmoded machines and superfluous workers are made redundant, as waste (including state expenditure on armaments) becomes an acceptable form of mopping up overaccumulation and as inflation eats away at buying power. This continual, incremental devaluation does not, however, mean capitalism has learned to equilibrate, thus avoiding more serious, system-threatening crises. Devaluation of a fully cathartic nature (of which the last Great Depression and world war are spectacular examples) is periodically required to destroy sufficient economic deadwood to permit a new process of accumulation to begin.

When overaccumulation becomes widespread, extreme forms of devaluation are invariably resisted (or deflected) by whatever local, regional, national or international alliances exist or are formed in specific areas under pressure. Hence overaccumulation has very important geographical and geopolitical implications in the uneven development of capitalism, as attempts are made to transfer the costs and burden of devaluation to different regions and nations or to push overaccumulated capital into the buildings (especially commercial real estate), infrastructure and other features of the 'built environment' as a last-ditch speculative venture. Moreover, the implications of overaccumulation for balance in different sectors of the economy – between branches of production (mining, agriculture, manufacturing, finance, etc.), between consumers and producers, and between capital goods (the means of production) and consumer goods (whether luxuries or necessities) – can become ominous. Indeed, because the rhythm of overaccumulation varies across the economy, severe imbalances between the different sectors and 'departments' of production (sometimes termed 'disproportionalities' or 'disarticulations') emerge and introduce threatening bottlenecks in the production and realisation of value, which further exacerbate the crisis. These processes enhance the control and speculative functions of finance. The argument, simply, is that as overaccumulation begins to set in, as structural bottlenecks emerge, and as profit rates fall in the productive sectors of an economy, *capitalists begin to shift their investable funds out of reinvestment in plant, equipment and labour power and instead seek refuge in financial assets.* To fulfil their new role as not only store of value but as investment outlet for overaccumulated capital, those financial assets must be increasingly capable of generating their own self-expansion, and also be protected (at least temporarily) against devaluation in the form of both financial crashes and inflation. Such emerging needs mean that financiers, who are after all competing against other profit-seeking capitalists for resources, induce a shift in the function of finance away from merely accommodating the circulation of capital through production, and increasingly towards both speculative and control functions. The speculative function attracts further flows of productive capital, and the control function expands to ensure the protection and the reproduction of financial markets. Where inflation may be a threat, the control functions of finance often result in high real interest rates and a reduction in the value of labour-power (and hence lower effective demand). Where bankruptcies threaten to spread as a result of overenthusiastic speculation, the control functions attempt to shift those costs elsewhere.

These, then, are the underlying core processes that generate crises, amplify uneven development and allow financiers an inordinate say over how, at the turn of the century, states are run throughout the world capitalist system, including its South African branch.

PART I

Power and Economic Discourses

1

Neoliberal Economic Constraints on Liberation

The argument: Democratic South Africa's inheritance included an economy that proved not only difficult to manage, but also to understand, particularly in relation to financial turbulence and global integration; yet post-apartheid policy-makers drew all the wrong lessons from 'international experience' and hence prepared to amplify rather than correct apartheid capitalism's main economic distortions.

UNCERTAIN CHANGE

The unbanning of South Africa's liberation organisations and release of Nelson Mandela in February 1990 provided a moment of uncertainty – perhaps five or six years' duration – when, it seemed to most observers, nearly any kind of political-economic future was possible. The existence of fluidity within and around the ANC heightened the country's already intense ideological and factional struggles. There was little doubt that an overhaul of the country's notoriously inefficient, skewed and stagnant economy was in store, but what forces would set the parameters during the crucial first half of the decade were by no means evident.

It was an auspicious time, for while still serving his last month in prison, Mandela insisted that Freedom Charter demands for 'the nationalisation of mines, banks and monopoly industries is the policy of the ANC and a change or modification of our views in this regard is inconceivable'. Mandela's statement was not dismissed as idle chatter on Diagonal Street. As *Business Day* glumly put it the next day, the statement 'will set back the hopes of those moving towards acceptance of majority rule in the belief that free enterprise and individual property rights would still be possible'.[1]

But such hopes – and extensive 'scenario planning' efforts to draw the ANC and some trade union leaders up the oft-cited 'learning curve' (which quickly turned out, instead, to be a steep forgetting curve for former shopfloor or streetwise activists) – were soon to be richly rewarded, as Chapter 2 shows. Indeed, not only were free enterprise and property rights enshrined in every major economic policy statement and the Constitution itself, full-blown neoliberal *compradorism* became the dominant (if not universal) phenomenon within the ANC policy-making elite. This is, indeed, the overall theme of *Elite Transition*.

Yet, as Chapters 3 and 4 document, neoliberalism could hardly be celebrated, given the rapid recognition of failure on the part of orthodox, market-oriented policy-makers in 'developmental' arenas, such as housing. In part, this recognition came from the intense community and labour struggles that continued to be fought. But rather than turn left in response to grassroots cries for help, governing elites dispensed with the *Reconstruction and Development Programme* (*RDP*) – an uneven and often internally contradictory document, to be sure – during the first two years of policy-making, and the Ministry (in the Office of President) and main politician responsible for the *RDP* were unceremoniously dumped in March 1996. Notwithstanding a rhetorical return to the *RDP* in 1998–99, by the time of the June 1999 election there were huge areas in which promised reforms were nowhere on the agenda, while other social policies explicitly reversed the *RDP*. Housing and urban municipal services may have been the most striking examples where ministers took advice which led to policies antithetical to their electoral mandate.

As Chapter 5 shows, the persuasive power of World Bank/IMF intellectual arguments – if not the institutions' consistency and competence – was partly to blame for the fact that a decades-old liberation movement disappointed its constituents' entirely reasonable aspirations within months of coming to state power. In turn, Chapter 6 argues, the international face of neoliberalism was greeted with healthy scepticism. But even if (at the time of writing) ongoing 'struggles within the struggle' – as optimists from progressive political, social and labour movements described their David to neoliberalism's

Goliath – jolted right-leaning ANC leaders into recognising the self-destructive path along which they continued stumbling, there was no discernible deviation from that path. This may yet change, of course.

But if a dreadful slide into the future is what we may learn from immediate post-apartheid lessons yet to be persuasively told, it is to South Africa's pre-1994 past that we can first turn for evidence of serious constraints to the growth of a distorted capitalism beyond its apartheid shell. For to understand the transitional period from 1990 until neoliberal orthodoxy was cemented – in the form of the June 1996 *Growth, Employment and Redistribution (Gear)* policy statement – requires a brief historical contemplation of the nineteenth- and twentieth-century background to the last three decades of local/global economic crisis, and the means by which the crisis was subsequently addressed.

A schematic overview of South Africa's economic dynamic is, then, the subject of this first chapter. In the course of exploring the country's inherited economic biases, we can also begin to document the lethal contemporary combination of stagnation, financial speculation and uneven geographical development, which, along with race and gender oppression, vividly demarcate apartheid capitalism's peculiar form of durable inequality.

Once we have recovered the structural basis for the 1970s–1980s stagnation, we can understand why, to the chagrin of many in the Democratic Movement, macroeconomic management during the 1989–93 late apartheid depression became a model for *post*-apartheid policy. As will become clear, two closely associated influences – turbulent financial markets and 'globalisation' – were extremely important in all of this. The broad drift into neoliberal policy-making in the economic and social spheres was, hence, not so much the surprise that residual progressive forces of the Democratic Movement would today suggest. For it is only by noting the *continuities*, not change, from the late apartheid to the post-apartheid economy, that we can move to new planes of analysis, advocacy and activism. Once the continuities are established in this chapter, we shall be positioned to explore the discourses of scenario planning that vividly (and vapidly) symbolised the liberation movement's compromise with economic power in Chapter 2.

ECONOMIC CRISIS

The long-term structural crisis in the South African economy – ultimately rooted in tendencies towards what can be termed the 'over-accumulation' of capital (see the Preface for an explanation) – is perhaps most baldly reflected, at surface level, in the persistent overcapacity and overproduction of (relatively uncompetitive) luxury manufactured goods for the (mainly white) upper-income consumer market, side-by-side with growing surpluses of unemployed black workers, heightened financial speculation and intensifying geographical unevenness. Looking more closely at the way the four main value-generating levels of the economy (here excluding services, which mainly distribute value rather than produce it) operate, we can briefly summarise the South African economy:

- The 'minerals–energy complex'[2] – comprising the core quarter of the economy since the late nineteenth century, encompassing gold, coal, petrochemicals, electricity generation, processed metals products, mining machinery and some other, closely related manufactured outputs – remains South Africa's economic base.
- Intermediate capital goods (especially machines that make other machines) remain underdeveloped.[3]
- Luxury goods are produced locally at close to world standards (if not prices), thanks to extremely high relative levels of (traditionally white) consumer demand based on extreme income inequality, decades of protective tariffs and the presence of major multinational corporate branch plants.[4]
- Basic needs industries are extremely sparse, witnessed by production of low-cost housing far below optimal capacity (see Chapter 4), dangerous and relatively costly transport, and the underproduction of cheap, simple appliances and clothing (which are increasingly imported), at the same time social services and the social wage have been set at exceptionally low levels for the country's majority, notwithstanding South Africa's upper middle-income per capita wealth.

These economic phenomena reflect as severe a case of uneven socio-economic development as exists anywhere on earth, and along with apartheid policies help explain why the top 5 per cent of South Africa's population consume more than the bottom 85 per cent, resulting in a Gini coefficient (the main measure of income disparity) of 0.61, matching Brazil and Nigeria as major countries with the worst levels of inequality.[5]

Thus the legacy of apartheid married to extremely skewed, concentrated capital accumulation left South Africa characterised by:

- dire poverty, with more than half the country's population living within households that earned, on average, below R300 per month during the 1990s, especially in rural areas (in particular, in former 'bantustan' homelands in the Eastern Cape, KwaZulu-Natal and the Northern Province), and with women and youth most vulnerable;
- ongoing racial bias in income distribution, as 95 per cent of the poor are black 'African,' and 4 per cent are 'coloured' (mixed race), with people from the white and Indian race categories comprising less than 1 per cent of the poor; and
- inadequate access to basic services, with fewer than one-third of Africans having internal taps, flush toilets, electricity and refuse removal.[6]

There are many other reflections of the irrational scale of inequality, and if gender imbalances were more rigorously recorded in official data, these would reflect even more shocking disparities. Yet South Africa has had the requisite institutional capacity within the state (sufficient, anyway, to build nuclear weapons) and the ongoing encouragement from powerful progressive forces in civil society (as vibrant as any in the world during the 1990s) to experiment with non-market, even anti-market, development strategies. Moreover, South Africa also suffers crime and violence of such magnitude that elites should logically find it in their class interest to share even a slightly greater flow of the national income (although some have concocted an argument that there is no causal link between poverty/unemployment and crime). South Africa's per capita Gross Domestic Product is approximately that of Chile, Brazil and Malaysia, and substantially higher than that of Poland or Thailand, and far higher than any other major African country. In short, the country should be in a position to make dramatic progress in the struggle against poverty and inequality.

But uneven development appears too deeply rooted to reverse inequality in any but marginal, unsustainable ways. Those roots were most powerfully dug in when the settler-colonial economy emerged during the nineteenth century, exacerbated by the discovery of diamonds in 1867 and gold in 1886, and by the role of key financial institutions in directing capital accumulation.[7] During the 1930s and 1940s more balance was achieved, as the economy partially delinked from global circuits.[8] As the depression-riddled and then war-saddled global economy played a less important role – aside from purchasing gold – from roughly 1933 to 1945, South Africa witnessed a significant burgeoning of secondary manufacturing industry (beyond the traditionally strong mining equipment sector). The annual GDP growth rate (8 per cent) was the fastest South Africa recorded in modern times. Moreover, the rate of growth of the black wage share rose more than 50 per cent during this period (from 11 per cent to 17 per cent of the total wage bill).[9]

As South Africa reintegrated into the world economy, racial capitalist biases were amplified (for example, the black wage share stagnated, reaching just 21 per cent by 1970). White, upper-class privilege was, hence, systematically generated not merely in the political (apartheid) sphere. The overall distortion of economic activity during the 1950s and 1960s became ingrained through the economy's overemphasis on deep-level minerals extraction and energy-related industrial development.

At the same time, protective tariffs encouraged luxury consumer goods producers to locate in South Africa, at the expense of both local capital goods manufacturing and the consumption of basic needs goods in relation to their potential. International merchants faced Pretoria's rather high 15 per cent tariff barriers on luxury consumer goods, compared with trade in machinery which was burdened with only a 2 per cent tariff. This encouraged transnational producers to locate in South Africa *en masse* during the 1950s and 1960s, and in turn exacerbated the bias towards local production of luxury consumer goods instead of capital goods (and hence left South Africa with an even greater dependence upon imported machines).

An economic 'crisis' – by which is usually meant a situation in which the normal functioning of the system cannot correct intrinsic problems, which instead require resolution beyond the logic of the system – surfaced during the 1970s and became acute during the late 1980s. Particularly in manufacturing, average profitability rates (earnings in relation to capital stock) fell steadily from 40 per cent during the 1950s to less than 15 per cent during the 1980s, and reinvestment dropped by 2 per cent each year during the 1980s.[10] By the trough of the subsequent 1989–93 depression, net fixed capital investment was down to just 1 per cent of GDP, in comparison to 16 per cent annually during the 1970s.

There are various explanations for this, some of which pin the blame upon rising wages[11] and others upon the breakdown of South Africa's 'racial Fordist' – to recall the phrase popularised in academic circles by trade union movement intellectuals[12] – institutions, norms and processes of capital accumulation. Theories of the political-economic crisis overlapped with those aimed at resolving the traditional 'race–class debate'. But what was perhaps most evident about the way the crisis played itself out was that, from the 1960s, 'unusually' high levels of machinery compared to workers – as the World Bank commented in its first major policy document on South Africa[13] – led to chronic overproduction, relative to the size of the local market.

STALLING AND SHIFTING THE CRISIS

This fundamental contradiction – captured by the idea of the 'over-accumulation of capital' – represents an eternal underlying tendency of capitalism. In South Africa the tensions of overaccumulation first emerged in the form of a massive glut in inventories of consumer goods in 1967. The glut forced liquid capital out of production and into the money and capital markets – hence a speculative Johannesburg Stock Exchange binge from 1967 to 1969. Then capital flows shifted noticeably once again. Initially, with the 1969–71 stock market crash, and fuelled by the dramatic rise in the international price of gold once the US ended its postwar linkage to the dollar,[14] an inordinate amount of capital subsequently flowed into geographical expansion – within and beyond South African borders – over the subsequent decade. In the process, reinvestment momentarily perked up with a new flood of capital directed at manufacturing automation, which increased from 1970 to 1973 by a 57 per cent faster annual rate than during the previous decade (which had itself experienced an unprecedented technological intensification of production).

But what soon became evident was that such expansion would accentuate, not pacify, the deeper tendencies towards both overaccumulation and uneven development. Some important vehicles of intensified uneven geographical development during the early 1970s included the internationalisation of the mining finance houses (which searched out new overseas acquisitions instead of reinvesting locally) and an enormous boom in the construction sector until 1974. When private sector investment slowed, the state took up some of the slack with unprecedented parastatal expansion (iron and steel, electricity, oil-from-coal, transport), outward-oriented investments such as Richards Bay and Sishen-Saldanha, the upgrade of SA Airways and a renewed commitment to world-class transport more generally, infrastructural improvements and wide new electricity grids and water/sanitation lines, and promotion of worsening urban and suburban sprawl. From 1970 to 1977, state spending in transport, storage and communications increased by 65 per cent each year in real terms beyond similar investments during the 1960s, and during the same period new infrastructure for electricity grids and water lines attracted 28 per cent more funds each year than during the 1960s.[15]

In short, capital, including parastatal corporations, suffered a growing problem of overaccumulation from the late 1960s, and thus searched and found a short-term 'spatial fix' – as this phenomenon has been termed[16] – during the 1970s. Geography temporarily came to capital's rescue as the basis for offloading overaccumulated capital. During the 1980s, other spatial tactics included greater labour mobility facilitated by taxi deregulation, a liberalised urbanisation policy, and the long-overdue entry of the private sector into mass township housing construction.

There was, additionally, apartheid's own supposed geographic antidote to the glut of domestic manufacturing capital: the homelands-inspired 'regional decentralisation' policies and subsidies which picked up steam during the 1970s, and which turned during the 1980s to three dozen specific 'deconcentration points'. Aside from the policy's political purpose, namely propping up the bantustans, decentralisation also played a (temporary) role as a form of spatial fix, by promoting a qualitative new degree of 'competition in laxity' (dramatically lower wages, tax holidays and other incentives) which fuelled capital mobility. Such mobility reached its peak in the mid- and late 1980s, in attempts to export cheap manufactured goods from deconcentration points resembling low-level export processing zones. Indeed, within a few years the percentage of manufacturing employment in the deconcentration points soared from 2 per cent to

18 per cent of the country's total, thanks to billions of rands in state subsidies (half the decentralised operations were unprofitable without state support).[17]

These stalling/shifting tactics – representing some of the many ways to move an overaccumulation crisis around through time and space without really resolving it – gave South Africa a privileged refuge from the full force of the global law of value throughout the difficult decades of global restructuring prior to South Africa's own political liberalisation. But by the mid-1980s, recession, intensifying sanctions, growing worker militancy and international competition led most firms, and particularly the decentralised manufacturing operations, to comprehend better the dark side of their geographical confinement.

That the political tensions created would have to be addressed more forthrightly, failing which the country would witness an economic free-fall and political anarchy, was finally understood by South African capitalists and the leading state 'econocrats' (who chewed away a substantial bite of power from the 'securocrats' during the late 1980s). For some, the 1989–93 depression was the definitive lesson about the limits to the local market, while for others the realisation had dawned earlier, during the balance of payments crises that followed the momentary early 1980s gold boom.[18] The more general worry gnawing away at white elites was that a siege economy could never reverse the declining rate of reinvestment and accompanying fall in the rate of corporate profit.

In contrast, smaller, more opportunistic firms initially reacted to stagnation and tightening sanctions by relocating operations to deconcentration points and turning their products inward to the domestic market during the late 1980s.[19] The fixed manufacturing investments of the major cities now came under even more acute pressure, leading to four decisive responses by urban capital's representatives (the Urban Foundation and Johannesburg Chamber of Commerce): a dramatic new commitment to shifting capital into township housing, through newly legal, individualised housing bonds (with strong advocacy against residual public housing programmes); energetic and ultimately successful lobbying against state decentralisation subsidies; the establishment of a broad corporate consensus favouring export-led growth policies; and the belated and rather grudging acknowledgement that one-person, one-vote democracy in a unitary state – that previously forbidden formula – would be acceptable in exchange for the lifting of sanctions and pliant post-apartheid economic policy-making. When several key Congress of South African Trade Unions (Cosatu) leaders and staff – later to become managers of industrial policy and labour relations within the new government – finally agreed to support an export-oriented modernisation strategy in 1992, under the guise of their own 'post-Fordist' rubric linking democracy and development, big business began to find itself allied with the Democratic Movement on behalf of more rapid political and economic liberalisation.

In sum, while the roots of the crisis were to be found in the skewed structure of production, the most striking symptoms included steadily declining profit rates, a substantial decline in the economy's growth rate from late 1974, a drop in manufacturing employment from 1975 and noticeable rise in the unemployment rate, and a substantial fall in private sector investment in plant and equipment from 1976. Parastatal firms were initially called in to take up the investment slack, but this required a dramatic increase in borrowing. Indeed, along with uneven geographical development, the untenable growth of financial markets during a period of productive sector decline was the economy's other most significant self-destructive phenomenon. The rise of finance, and its potential for catastrophe, deserve additional attention.

FINANCIAL POWER AND VULNERABILITY

During the late 1970s and early 1980s, a combination of local over-accumulation with an inflow of fresh, gold-related funds from overseas banks and the IMF together encouraged South African financiers – especially the inexperienced and overanxious Nedbank and Volkskas banks – to enter the international money markets. They had initially counted on the sustained strength of the rand, as the price of gold soared beginning in 1978 and as US interest rates rose to record levels (while SA rates stabilised). Then, from 1982 to 1984, the Johannesburg Stock Exchange kicked off one of the world's most remarkable bull markets, even during a decade characterised by outlandish speculation at the global bourses, while simultaneously the capital stock of corporate South Africa stagnated and a deep recession commenced.

The shift of flows from productive circuits of capital into financial circuits also coincided with South African borrowers increasing their debt loads, in a process which mirrored the international 'financial explosion'.[20] South Africa's private sector debt/GDP ratio had been stable for many years at 30 per cent, but in 1979 it began to rise dramatically, and reached 50 per cent a decade later, and 70 per cent by 1999. The dramatic rise of the real interest rate, particularly during 1998, was to make matters all the worse.

To exacerbate matters, deregulation of banking began in earnest during the early 1980s. The official De Kock Commission recommended lifting prudential requirements and credit and interest rate ceilings, and adopted a 'risk-based' approach to the 'capital adequacy' of a bank, in effect shifting regulation of bank activities from the state to the market. Tax amendments reduced bank tax liabilities to as low as 33 per cent of income by 1993, at a time the corporate tax rate had reached its maximum of 48 per cent. Increased capital flight was facilitated – often illegally (see Box 1.1) – by financial institutions, and from 1985 to 1992 amounted to an estimated 2.8 per cent of GDP in net terms (indeed, Zav Rustomjee estimated that during the period 1970–88 it was as high as 7 per cent of GDP), enough to have reversed the period of economic decline to one of marginal growth.

Flight capital had any number of routes out of SA, including false trade invoicing, bogus agents' fees and business commissions (such as is rampant in the platinum trade), debt swaps, retention of a portion of foreign borrowings in overseas accounts and dual exchange-rate 'roundtripping' between the commercial and financial rands. A 1992 study by the Bank of Lisbon (Johannesburg) suggested a problem with the smuggling of currencies and other collectibles. Foreign investment by SA companies also increased, as Anglo, Rembrandt (Richemont) and Liberty Life all relied increasingly upon their extensive international operations for increasing profit shares. Other major firms which followed abroad – Barlow Rand, Malbak and Sage – fared much worse, but that did not deter further interest. One of the most important instances of capital export was Gencor's purchase of Shell Oil's Billiton mining group; Finance Minister Derek Keys' resignation in mid-1994 to run Billiton was, some whispered, not unrelated to his controversial decision in 1993 to allow Gencor access to foreign exchange to make the deal.

The biggest firms did not become any more patriotic once apartheid had ended. By 1998, transfers of headquarters to London were announced by Anglo American Corporation, Liberty Life, SA Breweries (SAB) and Old Mutual – this in the immediate wake of colossal local victories for the latter two firms, namely Trade and Industry Minister Alec Erwin's 1998 denuding of both the Liquor Act and the Competition Act so as to allow SAB's beer monopoly (98 per cent market share and anti-competitive production–wholesale ties) to continue, and permission by Finance Minister Trevor Manuel for Mutual to end its status as a mutually-owned company and become a shareholder-owned entity. Mining houses were another vehicle for disinvestment during most of the 1990s, with widespread allegations of massive transfer pricing to shell companies in places like Zug, Switzerland.[21]

Box 1.1: Financial shenanigans

Highly regarded corporate personnel were partly to blame for the unfortunate combination of financial power and vulnerability that characterised South Africa's neoliberal economic transition. An unending stream of charlatan financiers from major banks, insurance houses and stockbroking firms began to ruin the reputation of their rest of their profession: Piet Badenhorst, Danie Cronje and so many other ABSA officials,[22] Frankel Max Pollack Vinderine's Greg Blank along with Old Mutual lead trader Colin Harper and portfolio managers Marco Celotti and David Schapiro,[23] Fundstrust's Jan Marais and Ansi Kamfer,[24] the Reserve Bank's Christoffel Lombard,[25] *ad nauseam*, were guilty between them of many billions of rands worth of financial scamming.

In 1994, the Witwatersrand Attorney-General investigating late 1980s foreign exchange activities of SA banks issued a report alleging fraud in every major transaction approved by banks and the Reserve Bank.[26] The Reserve Bank seemed to revel in a culture of sloth, and the Registrar of Financial Institutions, Hennie van Greuning, was unveiled as incompetent in the 1992 Cape Investment Bank fiasco and 1993 Masterbond prosecution (van Greuning soon left for Washington, DC, to help the World Bank design financial liberalisation, after Stals failed in early 1993 to jettison his unit to the Finance Department, reportedly to save Reserve Bank face).

Fraud came to dominate many business careers during the elite transition. In 1991 alone, more than 55,000 'economic crimes' took place, according to the Witwatersrand Attorney-General.[27] Corporate crime of the order of R6 billion a year was estimated by the Office for Serious Economic Offences, and South Africa was cited by Britain's Centre for International Documentation on Organised and Economic Crime as 'a prime target for future growth in international economic crime and money laundering'.[28] One widely cited police report estimated fraud costs in 1992 of the order of R374 billion, a figure so enormous that it beggared belief.[29]

Even at the industrial heart of the South African economy a man like Anglo chief executive Julian Ogilvie Thompson was reduced to a hapless financial shyster, when trying to market De Beers shares to dubious London stock market investors in mid-1992. Capturing Unita's diamonds (thus indirectly fuelling Angolan civil war) temporarily rescued De Beers, whose share price had crashed by more than 50 per cent. But the diamond market's decaying fundamentals – increased supply from Russia, diminished demand from shrinking East Asian luxury markets – proved uncomfortable during the SA depression (and again in 1998) and even Anglo's stable of newspapers turned angrily against Thompson for his dishonesty.[30]

As was the case globally, such neoliberal dynamics generated unprecedented financial profits. As former Reserve Bank deputy governor Jan Lombard put it in 1989, just as the interest rate spread began rising to extremely high levels, 'Profits in all industries showed a markedly declining trend over the past 12 years. In the sector finance, insurance, real estate and business services, however, the ratio fully recovered its lost ground since 1981 ... To my mind, such a trend for an economy in the position of South Africa is not a healthy one.'[31]

At the same time, total financial sector formal employment nearly doubled, from 106,000 in 1977 to 205,000 in 1996. The most impressive spurts in employment growth were 1978–85 (from 107,000 workers to 160,000), on the back of the gold boom and associated increase in credit growth, and 1987–90 (from 160,000 workers to 195,000) as deregulation unfolded and a variety of financial innovations were introduced. (Only in early 1996 did the banks announce plans to cut jobs – amounting to an estimated 10 per cent of staff – in order to introduce a new wave of labour-saving technology. Branch closures led to more losses.)

But notwithstanding high profits and nearly unparalleled job creation, there was a terrible boom–bust unevenness within the financial markets during the 1980s, as the case of mortgages ('bonds') for housing demonstrates. In the private market, only 10 per cent of the African population could afford to acquire homes (which for middle-income workers able to raise credit came at a minimum price of roughly R35,000 per house), while at the same time, as Chapter 4 shows, housing finance brimmed over in the white suburbs and massive inflows of funds to banks and institutional investors generated speculative investment pools that in turn could find few productive outlets.

To illustrate the scale of the contradictions, South Africa was second in the world (to the United States) in the percentage of bank assets held in the form of residential mortgage credit (39 per cent in 1990).[32] Yet of R50 billion in such loans on the banks' books during the early 1990s, just R8 billion (16 per cent) was invested in the township market (home to two in every five South Africans). Aside from a few townships that existed prior to the 1913 Land Act, Africans were only allowed to own urban homes – through a 'leasehold' system that soon became full title and the basis for collateralisation of credit – beginning in the late 1970s, at the time the state began phasing out new public housing construction.

Thus most of the bank townships loans were granted over just four years, until mid-1990, when a variety of factors – market saturation, an increase in nominal interest rates from 12.5 per cent (–6 per cent in real terms) to 21 per cent (+10 per cent), poor-quality construction and lack of community facilities, the retrenchment wave that accompanied the long depression, an upsurge of political violence in key areas, and a decline in township housing values leading to widespread 'negative equity' (in which bond value exceeds house price) – converged to end the flow of new loans and reduce repayment rates on outstanding loans. As late as 1996, it was estimated that of 200,000 township bonds, 40,000 were in default or deep arrears.

Meanwhile, capital market funds continued to swell by tens of billions of rands each year, thanks in large part to black worker pension contributions and insurance premiums. These funds were mainly invested in JSE shares and speculative construction of commercial property. In the latter case, overbuilding during the late 1980s quickly generated artificially high land prices in central business districts, and then 20 per cent vacancy rates by 1991 and a fully-fledged property market crash. Moreover, the banks began to suffer levels of arrears and defaults within their portfolios comprising company, consumer, housing, white farmer and black taxi loans which were unprecedented in recent history. In particular, they bore huge costs during the bankruptcies of major construction firms and several large conglomerates.[33]

The state's response was to deregulate and privatise even faster, push real interest rates to still higher levels and introduce a regressive Value Added Tax while lowering corporate taxes. The banks' response was to open more branches in the Cayman Islands, Panama, the Isle of Man, Guernsey, Jersey, Zurich and other hot money centres than in all South Africa's black townships combined (in fact, the banks closed most of their township branches after the housing finance crisis emerged in 1990; a mapping of offices closed and offshore subsidiaries opened would offer one of the most graphic capital-flow symbols of bank patriotism during South Africa's democratisation process). 'Get your money off Treasure Island', Standard Bank would brazenly advertise in the business section of the upmarket newspaper *Mail and Guardian*, with a mock parchment graphically showing the jungly hazards facing besieged local savers.[34] Thus during a crucial three-month period in late 1992, First National bought Henry Ansbacher bank for R300 million and in the process gained Panama, Guernsey and Cayman Island branches, while Standard Bank bought ANZ Grindlays (with several African subsidiaries) for R165 million. On the industrial front Anglo American and Royal bought the Del Monte food multinational for R1.8 billion and Sentrachem bought an Australian chemical company. The predictable result was a cataclysmic drop in the value of the financial rand, from 3.9 finrands to the dollar in August to 5.1 in November. The spread between the financial and commercial rand widened to 46 per cent, the worst differential since 1986.[35]

Some of these developments initially left South Africa's major banks badly exposed. In 1989, just as the depression began, *The Banker* magazine ranked South Africa's four major banks 290, 303, 412 and 439 in the world in terms of their assets (i.e. the amount of other people's funding they had converted into loans and investments) but just 482, 774, 743 and 540, respectively, in terms of the strength of their underlying capital (the banks' own wealth; the capital/asset ratio is the most common measure of the financial stability of a bank). Yet somehow little of this would be evident on the surface, and given the rise in JSE bank shares it didn't worry investors. The return on assets (the most common method of assessing bank profitability) rose most impressively for Standard Bank, for example: from 0.99 in 1991 to 1.09 in 1992 to 1.13 in 1993 to 1.30 in 1994 to 1.35 in 1995 – far in excess of international norms. First National Bank and Nedcor also steadily increased their earnings during the early 1990s, with only ABSA showing declining (though still substantial) returns on assets during the period. The banks also spent the early 1990s building luxuriant billion rand headquarters (such as Standard's Superblocks and First National Bank 'Bank City') and in unrivalled compensation packages for senior management.

How did the banks survive and prosper, and indeed rake in record profits (between R750 million and R1.25 billion for each of the four leading banks) during the 1989–93 depression? In past periods, such as the mid-1980s, financial panic or the late 1980s disinvestment wave when Standard Chartered and Barclays left, they were bailed out by larger investors: Old Mutual bought Nedbank, the Sanlam-Rembrandt empires supported Volkskas and Bankorp, Liberty Life bought Standard, and Anglo American bought Barclays (renaming it First National Bank).

During the early 1990s, new strategies evolved. The most obvious process was intensified concentration within the financial sector. The share of banking sector assets controlled by the four largest banks increased from 69 per cent in 1991 to 84 per cent in 1995. Some of the more sickly banks merged with each other (in the case of Volkskas and Bankorp in the ABSA group). They bought or converted building societies (in the case of Nedbank-Perm, NBS, Saambou and the United-Allied component of ABSA), which had the effect of taking depositors' capital built up over a century in some cases (augmented by generous tax breaks) and effectively privatising it solely on behalf of the present generation – a phenomenon repeated by the two giant mutual insurance companies, Old Mutual and Sanlam, in 1998–99. And the banks also increased their own business profitability by dramatically raising the 'spread' between what borrowers paid and what savers were rewarded. The four large banks rarely engaged in generalised price wars (i.e. the interest rate charged for a loan, or paid to a saver). Just before the depression began, the spread was 2.25 per cent; it quickly rose to more than twice that. Bankers also developed a naughty habit of violating the Usury Act on overdraft facilities, which generated a new cottage industry of small-time accountants calculating interest for angry bank clients. ABSA alone allegedly overcharged customers by R1 billion. The vast number of publicised consumer complaints against banks suggested a stunning level of officially condoned fraud, emblematised by the fact that the bureaucrat responsible for Usury Act enforcement was shipped to Pretoria's equivalent of Siberia and eventually fired in 1996.[36]

Also crucial to the management of financial crisis was the willingness of the Reserve Bank to accept responsibility for South African banking and corporate exposure in international markets. This took several forms, including an enormous 'lifeboat' for Bankorp when it began to fail in 1985; it was transferred to ABSA and increased to R1.125 billion – as a 'loan' to be repaid at 1 per cent interest – in part to help ABSA wind up extremely poor-quality assets tied to corrupt banking practice.[37] There was also Reserve Bank 'forward cover' protection, namely billions of rands in subsidies against the risk of currency devaluation – based on more than 100 billion rand of foreign loans by the late 1990s – essentially donated to those firms which could borrow internationally, notwithstanding the enormous cost involved (what with the sliding value of the rand). The initial rationale was that due to financial sanctions, the Reserve Bank needed continually to acquire foreign reserves.

Under Gerhard de Kock and prior governors, the Reserve Bank mainly served the needs of the National Party, manipulating credit to help wretched Afrikaner farmers and playing loose with monetary policy at key political junctures. Chris Stals took over from de Kock in 1989. Although he shifted dramatically to a tight money, deregulatory financial regime, Stals still approved the most egregious bail-out (moving from Bankorp to ABSA) and was ultimately responsible for ineffectual banking regulation, as evidenced by accelerating financial scams; systematic corruption in foreign exchange dealings; and mockery of the lender-of-last-resort function. However, for his skill at keeping interest rates at their highest levels in the country's history and for his role in deregulating currency controls, *Euromoney* magazine named Stals 'Central Banker of the Year' in 1995.

Thanks to the Reserve Bank's tight money policy, real interest rates on South African government bonds had reached more than 10 per cent by the mid-1990s, compared to less than 5 per cent in Britain and Germany, and approximately 3 per cent in the US, Japan and Australia. Such historically unprecedented real interest rates generated an enormous inflow of footloose foreign finance to South Africa during 1995, following the lifting of the finrand in March. It was not only the bond markets that prospered from the inflow. More than half the turnover on the Johannesburg Stock Exchange during 1995 was of foreign origin. But the hot money also soon wreaked havoc on the currency, for it drained out just as quickly when negative herd instincts emerged a year later, leading to a 25 per cent drop in the rand's value during the first four months of 1996 and a further 10 per cent decline by the year's end.

The currency crash also caught one bank (Standard) with its pants down. Having borrowed abroad in order to take advantage of the attractive interest rate difference – identical to the Nedbank and Volkskas blunders over a decade earlier – Standard had suddenly to compensate for the rising cost of repaying dollars with declining rands. An incident in which it led a general rate increase through 'price leadership' (Box 1.2), combined with innovative tactics devised by grassroots civic associations and residents' committees, showed that notwithstanding widespread consumer anger about banking power (Box 1.3), there was also a measure of vulnerability.[38]

But notwithstanding a hot rhetorical campaign by civic associations under the banner of the SA National Civic Organisation in 1992–93, there was insufficient vulnerability to compel the banks to defund homeland and apartheid agencies which operated huge, corruption-plagued military bureaucracies on high-cost overdraft lines of credit. (Finally, in early April 1994, the interim government of national unity threatened to have Mangosuthu Buthelezi's billion rand First National Bank accounts in the KwaZulu capital Ulundi frozen, which must have been a central reason for his retraction of the threatened Unilateral Declaration of Independence and election boycott.) The overpriced loans – much at unconscionable overdraft interest rates – that banks gleefully made to bantustan dictators during the 1980s still weighed heavily on the fiscus in the post-apartheid era, but frightened ANC economic policy-makers made no move to revoke or renegotiate the debt.

Box 1.2: The interest rate ratchet

By May 1996, the shortage of funds caused by the combination of capital flight and the rapidly depreciating currency catalysed a telling incident that marked both financial power and vulnerability: the four major banks simultaneously increased interest rates by 1 per cent, at the same time the inflation rate had dropped to just 5.5 per cent.

As was widely noted, the increase was unique because it did not directly follow a uniform rate rise in the 'Bank Rate' by the Reserve Bank. Instead, the impetus came from South Africa's largest bank – the Standard Bank, which had become badly exposed in international markets when it did not anticipate the currency crash – and was followed within an hour by the other banks. The underlying rationale most widely cited by the banks was a 'money market shortage', which was exacerbated by capital flight and the Reserve Bank's decision not to buy securities on the market and hence relieve the shortage.[39] This squeezed the banks' own profits intolerably, they insisted, although it was embarrassing that during the very week of the interest rate increase ABSA announced a 50 per cent rise in profits compared to the previous year.

The banks raised the public's hackles because they could not explain how, notwithstanding divergent cost structures and marketing policies, the rate increase was absolutely simultaneous and uniform (the money market shortages affected all the banks differently, depending upon their exposures, their growth strategies, their funding needs, etc.). A uniform basis for an increase would have been the case with a Reserve Bank rate increase; without a Bank Rate increase, the banks should not have reacted simultaneously and with the same increase. Some banks which were recording extremely high profits should have had the capacity to allow other banks to raise their rates, and then compete to win a larger market share.

The potential for competition was demonstrated late the following month, when differences between the banks on the housing bond rate did indeed emerge.[40] This flurry of competition, simultaneous to the decision by all banks to lower the general interest rate, was indicative of the banks' ability to compete on price terms when they so desired. But psychologically, it was probably important to the bankers that they not be seen to fold under intense

public criticism. Hence they delayed for several weeks the decision
to bring the interest rates back down 1 per cent, which tellingly
they also did practically in unison, within a day of each other.

Box 1.3: Banks and consumer alienation

South African banking consumers – especially homeowners –
complained bitterly about seemingly capricious interest rate
increases; a limited range of financial products; a legacy of poorly
designed, low-cost lending initiatives; a wave of foreclosures and
evictions; the decision in 1995 to raise interest rates for low-income
homeowners (at the same time that lower rates were being offered
to professionals); the 1995–98 spate of bank branch closures and
the simultaneous disowning of more than 1 million low-profit
savings accounts (notably by the Perm); and systematic 'red-lining'
(geographical discrimination) of black and desegregating of urban
neighbourhoods. Specifically, the South African National Civic
Organisation regularly criticised bankers during the early 1990s for
(in Sanco's words):

- 'cementing the geography of apartheid' by financing
  developers who built housing estates far away from the
  central cities, often in collusion with corrupt apartheid era
  councillors;
- financing 'fly-by-night developers' to put up shoddy housing
  (90 per cent of township houses had flaws, according to a
  Housing Consumer Protection Trust report), while bank
  valuers were sometimes paid to look the other way;
- charging relatively low rates of interest on housing bonds as
  a baiting technique to solicit marginal borrowers – those
  affected included thousands of pensioners and others aged
  65 and older who were encouraged to take out bonds to
  construct two rooms and a garage behind their matchbox
  houses, which in turn were collateralised on top of the new
  structure; as interest rates rose marginally, many hundreds
  of defaults occurred – and then when the interest rate soared
  by 1989, having nothing to offer those borrowers now
  unable to pay their bonds;

- failing to develop safety-net mechanisms to protect their own investments and enable working-class people to retain their homes, as the subsequent recession threw hundreds of thousands of workers out of their jobs, and as rising food prices and new VAT charges ate up monthly incomes;
- not catering for the vast majority of the South African population, both by failing to make available housing loans for less than R35,000 and by not having lending facilities and suitable housing loan products in rural areas where individual title deeds do not exist;
- making loans without adequate buyer education, with no scope for community participation and control, with no forms of civic empowerment, and with no options for co-operatives, land trusts or housing associations.[41]

In addition, consumer advice offices received more complaints about financial institutions than about any other sector of commerce. General consumer concerns about bank practices included misleading advertising, inadequate consumer education, lack of competition between banks, rising fees for financial transactions (even at automated teller machines), lack of access to bank facilities for township and rural financial services consumers, and lack of responsiveness to complaints.

Moreover, because banks largely failed to serve South Africa's lower-income consumers, there was a notable rise in loan sharks (*mashonisas*), fraudulent 'pyramid' schemes and other exploitative financiers (including touted NGO creditors) in township and rural markets. Credit available only at interest rates of 350 per cent per annum was not at all unusual for informal sector borrowers with no credit history. Notwithstanding a continual barrage of rhetoric about South Africa's poor savings rate, banks actively discouraged low- and moderate-income people from opening accounts.

None of these problems, identified around mass social struggles during the early 1990s, improved noticeably over the next few years. Notably, of the barrage of consumer financial protection interventions mandated as campaign promises in the *Reconstruction and Development Programme* in 1994, by the end of the ANC's first term in office not one had been implemented.

INDUSTRIAL DECLINE DURING THE RISE OF GLOBALISATION

The deep-rootedness of the 1970s–1980s overaccumulation problem became ever more obvious during the early 1990s, as regular predictions by leading economists of an imminent upturn consistently proved incorrect. This was particularly true regarding fixed investment. As *Business Day*'s Greta Steyn remarked in late 1992: 'a decade of local economic stagnation while world demand has been sluggish does not provide a rationale for private investment spending'.[42]

What new investment occurred was largely of the old-style capital-intensive, publicly subsidised variety. The R7.2 billion Alusaf project (supported by at least R700 million in taxpayer funds, not including extremely low-priced electricity) produced jobs at a cost of R3 million each (in comparison to the Small Business Development Corporation cost of R18,000 each),[43] while the R3 billion Columbus stainless steel plant generated no new net jobs. The movers and shakers behind Alusaf and Columbus included Anglo American, Sanlam and Gencor, the Industrial Development Corporation and Eskom. Such investments contradicted the labour-intensive, non-subsidised approach which appeared by then to have become a consensus position amongst even mainstream economists. The reality of business behaviour remained very different from either the optimal policy for a more balanced form of capitalist growth, or from what the models predicted.

By 1998, the continuity in industrial investment patterns was evident. A generous ANC government redirected the *RDP* Fund away from basic needs and – via the Department of Trade and Industry – towards 'corporate welfare' Spatial Development Initiatives (the Maputo Corridor, the Fish River SDI, Saldanha, etc.). Without much debate, billions of rands in taxpayer subsidies were committed to capital-intensive, electricity-hungry mega-projects such as the Mozal aluminium smelter in Maputo (benefiting Alusaf, part-owned by Gencor) and, near Port Elizabeth, Coega minerals processing – initially, a zinc smelter (first proposed by Billiton, Gencor's foreign subsidiary spinoff), but when that failed due to the global economic crisis, a stainless steel plant (tied to the controversial purchase of German submarines) – and a deep-water port (South Africa's third such port, while Port Elizabeth's existing port functioned perfectly well). However, the multi-billion rand projects entailed only a smattering of permanent jobs (fewer than 1,000 in each megaproject), plus expanding gluts in already declining world metals markets, as well as enormous ecological degradation.

Setting aside the white elephant projects which united the pre- and post-1994 white bureaucrats, monopoly capital and giant parastatal corporations, a shocking decline in other fixed investment added to shrinking domestic markets proved disastrous for many small and medium-sized enterprises. To illustrate, the only manufacturing sectors which claimed growth during 1992, at the trough of the business cycle, were plastic products, other chemical products, non-ferrous metal products and professional/scientific instruments. Worst hit were footwear, glass and textiles, which suffered large excess capacity problems. Major shakeouts were expected in heavier industrial sectors, particularly as the World Trade Organisation rules took full effect into the next century. The auto sector, for example, produced 300,000 vehicles annually during the early 1980s under conditions of relatively high import protection, while the early 1990s averaged less than 200,000.

The desperate need to shrink the scope of the industrial economy to restore efficiency and profitability could not be blamed on the advanced stage of class struggle in South Africa. For while large strikes occurred in several sectors, and Cosatu shop stewards maintained a salutary militancy and class-consciousness,[44] nevertheless, workers were forced to accept wage increases below inflation during much of the depression.[45] Moreover, from 1995 to 1997, strike days declined dramatically, and unit labour costs also fell substantially through the 1990s (largely due to the replacement of labour by capital).

On the other side of the class divide, monopoly capital appeared more collusive and anti-social than ever. Price fixing and agreements to allocate market shares were customary, and product lines of many key manufacturing sectors were dominated by a single firm. Monopoly capital was characterised by interlocking directorates, a tiny number of major corporate shareholders at the top of 'pyramid' groups (Anglo American, Rembrandt, Old Mutual, Sanlam, Liberty Life), and an incessant search for profits via short-term financial ratios (rather than long-term R&D). Although the immediate post-apartheid era saw some changes in the formal structure of ownership – a 'Black Economic Empowerment' fashion made it appear that by early 1998, prior to the April–September crash, 9 per cent of the stock market was black-controlled – this was at best superficial and fragile (at worst, a vehicle for systematic black disempowerment), permeated by underlying status quo power relations, corporate behaviour and performance (Box 1.4).

Meanwhile, on the international trading and investment front, South African manufacturers learned what minerals and agricultural exporters had found out the hard way over the past decades: the rules of the international trade game were simply not fair. After peaking in 1973, raw materials prices sunk to their lowest real level in recorded history by the early 1990s, with the result that yet more pressure was placed upon manufacturers to lead an export-oriented growth strategy.

Many manufacturers, though, were in no mood for such talk, and the more they learned about the rigours of foreign competition, particularly as globalisation became the economic fad term of the early 1990s, the more nervous they became. The SA Foreign Trade Organisation chief executive lamented exporters' 'dismal performance' during the 1980s – when South Africa slipped from 16th to 30th place in world rankings – but as the realisation began to creep in that foreign competition was extremely tough, its 'export confidence barometer' fell by 50 per cent from 1991 to 1992.[46] That was a crucial period, for of more than 600 manufacturers surveyed by the Department of Trade and Industry at the time, 43 per cent produced exclusively for the local market while another 42 per cent could export only 10 per cent or less of their production.[47]

Even Cosatu's post-Fordist economic advisers conceded in 1993 that 'Entry in external markets has been difficult, partly because of the growth of protectionist barriers in key, large economies and partly because of heightened competition. At the same time, most of the developing world (including South Africa) is being forced to open domestic markets to imports.'[48] Searching high and low for export-oriented industries, the World Bank went on the record with a claim that South Africa is 'able to compete internationally' at the high end of the clothing market, where South African 'wages were up to ten times lower than Korea, Taiwan, Hong Kong and Italy'.[49] Yet because of tough foreign competition, nearly every South African apparel manufacturer still produced at least 75 per cent of output for local markets.[50]

If South Africa's export strategy was not working, it was not because of a lack of incentives. Energy costs for export producers, for example, were priced artificially low (to the extent that bauxite was imported to South Africa for conversion into aluminium by Alusaf thanks solely to a very low Eskom electricity bill). The government's General Export Incentive Scheme cost the equivalent of a 2 per cent increase in the VAT rate, yet was 'relatively useless for boosting exports', according to officials from the General Agreement on Tariffs and Trade (GATT).[51] In short, comparative advantages were few and far between.

Box 1.4: Black economic disempowerment

There is a tendency in South African political discourse to blame the victims, and failed black entrepreneurs – an easy target for leftists – are no exception (ANC MP Ben Turok, for example, was among the most regular and belligerent of white petit-bourgeois critics of an aspirant black bourgeoisie). At one level, such disdain has been provoked, for the *nouveau-riche* character of Black Economic Empowerment (BEE) means that the objective sometimes degenerates – as in a 1996 endorsement by then deputy Trade and Industry Minister Phumzile Mlambo-Ngcuka (a former trade unionist) – into becoming, quite simply, 'filthy rich'.[52]

But matters are always more complicated in South Africa – letting the cat out of the bag, one *Star Business Report* journalist observed, 'The white establishment use black faces to gain access to the new government and often pay the blacks in the form of shares in their companies. So at the end of the day, it is a handful of black people that are being enriched.' The actual number? Controversial hawker-entreprenuer Lawrence Mavundla counted 300 people in Mlambo-Ngcuka's 'filthy rich' camp (not much of a new 'class' there) – whom he reckoned were already very well off – and argued that BEE as it was already understood by late 1996 was a 'sham'.[53]

Instead of disdain or envy, a more appropriate sentiment might be *pity*, for if ever there was a case that white South African elites laid a neoliberal ambush for their successors, BEE is it. The trajectory was hinted at by political scientist Sam Nolutshungu during the early 1980s, when he described 'the inability of the system of dominance to provide terms of black submission to the social order that collaborating black classes could themselves uphold, and, in their turn, purvey to others persuasively'. Thus, he continued, 'It is in recognition of this fact that the regime now seeks to incorporate the black elites, a measure which, at this late hour, and in the manner of its conception and execution, more resembles a strategy of counter-insurgency than a commitment to fundamental reform.'[54] At a political level, the mass democratic organisations prevented Pretoria's co-option strategy from proceeding very far, and in any event collaborating classes were given few real opportunities for accumulation, aside from homeland patronage, until later in the 1980s.

At that point in late apartheid's mutation, the most aggressive of BEE hucksters took over: white free-market propagandists, desperate for allies. Billboard images erected during the 1980s by the public–private Small Business Development Corporation depicted 70,000 kombi-taxi drivers as the economic motors of the New South Africa. 'Free Enterprise is Working!' the billboards shouted. The Johannesburg *Star* was an important site of liberal ideological signposting, with journalist Patrick Laurence waxing eloquent in 1989 that, 'The robust, competitive taxi drivers can be seen as evidence that capitalism is alive and well, and that even within apartheid South Africa, where for decades Black business was shackled, the capitalist ethos is strong and growing.' Likewise, John Kane-Berman, a director of the SA Institute of Race Relations (which was in the process of transforming from a liberal to neoliberal institution, in a manner that later characterised the Democratic Party), would in 1990 describe the black kombi-taxi industry as 'the most dramatic black success story so far' – though three years later, after a taxi flare-up in Johannesburg's central business district, which left four people dead and terrified the occupants of downtown financial institutions and mining houses, he admitted that the industry was better termed a 'débâcle'. Indeed, after that incident, *Financial Mail* editorialists finally voiced concern that, 'It will be tragic if many black small businessmen [kombi owners] burn their fingers on their first encounter with capitalism.'[55]

The sad reality was that the first organic encounters that many South Africans had with petty capital accumulation – the sale of goods and services in township and rural spheres previously unexplored, prohibited or severely distorted by large-scale capitalists – were of severe over-trading (overaccumulation). Loan defaults, bankruptcies and other evidence of market failure emerged especially in the high-profile areas – taxi transport, commerce (*spaza* shops), finance and construction – that had once been the subject of so much enthusiasm and opportunism. Notwithstanding some successes, such as a 1990 battle *shebeen* (informal tavern) owners won against SA Breweries – which controlled nearly the entire beer market – over the cost of wholesale beer, the informal sector imploded with tensions. This in turn had enormous destructive effects on all aspects of life in inner-cities, townships and rural areas.

For example, accidents stemming from speeding and reckless taxi driving, resulting in the deaths of thousands of South Africans each year, were often a function of taxi-owners pushing their workers in order to repay auto loans whose interest rate had soared from 17 per cent in the late 1980s to more than 30 per cent in the early 1990s (so concluded even the Goldstone Commission in 1993). And yet passengers waited in excess of an hour, often two, to get from Alexandra Township to downtown Johannesburg on weekday mornings, for there were too few taxis during rush hours, but too many to make profits during the off-peak periods. However, instead of inter-firm competition taking the form of price discounts to attract customers, the taxi fleet owners often authorised gun battles in order to monopolise prime routes. Meshack Khosa described these contradictions more formally in an Oxford dissertation: 'Unavoidably, crises associated with capitalist accumulation are evident in the industry', namely record levels of default on taxi loans; over-supply of vehicles in the taxi ranks; desperate monopoly pricing practices; intensified exploitation of labour; driver speed-up; and violent taxi feuds, which all reflect the growing intensity of the crisis.[56]

Likewise for hawkers and township *spaza* shops, which reportedly employed 3 million blacks (including a high proportion of women), competition in both township and city began to appear ruinous during the early 1990s.[57] As an example, the African Council of Hawkers and Informal Businesses made news when its president, Mavundla, periodically threatened the new wave of successful Taiwanese, Zimbabwean and other foreign hawkers operating in the Johannesburg inner-city, forcing many to flee. There was only mild encouragement from Erwin's post-apartheid Trade and Industry Ministry (though the responsibility may have been Mlambo-Ngcuka's), with far more embarrassments in the field of small business promotion than successes.[58]

Another strategy would have been black petit-bourgeois class formation according to, say, the model of Zimbabwe and some other major African states. (Harare's black bureaucrats swelled six-fold over a decade, from a base of roughly 20,000 at independence, and during the 1980s represented Robert Mugabe's most loyal social base.) But hiring more civil servants as a politico-bureaucratic route to small-scale accumulation, was potholed by neoliberalism. The shrinkage of the national and especially provincial civil services mandated by *Gear* began with 100,000 civil service job cuts from 1994 to 1999. (In this context, black directors-general in the Departments of Public Administration, Public Works and Home Affairs resigned in 1998–99 to pursue business interests, with the latter, Albert Mokoena, already doing so on the job by apparently helping Zambian basketball players working for his for-profit team jump corruptly through immigration hoops.)

Under such difficult circumstances, a class consciousness was distinctly lacking amongst those involved in BEE, notwithstanding much bemused publicity about new conspicuous consumption norms (and various slick periodicals devoted to BEE). For example, the SA Black Taxi Association reflected the overaccumulation problem when it fragmented badly during the early 1990s, while the marketing company set up to promote BEE (including taxis, savings clubs (*stokvels*), burial societies, *spaza* shops, and the like) – the Foundation for African Business and Consumer Services (Fabcos) – retrenched more than 100 workers in November 1992 during one of its intermittent crises. Commented a then respected consultant, Eugene Nyati, Fabcos and the National African Chamber of Commerce had 'failed to transcend narrow sectarian rivalries'. Black businessmen, Nyati contended, were too guilty of 'snobbery' to act *as a class*: 'They rely too much on, and expect too much from, an impressive curriculum vitae. It often becomes an alternative to competence and commitment.'[59]

Such criticisms were yet more vocal by the turn of the century, when it came to the serious BEE money: the enormously debt-ridden ('leveraged') construction of pyramid arrangements facilitated by fee-hungry, white-controlled merchant banks. The best single case of BEE via pyramid conglomerate shareholdings was generally acknowledged to be Don Ncube's Real Africa Holdings (supported by African Life insurance and bolstered by Real Africa Durolink investment/merchant banking), which adopted a classic insurance-based acquisition strategy borrowed from Afrikaners (but under Ncube, a long-time Anglo American Corporation apprentice, turning to information technology and privatised education). Yet Real Africa still traded at a major discount to underlying asset value in 1999.

In the same spirit, in 1993 Sanlam sold a controlling stake in Metropolitan Life to a black consortium – New Africa Investments Limited (Nail) – led by Soweto civic activist (and Mandela physician) Dr Nthato Motlana, following Motlana's flirtation with Anglo American's Southern Life on a similar deal. (Metlife was ripe for unloading because of chronic labour problems.) Motlana added to his financial stable the African Merchant Bank and Theta's usury-busting Theta micro-lending activities, before acquiring control of the former mining conglomerate Johnnic, which meant diluted control of Times Media Limited (South Africa's major newspaper publisher) and South African Breweries.

But more and more shady deals were done in the mid-1990s using investment trusts and holding companies. By the late 1990s, more and more high-profile black businesses – Pepsi, National Sorghum Breweries, African Bank (as well as Community Bank) – had gone effectively bankrupt when business plans, trading conditions or the cost of borrowing backfired on the highly leveraged deals. The venerable Johannesburg Consolidated Investments (JCI), bought on credit by a consortium led by Mzi Khumalo, soon collapsed (requiring substantial asset-stripping to pay creditors and a full unbundling) partly due to declining gold prices and rising real interest rates, but also because shareholders revolted against Khumalo's nakedly self-interested investment of hundreds of millions of rands in a family-controlled firm unrelated to JCI's business. (The former Robben Island prisoner and Umkhonto we Sizwe fighter took his first stumble when he tried unsuccessfully to fire 23,000 JCI mineworkers, and after the mining fiasco was soon under the business microscope again when a flashy Malaysian investor, Samsudin, furiously accused him of starting a run on the Durban-based New Republic Bank – which effectively killed the bank, driving it into Reserve Bank curatorship – so as to lower its share value in an anticipated purchase by Khumalo.)

By April 1998, BEE pyramid schemes found themselves holding the highest priced shares (measured by the price–earnings ratio) in South African history, and they continued to buy new ones. But they were paying for those shares with the highest priced debt ever. Then, from June to August, the Bank Rate soared by another 7 per cent and the overall Johannesburg Stock Exchange index plummeted by 40 per cent from April to September. Some shares were hit harder than others, with Motlana's Nail and other BEE counters suffering particularly severe corrections. Nail-controlled Johnnic had reached nearly R70 per share in April 1998, but it subsequently crashed to R21 a few months later and by mid-1999 the price was still only R35. This was a huge and embarrassing (and for many investors devastating) discount on the R60 per share for which former ANC general-secretary, former National Union of Mineworkers leader and former lead constitutional negotiator Cyril Ramaphosa had earlier marketed the company to ordinary black consumers (through the 'Ikageng' share purchase scheme).[60]

There were similar scandals, as in 1999 when Ramaphosa's ex-colleagues at Nail – Motlana, Jonty Sandler (a white promoter still suffering from a tarnished reputation after having collapsed a Standard Bank-financed property complex near Soweto during the late 1980s), Dikgang Moseneke (once a militant 'one-settler, one bullet' Pan Africanist Congress leader) and Zwelakhe Sisulu (formerly head of the leftist New Nation newspaper and then of SA Broadcasting Corporation) – agreed to give themselves R35 million each in personal bonuses for good performance. That this covered the period of the massive share drop was extraordinary cheek, and all fingers pointed to Sandler (and his influence over Motlana). Forced to recant by a bolshie board of directors (mainly led by white-controlled financial institutions), the disgraced Sandler and mortified Motlana were forced into early retirement (taking more than R50 million each as parting gifts when they traded in their shares). Earlier in 1999, Ramaphosa had been forced out of Nail by his partners and went to a banking-based conglomerate, after turning down the forthcoming but ill-fated 'pay day' due to substantial disputes over company strategy (his old adversary Mbeki publicly denied having anything to do with the firing – which, though probably true, was nevertheless revealing).

In addition, smaller-scale reversions of leftists to black capitalist disempowerment included the shocking political investment – for not much actual money could have been involved – by Moses Mayekiso, representing the SA National Civic Organisation's impoverished investment company Sanco Holdings, in the Biwater

Corporation bid to privatise the water supply in the city of Nelspruit. (The British firm Biwater, on whose board of directors Margaret Thatcher sat, was accused by South African and international trade unions of massive corruption and mismanagement in its other international operations, and the company replied with unsuccessful libel lawsuits.)

Trade union investment funds were also poorly conceptualised, with high-profile ex-socialist unionists Marcel Golding and Johnny Copelyn (another white man nicely empowered by BEE) getting involved in easy money casinos, cellphone and television deals – but also realising that by 1999 they had added no value to investments like Pepsi, information technology and financial services. Their only real value was fronting for massive mineworker and clothing worker pension funds (for which they paid themselves generous individual finder fees, quickly becoming multi-millionaires). But in television, for instance, the Golding-Copelyn investment company (Hoskens) pushed a harder line on commer-cialisation (hence further Americanising South African culture), and their other BEE partners quit in a huff.

The privatisation of state transport services was another example where trade union bureaucrats dabbling in investment vehicles undermined their own workers, for favouritism by Transnet in giving out shares to the SA Railworkers and Harbour Workers Union apparently softened up the union so much that the parastatal's managing director, Saki Makazoma, felt sufficiently confident to announce the firing of 37,000 workers in mid-1999 as commercialisation and privatisation stepped up pace. A similar embarrassment had befallen the first major trade union foray into BEE, when the mineworkers' fund invested in five mines that were subsequently unveiled as lemons (though angry retrenched workers disagreed), leaving union president James Motlatsi only one other way to embrace BEE: controversially joining the board of Anglo American Corporation. Finally, Cosatu's federation empowerment fund (Kopano ke Maatla) had to pull out shamefacedly of the R100 million privatisation of Aventura Resorts – after claiming to dubious members they aimed to turn the kitsch Afrikaner retreats into working-class recreational settings – because their Malaysian partner (Samsudin again) was wiped out by Khumalo and the 1997–98 Asian economic crisis. But business failure was not a monopoly of ex-leftists, as 1999 listings and fundraising by holding companies Brimstone, Women's Investment Portfolio, Sekunjalo, Pamodzi all fared miserably and BEE became widely ridiculed.

Overall, the conditions for BEE during the 1990s compared rather unfavourably, to put it mildly, with what advocates of Afrikaans economic empowerment a half-century earlier encountered: vibrant macroeconomic growth (not the 1990s depression followed by fragile growth and over-traded markets); high barriers against international competition (not excessive late and post-apartheid trade liberalisation); relative competitiveness in infant industries (not the English–Afrikaans monopolisation encountered by contemporary black firms); ethnic buying loyalty (not the suffocating marketing of contemporary global brandnames and the stillborn 'buy-black' campaign); the power and patronage potential of a newly acquired state and ambitious politicians (not the relative shrinkage and frightened withering from market interventions practiced by ANC leaders); the relatively low price of stock market shares (not the highest price/earnings ratios ever); and a low real rate of interest (not the highest in the country's history) for borrowing to purchase shares or make productive investments.

In short, aspirant elites who decided to join the system rather than fight found a perpetually stagnant economy, an increasingly neoliberal state with less reach and ambition than at any other time in living memory, the highest priced stock market shares and the highest real interest rates in the country's history. Frantz Fanon wrote about this dilemma three decades earlier: 'In its beginnings, the national bourgeoisie of the colonial country identifies itself with the decadence of the bourgeoisie of the West. We need not think that it is jumping ahead; it is in fact beginning at the end. It is already senile before it has come to know the petualance, the fearlessness, or the will to succeed of youth.' Thus by mid-1999, a worried *Financial Mail* editorialised (with its front-page headline, 'Mbeki Wins as ... Empowerment Fails'), 'The model is flawed. Some individuals are wealthier, but few jobs have been created. Where there should be new productive capacity, there is massive debt. And at stake is not merely the fortunes of a few companies, but the very legitimacy of the capitalist system.'[61]

COMPARATIVE DISADVANTAGES

Why, then, could South African manufacturers not compete? Some economists claimed that protectionism within the rest of the South African economy generated a bias against exports (due to higher materials prices), yet a World Bank report observed that in comparison to 31 other developing countries, a variety of exemptions and special arrangements within the South African tariff structure resulted in the lowest 'effective tariff take' of all the countries.[62] In 1992, the World Economic Forum and the International Management Institute (both based in Switzerland) studied the economic competitiveness of 22 industrialised and 14 'newly industrialised economies' and ranked South Africa 29th overall. Amongst the 14 countries in the latter category, the sectors where South Africa showed a comparative advantage were finance (ranked fourth) and science and technology (fifth), neither of which could claim much contact with the majority of the South African population. With respect to education, equal opportunity in jobs, and 'worker motivation', South Africa was worst of all.[63]

With the onset of GATT, South Africa's international competitiveness continued to degenerate, as the country perennially scored in the bottom 10 per cent of more than 50 countries surveyed. With tariffs scheduled to fall by 36 per cent due to GATT, hence providing relatively lower-cost imports, the differential effects would exacerbate the country's unevenness. According to a report by the conservative parastatal Industrial Development Corporation, GATT 'would benefit the rich the most'.[64] Even agriculture would take a knock, for GATT had rejected Pretoria's initial submission in September 1993 on the grounds that maize, wheat and meat are still too shielded from cheaper imports. A second GATT submission two months later bombed out due to still excessive clothing and textile industry tariffs, which led Cape Town clothing firms to terminate hundreds more jobs immediately. Overall, according to a 1993 report by the World Bank and the OECD, GATT would cost South Africa $400 million in net annual lost trade revenues by the year 2002 (due to declining prices of exports), not including the social costs of associated unemployment and adjustment, or the lost import tariff revenues (equivalent to a 1 per cent increase in the Value Added Tax).[65]

Foreign investors understood that under such conditions, South Africa would not offer the growing market they needed. There were paradoxical experiences, in any case, for thanks to monopolistic conditions in local markets, the average US manufacturing multinational earned huge profits just before the early 1990s depression began (8.3 per cent after-tax return on investment in 1988, compared with 6.5 per cent in Latin America, 5.5 per cent in Asia and 4.9 per cent in Western Europe).[66] Nevertheless, there was no real scope for substantial additional foreign investment in the saturated local market, unless and until South Africa realised substantial growth in domestic demand.

Anti-apartheid pressure had contributed to multinational corporate disinvestment, but the dwindling of interest in South Africa had actually begun during the early 1970s when overaccumulation become increasingly evident, as total foreign direct investment (measured in 1985 rands) fell from R31 billion in 1973 to R26 billion in 1983 and R22 billion in 1992. As even Sanlam's neoliberal 'scenario planning' exercise cautioned, 'It would not be wise to overestimate the foreign investment potential.'[67]

But would political reform and economic liberalisation not turn matters around? In the wake of the 1994 election, expectations of enormous improvement went unfulfilled. Until the currency crashed in 1996, South Africa faced a persistent and worrying trade deficit. Partly this was a function of the fact that notwithstanding his close personal friendship with ANC economic policy chief Trevor Manuel, the late US Commerce Secretary Ron Brown rejected South Africa's request to be classified as a 'developing country'.[68] Partly as a result, South Africa lost preferential trade possibilities and it consistently imported far more from the US than it sold there. Similarly, the European Union used hard-sell tactics to promote what was recognised as an extremely exploitative free trade agreement with South Africa in 1999.

Officials from the Departments of Finance and of Trade and Industry had also decided to please wealthy whites by permitting a steady inflow of luxury consumer goods, and even removed an import tariff in 1996 that had previously served to dampen demand for luxury goods. And rather than building more equitable trading ties with Southern African countries, Pretoria bowed to the wishes of powerful industrialists by pushing hard for regional exports but blocking imports (for example, by refusing to renew most favoured nation trade status with Zimbabwe), in the process profoundly alienating allies who had long sheltered the ANC in exile (see Chapter 6). Meanwhile, during his 1994–96 stint as Trade and Industry Minister, Manuel pulled down the tariff walls that had kept out imports from Europe and the US far faster that the World Trade Organisation (WTO, GATT's successor) required. Hence deindustrialisation hit key sectors – including clothing, electronics and appliances – once tipped as potential export success stories.

Ironically, although ANC policy-makers bent over backwards to force South Africa into the global markets, vested interests still maintained residual clout. In 1995, pressure from Anglo American led to steel tariffs being raised high enough to justify new (highly subsidised) investments. In mid-1996 the US Trade Representative condemned South Africa not only for violating 'the spirit of the WTO', but also for lack of transparency in tendering and 'consistent misappropriation of internationally-known trademarks' (software piracy was fairly rife).

A shocking but revealing case emerged when pharmaceutical companies 'hired' (through campaign contributions) dozens of US Members of Congress and even Vice-President Al Gore to try, in 1998–99, to force the South African Health Ministry to end not only its attempt – in the 1997 Medicines Act – to import cheap anti-viral HIV/AIDS and other medicines (and license them locally in South Africa instead of relying upon the products of multinational drug companies), but South African public advocacy through the World Health Organisation. The State Department described its own (and Gore's) tactics against South African medicines sovereignty as a 'full court press' in a 1999 report. Thus, for all its talk of supporting the newly liberated country, the US was keen to teach South Africa tough lessons in international economic power.[69]

CONCLUSION: FROM ACCUMULATION CRISIS TO POLICY WHITEWASH

By the late 1980s, notwithstanding South Africa's state of semi-siege and hence some residual interest in an inward-oriented economic strategy, neoliberalism was inexorably adopted as the basis for economic policy-making, and enhanced the profitability of financiers while destroying industrial capacity. Uneven development meant that even if there was growth, it would not succeed in linking the production and consumption sectors. Industrial development remained stymied by the limits of the market (the overaccumulation problem) and by the extremely distorted productive infrastructure in the country, through which linkages and articulations between different sectors (capital goods and consumer goods, for example) were perpetually underdeveloped or bottlenecked. The route to profits, under such conditions, wound its way through financial speculation, capital flight, big but rare chunks of extremely capital-intensive investment and a desperate hope that South Africa could become internationally competitive, notwithstanding growing evidence to the contrary.

The next chapter shows how important it was for big capital to have the ANC and labour acquiesce to this accumulation project. Would it work? Retroactively in 1996, Trade and Industry Minister Alec Erwin's selective memory confirmed how easily that consent was won, at least amongst a handful of elites:

> In 1990, this was an economy heading for a major train crash. It was stagnant, shedding employment, insular and characterised by conflict. Debt was rapidly rising as was public sector employment. However the economic reform process did not start in April 1994. It began inching forward from 1992, propelled by the civil society process [i.e. demands for corporatism] outlined above, and when the ANC became virtual de facto government in the latter half of 1993 and the leader of the Government of National Unity in 1994, this reform intensified and gathered pace.[70]

This recollection, made to a *Business Day* banquet in mid-1996 (and then published in the *African Communist* as well as *Business Day*), was capped with the comment: 'For me, Gramsci's "pessimism of the intellect" allows common sense and good analysis to prevail, but it is "the optimism of the will" that generates noble efforts and successes.'

Erwin's intellect was not in the same league as Gramsci's, and, even before *Gear* became thoroughly discredited, allowed the minister optimistically to rejig reality while gratifying corporate South Africa.[71] For if not corporate profitability – which revived nicely after 1993 – other aspects of the South African transition continued to suffer major train smashes, including the currency in 1996; employment generation (negligible during the first two years of the upturn, and then actually negative by 1996); many *Reconstruction and Development Programme* promises (Chapter 3); housing construction (Chapter 4) and the like. The economy remained stagnant (in historical terms), with the peak annual growth rate just above 3 per cent before reversing into a steady slide to recession by late 1998. The formal (non-agricultural) sector continued to shed jobs at a horrifying rate. And if South Africa could no longer be described as 'insular', this was not a particularly good development for tens of thousands of retrenched manufacturing workers, or for the balance of payments. Economic conflict continued through the transition – as witnessed not only in myriad labour and community struggles, but also by Erwin's ultimately unsuccessful efforts to sell the *Gear* strategy – though as the next chapter suggests, attempts to suppress strife through social contracts were actively explored. The debt burden still rose inexorably, for consumers, corporations and government. So too, in the immediate post-apartheid era, did the numbers of public sector employees – though for someone quoting Gramsci that was surely a curious signal of an imminent train crash – and indeed without the creation of increased civil service jobs, unemployment would have been much more severe.

Erwin appeared to be living in a different South Africa entirely. Illustrating the neoliberal constraints on economic liberation that he and his colleagues were responsible for imposing, data released in the March 1997 Budget Review revealed that *Gear* was already evidently failing within months of its June 1996 launch. Economic growth in 1996 was more than 10 per cent lower than what *Gear* predicted, and fixed investment nearly 20 per cent lower. The real value of the rand fell by 16 per cent in 1996, far worse than the 8.5 per cent decline predicted in *Gear* at mid-year. The Reserve Bank's main interest rate was pushed up by 2 per cent during 1996, reaching 17 per cent by year-end, leaving an average real (after-inflation) rate of interest far higher than *Gear*'s prediction. Worst of all, 71,000 jobs were lost in 1996, a far cry from the 126,000 new jobs predicted in *Gear* in June that year. Bitter complaints from government's progressive social partners were heard, but neither Erwin nor other ANC leaders gave official recognition of the damage being done by the downshifting of macroeconomic performance. Things were to get worse, not better, in subsequent years, as the concluding chapter points out.

In short, the country's economy continued to face an accumulation crisis of serious proportions, characterised by productive sector stagnation and financial speculation, under conditions of state-led monetarist austerity and substantial capital flight, egged on by the most parasitical forces of globalisation. An example of the process by which ANC elites degenerated into promoting neoliberal economic policies which exacerbated conditions of uneven development, is offered in the next chapter.

2

Social Contract Scenarios

The argument: One of the main ways – certainly the most transparent, at a time of prolific, murky, behind-the-scenes deal-making – in which key ANC leaders took a neoliberal turn was their convergence with business representatives in endorsing a social contract capitalism which promised much; and thus if the underlying appeals for 'moderation' from both Left and Right were largely spurious, the discourse of scenario planning nevertheless reveals much about the necessary banalities of an elite transition.

SCENARIO PLUNDERING

With neoliberalism failing to deliver the goods throughout the early 1990s, it should have been easy to marshall a broad alliance within the ANC against the inherited macroeconomic policy. That the core ANC leaders held firm in favour of more neoliberalism during the mid-1990s suggests an extraordinary disjuncture with the past. Understanding this disjuncture requires delving beyond issues of 'structure' (the balance of forces in the economy and society) and into the particular way in which 'agency' (ANC leadership) was shaped.

This chapter examines one of the most important *modus operandi* – certainly the best documented and most telling of the transitional 'black boxes' that today we can peer into – for the destruction of progressive economic and social policy aspirations. As shown in subsequent chapters, prospects for a far more radical transformation of the relations of production and reproduction had been forcefully mooted by the leading organisations of poor and working-class people:

parts of the ANC and SA Communist Party, the Cosatu trade union federation and its component unions, the loose network of urban community groups known as the SA National Civic Organisation, the ANC-aligned women's movement, student and youth organisations, rural groups, a network of primary health clinics and others. By the late 1980s, these social movements and their technical supporters had generated excellent critiques of late apartheid rule and visions of thoroughgoing transformation. For neoliberal strategists, it would be crucial to distinguish conclusively such movements' concerns about sectoral policies from the broader economic policy problems that would confront the first democratic government.

In short, it was critical for status quo forces to establish an artificial distinction between the progressive micro-social policies and what came to be known, ironically, as 'sound' macroeconomic policy, in part by building a myth: the feasibility of combining a social welfare state in the developmental sphere with neoliberalism in the economic sphere. The *RDP* embodies this conceptual feat, although in practice, as shown below (in Chapter 3), the *RDP* chapter 'Meeting Basic Needs' was largely ignored, while the conservative parts of the chapter on 'Building the Economy' were amplified.[1]

But this worst of all possible outcomes was not just a function of unfavourable power relations in the wake of the *RDP*'s universal adoption by the main Government of National Unity partners in May 1994. It should become evident in this chapter that the ground for a massive basic needs crop failure was sown during the period 1990–93, and that a large part of the drought experienced in the realm of macro-economic policy – which would, by 1996, decisively rule out the implementation of *RDP* social promises – stemmed from intellectual retreat by select ANC leaders.

The point, of course, is not to focus merely on individual proclivities. Instead, this chapter addresses a critical *process* related to the macro-economic compromise that occurred inside the Democratic Movement policy-making elite as views hardened during 1992–93: the corruption of decades-old redistributive economic ambitions through a series of 'scenario planning' exercises. Aside from the brief moments of hope in 1994 when the *RDP* was drafted and adopted, the residues of this process were very much in evidence in subsequent years as well.

Focusing our review of macroeconomic development debates in this manner may help us understand not only some of the issues involved, but why progressive components of the *RDP* never gained the practical momentum that some advocates (including this author) had naively thought possible, and in particular why the macroeconomic perspective of Movement technocrats shifted so surely from ideas of radical restructuring grounded in the 1955 Freedom Charter, to state-led Keynesian managerialism (the sentiment at a 1990 ANC–Cosatu economics conference in Harare), to what became unabashed home-grown structural adjustment along neoliberal lines. For alongside the analytical failure of nerve was a political retreat, paved with consensus formation in cosy seminars sponsored by business-oriented think-tanks, of which Anglo American, Old Mutual/Nedcor and Sanlam stand out.

THE SCENARIO OF ELITE COMPROMISE

The scenario exercises revealed much through what they assumed, what they left out and how they drew the links between the status quo and a future ideal-type economy. To revisit the broader economic compromise in this manner allows us to ask explicitly, and begin to answer, some thorny questions.

How was it, in the second half of 1993, that one of the world's most militant trade unions bodies, Cosatu, endorsed the General Agreement on Tariffs and Trade in the tripartite National Economic Forum? Why did 'pacts', 'compacts', 'accords', 'social contracts' and the like occupy so much of the Democratic Movement's energy in the early 1990s? How did mediocre hucksters of neoliberalism flatter and cajole so many formerly tough-minded working-class leaders and progressive thinkers into abdicating basic principles? In short, how was it that scenario planning became the empirical basis for corporatist deal-making in the sphere of macroeconomic policy?

These deals were sometimes concrete, serving 'insider' beneficiaries and contributing to the formation of a labour aristocracy. But mainly the social contracts were conceptual in nature, serving small armies of consultants, building castles in the sky. In either form they were a pale reflection of the elite pacts which defined relations between big capital, big labour and big government in the postwar industrialised West. Indeed, under South Africa's prevailing conditions, the search for an abstract social contract based on an expression of General Will instead degenerated into a form characteristic of faltering economies on the world's semi-periphery: corporatism mixed with elements of populism, patronage politics and neoliberalism. Many progressive thinkers were, in the process, hoodwinked, while labour and social movements risked emasculation.

What do these categories mean in the New South Africa? They become clear by considering the various elite perspectives on pacting, which included purely ideological brainstorms as well as practical efforts aimed at toning down mass action strategies and tactics. Above all, the early 1990s required from South Africa's elites a special effort: they had to learn each other's basic objectives, philosophy and discourses, and they had to begin to make concessions – mainly rhetorical, but to some degree concrete – to build trust between negotiating parties with once vigorously opposed interests. Gradually, across many sectors of society, a kind of 'coerced harmony' was imposed (to borrow the phrase that the left-wing journalist Alexander Cockburn coined of the Clinton Administration's strategy for denuding US social movements).

Scenario planning brainstorms became commonplace for precisely this reason. As described by the liberal political scientists Heribert Adam and Kogila Moodley, 'All these were useful exercises in opening the apartheid mind among whites and blacks alike. Political scenarios can challenge frozen mental maps and stimulate alternative, innovative thoughts and policies for coping with apartheid's fallout.'[2]

Within the corporate world, the scenario methodology initially aimed at 'allowing senior managers to consider and evaluate the [scenario] analysis and likewise the conclusions and implications', according to Nedcor/Old Mutual's Bob Tucker, in the scenario book *Prospects for Successful Transition*,[3] by 'identifying major forces influencing the South African political economy, identifying the major uncertainties, and then structuring the findings into alternative paths of evolution'. In addition, the ascendant discipline of strategic planning and the study of isolated 'megatrends' which affect the corporate operating environment were pursued in close proximity to scenario planning.

Were such exercises merely attempts to discern the class interest of the most enlightened (or most exposed) firms, as they initially appeared? No, what was of greatest curiosity to the casual observer was the evolution of the scenario plan from corporate survival strategy to social contract parable, for here noxious social myths could be more readily born and bred. Beginning in late 1990, successive generations of scenario plans were typically brought to the public's attention first by excited rumours of the planners' arduous, behind closed doors bull sessions; then by selected leakage to the business press (often by hushed reference to the confidential, highly sensitive nature of the process); next by reference to the impressive and diverse collection of New SA elites who enthusiastically received early viewings of the scenario results; then through more presentations to sundry audiences in the corporate network; and finally through the ubiquitous video package and in print.

Who carried out this cutting-edge PR work, and why? In mega-corps which consider social engineering a logical extension of marketing, semi-charismatic individuals often pushed through an otherwise anonymous surface: Clem Sunter, Bob Tucker and Lawrence Schlemmer, respectively, from the Anglo American, Nedcor/Old Mutual and Sanlam scenario planning projects. But even without three such wise men, social blueprints would still have emerged. After Tucker's mid-1990 breakthrough into the progressive intelligentsia, it wasn't long before there was a rush to scenario planning by assorted characters and institutions of the Centre-Left.

Yet increasingly, the scenario exercises reflected the desire of the masters and carefully hand-picked participants to come up with a *deal* – rather than with good analysis. As a result, the universal characteristic of scenario planning was a failure to grapple with problems which are very hard indeed to resolve. Instead, the cliché-ridden scenarios became increasingly stylised and niche-marketed. The vocabulary levitated from low and high roads (Sunter) to encompass flights of flamingos, lame ducks and ostriches (found in the University of Western Cape *Mont Fleur Scenarios*).[4] Most scenario planners let racy metaphors overwhelm nuts-and-bolts policy calculations. In her evaluation of the first Nedcor/Old Mutual scenarios, University of Cape Town economist Nicoli Nattrass was caustic: 'The plan lacks integrity in the presentation. The road show dazzles rather than informs, sensationalises rather than analyses, and constructs false expectations by not drawing out the full implications of what is proposed.'[5] Contrast this with then ANC general secretary Cyril Ramaphosa's back-cover blurb – 'This book provides a sanguine yet unromantic glimpse into future possibilities' – and one senses the need for some sort of discourse-analytic critique of the budding literature.

CORPORATE SCENARIOS

The die was cast in the mid-1980s at 44 Main Street, Johannesburg – Anglo American Corporation headquarters – by consultant Pierre Wack, Shell Oil's Paris-based scenario 'doyen'. Wack helped Sunter launch what became a series of books on public policy from Anglo's point of view. The discipline of scenario planning matured slowly, as Sunter's book/video, *The World and South Africa in the 1980s*, offered up a novel combination of bold but wildly inaccurate predictions for global geopolitics, an apparent fear of full-blown democracy (and indeed trepidation of even mentioning the ANC), and fairly accurate projections of SA's forthcoming negotiations politics.[6] To illustrate: in 1987 Sunter left out Western Europe from the early projections because it was not to be one of the 'three main actors' of the 1990s (these being the US, Japan and Russia), and thus failed to foresee such structural cracks as the European Community currency turmoil which, ironically, revitalised the Anglo gold division (headed by Sunter) at a time, in 1993, when a mine closure wave appeared imminent. And Sunter's awe at Japanese financial fortitude in the 1980s offered no scope for understanding the 50 per cent crash in the Tokyo Stock Exchange index in 1990 and subsequent decade of stagnation. Moreover, the technological determinism which characterised Sunter's global economic analysis proved impotent in the face of more deep-rooted tendencies to stagnation. Many of Sunter's scenarios were clearly off-course.

What, then, was the real point? Was scenario planning an in-house amusement and intended primarily to shape outside public opinion? If so, SA's political future was all the more muddled for it. For what stands out is that, as late as 1987, Sunter avoided any projection or endorsement of one-person, one-vote federalism (the eventual outcome). Nevertheless, while he whinged excessively about the ill-effects of sanctions as a route to change (though it was arguably an essential component of the elite transition), Sunter's single-minded pursuit of negotiations was prescient. 'South Africa is an industrialised society, and in the heart of that society lies the model for the future', he asserted, based on his experiences with Anglo's trade unions. 'Negotiation works. Rhetoric is dropped, reality prevails and in the end the companies concerned go on producing the minerals, goods and services.'

The way Sunter expanded on this theme in an interview I conducted at the time of the 1994 election was revealing:

> In the mid-1980s there was still a political belief that one side could impose the future on the other side. I think we have been vindicated by saying it had to be negotiations. And I think we have also been vindicated by saying that the chemistry of negotiation changes people's perception in the negotiating forum. The devil's horns disappear from people as they see each other as ordinary people on the other side of the table. I just know from previous experiences that the chemistry really does change if you are sitting opposite union leaders and have a cup of tea with them and get to know them a little personally. In my case it was with Cyril Ramaphosa and Marcel Golding. You see them as reasonable guys and they've got their priorities and you've got yours. It's much easier to try and find a plausible compromise between those conflicting interests if you know the people.[7]

In Sunter's wake, the first of several aggressive attempts to forge an overarching social contract between the then National Party government, big business, the ANC, labour and organised community groups emerged from the bowels of high finance. In mid- and late 1990, three enormous institutions – Old Mutual insurance, Nedbank and the Perm building society, all closely linked through ownership and director relations – generated what Tucker (then the Perm MD) termed a 'compact'. This first, relatively clumsy effort was to marry basic needs economics with highly selective strategies of Far East newly industrialised countries. The compact not only mooted a broad transition away from authoritarianism, violence and racial segregation, but contended it should occur through conventional economic policies. When published in 1993 in Nedcor/Old Mutual's *Prospects for Successful Transition*, Tucker's scenario planners called for 'a black/white coalition government which would achieve considerable redistribution through high and sustained growth in a market-oriented economy, and which would respect the macrobalances so essential to sound economic growth'.

How did this position emerge? In the middle of 1990, Tucker assembled an eminent group of economists and political thinkers (including several from the ranks of the Democratic Movement), and spent R1.7 million of his institutions' funds on scenario planning brainstorms. The team took as its starting point rather stereotypical views expressed by 40 Nedbank executives who, as part of the scenario planning project, were interviewed for two hours each about what they wanted to see in a post-apartheid society. Onto an utterly orthodox framework, Tucker managed to weld a few progressive positions. This eclecticism permitted him to present scenario planning to groups as diverse as the cabinet, the ANC national executive, Anglo American, Cosatu's leadership and its 'Economic Trends' group, the ANC Department of Economic Planning, and the like. State President F.W. de Klerk was said to be especially keen.

Tellingly, however, presentations of *Prospects* were not made to opposing combinations of these audiences. And persuading big business of the merits of social investment taxes (such as 'prescribed asset requirements') and other deals with the ANC and Cosatu would not be an easy task. Tucker's team concluded, nevertheless, that a compact was in everyone's interests. And the time for reforms in the social structure, they concluded, was before not after the formal transition. In all these respects, South Africa would be lucky to emulate other 'successes': Colombia (1958), Venezuela (1960), Spain (1976), Turkey (1985) and Chile (1989).

The harsh reality, though, was that by the time scenario planning reached vogue status in the early 1990s, intractable township strife and the spreading slump in the manufacturing-mining-agriculture sectors appeared as insurmountable barriers to a successful social democratic transition, leaving open only the hope of forging the compact of progressive and establishment leadership. The wider society would be brought aboard only gradually.

One illustration of this failure was the manner in which Tucker dealt with racial integration, a vital component of any genuine social compact. In search of insights, the scenario team turned to a reading of the US experience of deracialisation and supposed 'underclass' formation which emphasised the (unfortunate) demise of conservative cultural values. Here, prodded by Tucker's Harvard Business School collaborator, Bruce Scott, the analysis ventured perilously close to 'blaming the victim' in classic neoconservative style. Yet Tucker sold this line of thinking to several serious Democratic Movement analysts.[8]

The argument advanced was that modernisation absorbed into US industrial society a range of minority communities – especially migrant job-seekers from the Deep South states – who failed to adjust to the demands of capitalist urban life. Without an inbred Protestant ethic (and hence impoverished because of their failure to work hard), these wretched communities became the hapless beneficiaries of liberal-driven welfarism. This, in turn, exacerbated poverty and dependence instead of eradicating it. When, from 1964, civil rights were introduced, the supposed middle-class 'role models' fled the ghettos and left behind the underclass to rot in a quagmire of crime, drugs and AIDS. There was no mention of the effects of continuing institutional racism in the US, the flight of urban manufacturing employment, the role of banks' widespread discrimination against inner-city home-buyers of all races ('red-lining'), pervasive unethical tactics of estate agents ('block-busting'), or of the way structural economic crisis destroyed other foundations of African-American communities. All of these were lessons South Africa would learn at first-hand in coming years, and indeed here it was impossible not to tease Tucker, who along with other local bankers was at that precise moment initiating red-lining in inner-city Johannesburg, ensuring its rapid metamorphosis from urban emblem of the desegregated New South Africa into the South Bronx.

On the other hand, Tucker stunned his audiences with the most ambitious housing programme yet mooted in South Africa. Through extensive new state subsidies, he suggested that 400,000 new sites could be serviced with electricity each year until at least 1995, adorned with 200,000 cheap (less than R15,000) houses and 200,000 self-help shack structures. Tucker was sensitive to criticisms that he and top Eskom management (also represented on the team) were 'talking to their own book', constructing a plan that best suited their own interests. So the Perm chief tried to link a construction job corps and other demand-side factors to a 'kick-start' for the entire economy, not just financial and landed capital. That kick-start, he argued, would be exhausted by 1994, and then the standard manu-facturing export thrust would move into gear.

Then there was the projection of an additional 200,000 low-cost houses constructed per year, but with home loans carrying 'positive real interest rates' (above the inflation rate). This latter rule epitomised the philosophy of sound 'macro-balances', a philosophy which, since the sado-monetarists took over the Reserve Bank in the late 1980s, proved thoroughly crippling to industry and to consumers. The mean-spirited object here was 'getting the government out of the housing business thus ending the difficulties arising from cost differences between subsidised government housing and that provided by the private sector'. This approach ignored the fact that without subsidies for actual housing structures, inadequate affordability prevents the vast majority of blacks from gaining access to conventional financing.

As for the 'gear-shift' into manufacturing exports proposed in *Prospects*, Tucker and his advisers simply assumed that producing labour-intensive goods for local consumption was, in the near term, a dead-end. But the export-led model was simply not convincing on its own terms. 'World scenario one' forecast, for example, that a 'credit crunch in United States and decrease in real estate prices in Japan [would] lead to credit inflation'. This *non sequitur* conflicted with another odd projection: 'Even under the least favourable conditions that we envisaged, manufactured exports would grow at a rate of about 6 per cent per year.' In other words, Tucker posited 'a pessimistic scenario driven primarily by financial crises' whose 'potential consequences' were 'severe', yet which miraculously would not impede international trade.

In the even more optimistic 'World scenario two', financial setbacks were unnoticed and global economic growth would accelerate on the basis of Japanese-inspired technological change (alone!), with trade up 10 per cent per annum. World scenario one was more likely in the short term, said Tucker, and World scenario two in the long term. 'In either case, however, the big opportunity [for South Africa] was in manufactured exports.' In reality, as noted in the previous chapter, even with the help of billions of rands in government subsidies squandered through the General Export Incentive Scheme, manufacturers themselves were deeply ambivalent about foreign markets, and the complete lack of specificity in *Prospects* as to which manufacturing sectors would successfully export was telling.

Tucker deserved credit for holding on to the basic needs kick-start argument against conventional wisdom, and *Prospects* gave joy to the progressive cause by legitimising prescribed asset requirements against financial capital (it was considered remarkable that Old Mutual allowed this through); by advocating urban land taxes 'to slow the development of shopping centres and office buildings' (again, precisely against the interests of Mutual); by criticising big business (especially the dinosaur conglomerate Barlow Rand, a Mutual subsidiary) for failing to invest in R&D; and by generally raising an alarm about SA's future, which many keen observers believed to be well founded.

Thus for some progressive technocrat-participants and audiences, the initiation into scenario planning provided a confidence boost. Tucker readily chipped a crack into the armour of smug self-satisfaction that characterised the occupants of the economy's commanding heights during the early 1990s. But as we shall see, this crack neither spread sufficiently to open significant new opportunities for progressives, to force capital into full social-contract mode, nor even to compel Old Mutual and its subsidiaries to clean up their own acts. More predictably, perhaps, Sanlam's social contract parable was – in contrast to *Prospects* – frank enough to spell out how to accomplish elite pacting without the burden of pretending to achieve a social compact in an inherently infeasible situation.

By 1993 the Afrikaner insurance-based conglomerate sponsored a scenario exercise, but unlike Tucker's crew (indeed, as a direct rebuttal), projected a sedate version of SA's political and economic future. The most painfully honest of the scenario efforts, *Platform for Investment*, was credited mainly to Sanlam, but was also erected by stockbrokers Frankel Max Pollak Vinderine (Sidney Frankel served as chair), accountants Ernst & Young and the Human Sciences Research Council (HSRC, a Pretoria parastatal which once specialised in apartheid social engineering), under the guidance of Schlemmer (former adviser to Inkatha and the National Party).[9] The *Platform*'s conservative foundation stone was this principle: 'We will not fall into the traps of alarmism or emotionally driven simplification.' Indeed, the worst nightmare was that continuing economic decline might appear to 'necessitate desperate, quick-fix policy measures'. The message was simple: calm down.

Since 'external [international] pressure on the major parties is formidable', a negotiated settlement between the ANC and National Party should have sufficient fibre to withstand further internal decay. Revolutionary agendas were powerful, 'but losing impetus and risk being sidelined'. As a result, 'fragmentation and chaos' could be avoided by the simple recognition that 'no major power faction can seriously calculate on gaining more than it will lose by attempting to eliminate opponents'.

Looking for a metaphor for the political deal, *Platform* wavered between 'stressed but sustained power-sharing' (also known as 'separate bedrooms') and 'co-operative alliance' ('separate beds'). Somewhere in the same bedroom – with capital and flexible National Party bureaucrats comfortably in bed with a few black elites, one presumed, and ANC progressives on the floor – existed the likely outcome: 'forced marriage'. But, asked *Platform*, 'Will power-sharing gain mass acceptance?' Although rank-and-file voters were 'politically moderate' and supported ANC-NP power-sharing, the answer was no, as grassroots activists in the ANC and its allies would 'react against compromises by their leaders'.

What response, then? There existed within the unemployed masses 'people of revolutionary sentiment, but these people are found among the employed and among students as well. Therefore panic measures and high risk strategies to address unemployment which are not sustainable are inappropriate.' After all, 'it is not the downtrodden, starving "down and outers" – the worms that turn – who start revolutions, but people who await a better life but then suddenly find their aspirations frustrated. Most unemployed people have depressed aspirations.' So, hinted *Platform*, just ignore them.

The ANC's moderate leaders would probably hold steady, and 'highly disruptive redistributionist strategies are unlikely'. Business and labour would discover a 'corporatist' outcome, since 'Cosatu's socialism is generally non-Marxist and moderating'. To this end the National Economic Forum 'will be as important as a political settlement. Business must be at the bargaining table. Work single-mindedly to promote the forum and to protect its influence on policies.' And promote *compradorism*:

> Once in an interim government the ANC's close association with the labour movement and with progressive NGOs will have to be loosened, allowing it to become more balanced in its approach. There is already a close working relationship between the ANC, the World Bank, the Development Bank of Southern Africa, the Consultative Business Movement and other organisations which are painstakingly pointing out the longer run costs of many redis-tributive strategies.

One may disagree with components, but the whole had a consistency that is admirable. There were, certainly, gaping flaws in *Platform's* construction; for example, of the 130 prominent interviewees, just five were Africans. And while *Platform*'s central tenet was that 'the future is not as black [*sic*] as it seems', this was a case of telling business what it wanted to hear, rather than what it needed to consider. Notwithstanding their certainty about the resilience of the forthcoming deal – a deal relatively devoid of socio-economic concessions – the *Platform* team merely rearranged the deckchairs on the SA *Titanic*. In contrast, some of the workers toiling below decks, arms chained to outmoded oars which could barely drive the increasingly sluggish slaver, expected much more than a status quo scenario from those intellectual representatives of the proletariat who were invited to drink in the captain's cabin above.

LABOUR SCENARIOS

Nattrass was right that retailing overpowered rigour in the Nedcor/Old Mutual scenarios, but in all fairness there were certain advantages to presenting SA's future in terms of catchy heuristic devices. For example, many progressive economists across the globe had taken to describing mass production/mass consumption systems as 'Fordist' and to projecting a 'post-Fordist' epoch characterised by an emphasis on product quality, variety and differentiation, speed of innovation, increased workplace democracy ('team concept', 'quality circles'), and Japanese-style production and inventory control techniques ('Just-In-Time', also a favourite of Nedcor/Old Mutual).

Inspired by a growing literature in 'flexible specialisation' and a popular academic offshoot of Marxism known as French Regulation Theory, and having established a new moniker for apartheid capitalism – racial Fordism – Cosatu's academic allies began developing scenarios for a future economic growth path ('the regime of accumulation'), characterised by very different institutions, norms and practices ('the mode of regulation'). Specifically, the arrival in 1990 of Raphael Kaplinksy of Sussex University, to co-direct Cosatu's Industrial Strategy Project (ISP), helped inaugurate post-Fordist thinking in South Africa.

There was some overlap here with Tucker's *Prospects*, which never reached the sophistication of ISP, but for which the Cosatu researchers were known to have developed great ideological fondness. For on the one hand, Kaplinsky and three local colleagues shared the post-Fordist critique of monopolistic inefficiencies and its fascination with skills upgrading – which are, no doubt, both vital components in any progressive labour strategy.[10] Kaplinsky et al.'s appraisal of corporate structure was often incisive and the overall objective laudable (if purely reformist): 'an alternative agenda in which high productivity is associated with living wages, and [which] involves the active participation of the labour force in production' (probably referring here to *planning* of production).

But, on the other hand, like Tucker and post-Fordists everywhere, the four also tended to place inordinate stock in international competitiveness (the most important ISP report summary was entitled 'Meeting the Global Challenge'). Here it is worth recording that Kaplinsky's influential early papers on post-Fordism in South Africa – 'Is and What is Post-Fordism' (*sic*) and 'A Policy Agenda for Post-Apartheid South Africa' – generated a sole (unintentionally comical) example of SA's possible comparative advantage in manufacturing exports: swimming pool filtration systems ('creepy crawlers').[11]

Was this an intelligent basis upon which to develop a trade union economic strategy? Cosatu leaders were apparently misled as they commissioned more and more work from ISP researchers, even when faced with Kaplinsky's admission (in the second paper) that 'It may seem crazy for a post-apartheid state to target the export sector in the face of the economy's present problems in meeting basic needs.' Quite right, but Kaplinsky et al. ploughed ahead anyway, with one concession after the next to the neoliberal agenda.

Thus even after several years spent studying global gluts in swimming pool filtration system (and related) markets, the ISP team recorded their agreement 'with most of the World Bank proposals for trade policy reform'. Granted, such proposals were at that stage (mid-1993) much less severe than what the Bank imposed upon the rest of Africa. Yet the shared ISP/Bank commitment to 'outward orientation' was dubious in view of the ongoing failure of SA's export-led growth strategies, not to mention SA's tough labour movement, relatively high wages (by international standards) and durable uncompetitiveness (see Chapter 1).

Simply stated, it was very hard to see how outward orientation serves labour's interests. Consider a conclusion from the 1993 study of South Africa's trade prospects by staff of the GATT: 'Export-led growth, while beneficial to the balance of payments, is unlikely to immediately affect levels of unemployment, given the capital intensity of the export sector, unless labour-intensive downstream industries can be developed.'[12] If the main beneficiaries of the late apartheid government's evolving industrial policy – the gargantuan Columbus stainless steel and Alusaf aluminium projects – were any indication of such downstreaming investment, prospects were indeed very bleak.

Worse, neither Cosatu's post-Fordist ISP economists nor the ANC offered anything that made more sense from the standpoint of export revenues.

Instead, the implications of the ISP research were not unveiled until an incident in September 1994. Over a year earlier, during National Economic Forum negotiations on GATT, an ISP researcher and then Cosatu representative Alec Erwin agreed – on behalf of tens of thousands of auto workers – to a substantial lowering of protective tariffs enjoyed by the motor industry (from 110 per cent to 85 per cent in 1994). The deal in the Motor Industry Task Force was not publicised until a year later when it took effect, at the most crucial moment in the first-ever national auto strike by the National Union of Metalworkers (Numsa). The Trade Minister, Trevor Manuel, took intense heat from Numsa general-secretary Enoch Godongwana (later Eastern Cape Economic Minister) who, in the immediate aftermath of the surprise tariff announcement (a boon to the car-makers' cost-cutting drive), was forced to wind up the strike. But Manuel angrily replied, correctly, that Erwin (then Numsa's education officer) had been party to the tariff agreement several months earlier.[13] This was news to most Numsa auto workers, reflecting how thinly through the ranks the Cosatu leaders' acquiescence to GATT had spread. Even one of the most conservative of major Cosatu affiliates, the SA Clothing and Textile Workers Union, attacked trade liberalisation with a vengeance that stunned labour-watchers (especially Manuel, who took the brunt of a Cape Town demonstration against a Malaysian trade mission in August 1994).

A different dialect of the same post-Fordist discourse was heard from a formerly hard-boiled Marxist scholar, Duncan Innes, who in his *Innes Labour Brief* (sold mainly to industrial relations executives) commented, 'A brain-elite has emerged as the new aristocracy of labour in the post-Fordist era in the more developed capitalist countries.' Concomitantly, said Innes, industrial jobs were fleeing the advanced capitalist world; 'the corresponding rise of Fordist structures in semi-peripheral countries holds further promise for South African trade unions ... A "new era" for trade unionism and industrial relations in South Africa has dawned and will take root during this decade.'[14] Characteristically, Innes was rather too glib, given the saturation of Fordist processes and products in SA; and he never grappled with the much richer ISP arguments about how to establish post-racial Fordism. But his megatrend intervention does lead us to ask further questions:

- Who was right, those (from ISP) arguing that the new era is post-Fordist and thus open to the dangers and inducements of radical restructuring along ISP lines; or those (like Innes) arguing for a revival of South Africa as a semi-peripheral Fordist producer where growth stems from changes mainly in the sphere of industrial relations?
- Was there any use at all in such heuristic devices if workers were left with such basic interpretive differences and such dismal strategic options?
- Would workers not have been better served by questioning both international capitalist Fordism and international capitalist post-Fordism, in favour of international labour solidarity and sub-regional economic self-reliance?

Indeed, this latter option was precisely what the continent's pre-eminent economist, Samir Amin, posited in early 1993:

We have to be clear about the goals. Should it be to become a competitive exporter as rapidly as possible? I think not. Rather, it should be to achieve the changes associated with redistribution of income: more popular consumption items, greater capacity to establish better productive systems in the rural areas, to meet popular needs in housing and the like, and less wasteful consumption by the minority ... Until then, the political economy of genuine democratisation implies what one might call 'delinking', turning the economy inward to ensure that the democratisation process is thoroughgoing and not just cosmetic.[15]

Sadly, such common-sense thinking was lacking within Cosatu prior to May 1994, when many of the post-Fordists, led by Erwin and Jay Naidoo, migrated into government. Added to organised labour's generally weak response to the retrenchment massacre underway across most industrial sectors, the forces of neoliberalism had begun to blockade Amin's more humane route. But, scenario cynics asked, wasn't such disempowerment of the working class – through self-made export-led fantasies which fit nicely into corporate-liberal pipe-dreams – precisely the point of scenario planning? And didn't such intellectual pessimism quickly become labour's practice as well? Responding to the difficult structural conditions, some in Cosatu turned to concessions in industry-wide negotiations – the corporatism so pleasing to the likes of Sanlam's planners – which, in the 1980s, would have been vigorously repulsed by a more muscular and self-interested labour leadership. 'What is required', the four ISP authors concluded in 1993, 'is to identify a structured forum in which these strategic discussions can be pursued across the spectrum of industrial activity without at the same time becoming swamped in a wider agenda of class conflict.'[16]

There was the caveat, pointed out by union intellectual Jeremy Baskin in a 1993 Centre for Policy Studies paper, that local capitalists were apparently not yet ready to take the corporatist turn due to continuing inter-capitalist competition and confusion.[17] If a corporatist sentiment was to be located, it would be within the Consultative Business Movement (CBM), home to SA's most PR-conscious firms (PG Bison, Premier, Southern Life, Upjohn and Shell). And, as might be expected, scenario planning helped nourish that self-interest, according to CBM, as witnessed by the 'significant difference in perceptions between members of management who have not been exposed to a detailed micro- and macroscenario covering South Africa's economic, social and political conditions, and those who have. There is a tendency to complacency among those who have not been so exposed.'

To remedy matters CBM conducted a series of 'Role of Business in Transition' workshops in mid-1992, and the manual that resulted, *Managing Change*, offers important insights. For instance, beginning in 1985, Eskom went through a change process involving a new company, Mission, Strategy and Philosophy, scenarios and problem-solving involving half the workforce, voluntary quality circles, team bonuses, a suggestion scheme, performance-based bonuses, and the like. As *Managing Change* reports, 'Employees start questioning and making decisions in terms of their new authority. Company leadership learns that their role is now to facilitate. Autocratic rule is no longer acceptable as part of the culture.'[18]

All this certainly sounded appealing, but again, cynics – including increasing numbers of workers and trade unions in increasingly Japanised countries such as the US and Canada (notably the influential Sam Ginden of the Canadian Auto Workers) – told their Cosatu comrades that a good deal of what was going on under post-

Fordism was simple 'speed-up', with the added dimension that workers now squealed on each other. Moreover, while these measures were being developed during the late 1980s and early 1990s, Eskom cut its workforce by a third (from 66,000 to 40,000) even while three-quarters of its potential black consumers had no household electricity due to lack of connections, and while the company spewed untold volumes of poison into the environment. (Eskom's own auditors remarked on the company's failure to abide by weak internal pollution controls.)

This is not to gainsay CBM's most sincere reforms, but simply to warn that scenario planners from Cosatu who enthused about the glamorous side of post-Fordist shopfloor change may have been woefully ignorant of the brutal processes and recalcitrant attitudes elsewhere in the corporate scene.

SOCIAL DEMOCRATIC SCENARIOS

The same naivety was evident when moving from the shopfloor to the scale of macroeconomics. Even as industrial retrenchments intensified and as those predicting a date for the long-awaited economic upturn were proved wrong again and again, yet more visionary macro-scenarios emerged, now explicitly aimed at generating a social democratic compromise. The two most important were the UWC Institute for Social Development-sponsored *Mont Fleur* scenarios (run by Professor Peter le Roux and facilitated by another Shell man) and the recommendations of Nedcor/Old Mutual's 'Professional Economists Panel'.[19]

Leaving the comfort of pedestrian clichés, le Roux and his *Mont Fleur* team – including influential ANC leaders Trevor Manuel and Tito Mboweni – took to the air with a 'Flamingo' scenario that outflew 'Icarus', the 'Ostrich' and the 'Lame Duck' in a contest rigged from the start. For those sceptical of *Mont Fleur*'s comic-book presentation, it might be said that the process was more important than the product. It was not very meaningful, in other words, that flamingos 'take off slowly, fly high and fly together' – in South Africa's case, by achieving a 'decisive political settlement' and 'good government' which 'observes macroeconomic constraints', leading to real income gains for wealthier South Africans of 1–3 per cent per year and 6–9 per cent for poorer classes 'mainly because of the increase in formal sector employment' (*sic*). Nor was full consensus very important, since over the long term 'some members of the team favoured free market-oriented policies. Other members of the team favoured more radical forms of redistribution.' The team unearthed no basic contradictions – aside from lack of political will – in this win–win scenario, and for that reason no one took the flamingos' flight-path seriously.

Instead, insiders conceded, the subtext throughout the *Mont Fleur* process was the maiming of poor Icarus, who initially soared in trying to meet vast working-class expectations but ended up aiming too high and self-destructing. Nubile observers may have gushed over the metaphorical wizardry. But what was really at issue here was the fundamental Democratic Movement tenet of 'Growth through Redistribution'. Icarus – 'the macroeconomic populist' – crashed not only against *Mont Fleur*; the first Nedcor/Old Mutual scenario scheme also labelled populism 'the worst option of all'. All the same, *Mont Fleur* as a piece of packaging (especially the video) was more insidious than any other scenario package.

Nedcor/Old Mutual's new Professional Economists Panel (PEP) was also presented via a *Weekly Mail* insert whose banner headlined screamed 'Consensus!' But what an odd consensus it must have been, considering the following IMF-style parameter: 'Neither individual proposals nor the package as a whole should result in any additional taxation or any increase in government expenditure overall.' How did PEP, which included such noted progressive intellectuals as Neva Makgetla and Devan Pillay, as well as the Free Market Foundation, accomplish euthanasia of Keynesian doctrine so easily? Maybe PEP's financier-sponsors felt the 1930s economist John Maynard Keynes (credited for saving capitalism from its worst excesses) deserved it – for his 'euthanasia of the rentiers' sloganeering – but this goes to show the particularly obnoxious role of bankers in scenario planning, in part because, in spite of their hard-nosed reputations, they can be awfully silly. Consider this 1989 forecast by Chris van Wyk – chief executive of the already scandal-ridden, decomposing Bankorp, later a member of PEP's (all-white) Drafting Committee – from an unpublished background paper used by the first Nedcor/Old Mutual scenario team:

Looking at the lean and fit condition in which South Africa is entering the 1990s, looking at the way in which we have survived the extreme economic punishment and adversity to which we have been subjected in recent years, at the vastly improved ordering of priorities and way of doing things in Government nowadays, at the prospect of peace and good relations spreading through Southern Africa, at the way in which the business sector is outlaying vast sums in new investment for future growth this year, looking also at the positive medium-term prospects for the world economy on which South Africa so closely depends, I am truly heartened.

In 1993, Chris van Wyk would have been hard put to explain to PEP colleagues the four-year-old recession; the massive government financial corruption which was being rooted out in the early 1990s; renewed post-electoral warfare in Angola (supported by diverse SA-based actors); the crash in South Africa's fixed capital investment (down to 1 per cent of GDP in net terms in 1992, from 16 per cent in the 1970s); and the sluggish world economy.

Unlike *Prospects*, there was practically no formal research undertaken during the PEP deliberations, which partly explains why the highest priority item in the PEP menu of recommendations was the free transfer of matchbox housing to existing residents. Development practitioners knew that transferring houses to present owners was not easy, in part because there were extraordinary controversies over disputed claims to housing and land in many townships.[20] PEP's market-oriented rationale for the transfer of housing proposal was to 'remove the maintenance burden from the public sector' and to place more of the financial responsibility for living in dangerous and filthy townships upon poor people.

The second PEP recommendation, an Independent Reserve Bank, was also devoid of critical analysis and reflected a desire to keep monetary policy quarantined from any democratic inputs: 'Bank officials must not fear removal from office for politically unpopular monetary policies', i.e. thwarting 'massive pressures to increase government social spending' with very high interest rates. Here PEP flatly contradicted an earlier commitment to develop 'institutions which will have the legitimacy through multiple stakeholder participation to develop economic policy more acceptable to all and thus more likely to be implemented'.

Certainly, some PEP recommendations were valuable to progressive strategists: a Freedom of Information Act, audits and codes of conduct for the civil service (but no mention of affirmative action); restructured security forces (but no immediate overall budget cut) and media (but no subsidy support to fledgling publications or community radio); and a unified industrial policy agency along the lines of Japan's MITI parastatal. But PEP's goal of an 'internationally competitive economic orientation and culture' entailed spending more on export promotion (and presumably less then on social welfare) and introducing export processing zones (whose experience elsewhere was central to heightening gender superexploitation and poverty).[21] In the wake of palpitations caused by Nedcor/Old Mutual's earlier diagnosis and the Tucker prescriptions, the PEP doctors' pre-Keynesian consensus was a real anticlimax.

Box 2.1: Unforeseen scenarios

Pierre Wack of Shell once commented: 'You can test the value of scenarios by asking two questions: 1) What did they leave out? 2) Did they lead to action?'[22]

First, then, historians of South Africa's mid-1990s chaos will no doubt chide scenario planners for, as Nattrass put it, 'not drawing out the full implications of what is proposed'. The Sanlam *Platform* shakily avoided manufacturers' own growing unease about exporting into international markets, the overextension of the financial system and the likely shake-out of yet more hundreds of thousands of jobs. Nedcor/Old Mutual's *Prospects* was a mixed bag.

No scenario really grappled with the country's traditional economic Achilles' heel: overproduction of luxury goods as a result of high import barriers and the capital-intensive technologies of multinational corporate producers. Add this to other self-destructive features of South African capitalism – massive capital flight, under-production of both machines and basic needs goods, and those speculative financial bubbles which were allowed to grow unhampered by sensible regulation – and there appeared few routes to industrial and financial restructuring short of deflation. Indeed, deflation characterised the period the scenarios were being developed, but was by no means finished. The entrance of South Africa into the world economy could easily make the early 1990s dislocations appear as a picnic.

Consider Wack's second criterion: would the South African elites' scenarios lead to action? Yes they could and should, proclaimed Robin Lee of Nedcor/Old Mutual in an unpublished background paper:

> Scenarios for firms which are as large and as important in the SA economy as the sponsors of this project have an added element of challenge. The sponsors are large enough to have an impact on alternative outcomes through their own behaviour, and conceivably through persuading others in business and/or government. The sponsoring firms are therefore actors and not just spectators or 'scenario consumers'.

But the actors were playing a different role. While in 1991 Nedcor/Old Mutual's consultant from Harvard Business School, Bruce Scott, was lambasting epidemic financial fraud as part of his critique of licentious US cultural values (somehow, he alleged, transmitted through the 1960s student and anti-war movements), he failed to draw to the attention of his audiences the fact that insider trading, stock manipulation and foreign exchange fraud were under investigation at the top ranks of Old Mutual. Between Mutual, Nedbank and the Perm, there were few institutions so wedded to the most parasitic and self-destructive tendencies of the SA economy – speculation in overvalued JSE shares and postmodern real estate, and international capital transfers. Tucker, though a true Christian liberal and clearly the most proactive establishment player, was nevertheless faced with the prospect of throwing stones from his own glass house.[23]

But the scenario planning game was not meant to challenge the norms and practices of South Africa's elites, as much as it was to deradicalise further the politicians and technocrats of the democratic movement, precisely in order to prepare them to join the elite. By mid-1993, when an election date was finally set, this task was largely complete – or as advanced as it could become without sinking participants into boredom – and the scenario planning fad finally, thankfully, petered out.[24]

THE NARROWING OF ECONOMIC POLICY DISCOURSE

What influence did all this scenario planning have on macroeconomic policy formulation, if not on the behaviour of particular sponsors

(Box 2.1)? One could point to the role of men like Manuel in Mont Fleur, attempts by Makgetla to swing the Professional Economists Panel in a more progressive direction, or the way in which complex dynamics within the trade unions and society as a whole were reduced to caricatures by opinion-makers. What is important here is that the process was remarkably successful in drawing in political elites and taming some of their once-radical technical supporters, leaving dissidents outside the net.

This was well illustrated in the way in which ANC–Cosatu policy formulation – which began at a Harare conference in 1990 – gradually but inexorably fell apart, leaving crucial debates unresolved in 1993, when dominant neoliberal forces inside and outside the state mobilised and won the most decisive battles.[25] In late 1993, contestation over ANC pronouncements on the economy represented a last gasp for progressives and coincided with arguments concerning one of the more controversial compromises of the Kempton Park Interim Constitution negotiations: independence for the Reserve Bank. Shortly after that compromise had been reached, Vella Pillay of the ANC/Democratic Movement's 'MacroEconomic Research Group' (Merg) – a collection of many dozens of left-leaning economists who published a Keynesian programme, *Making Democracy Work*, in November 1993[26] – publicly recommended a reversal of the independence decision ('combined with rules requiring monetary policy to be carried out in a medium term framework', a provision that should have appeased monetarist watchdogs).

After all, the Reserve Bank was owned by private shareholders. According to the Merg report, 'The fact that Reserve Bank independence removes it from direct control by elected bodies is one reason some of its South African advocates support independence.' But if autonomy for the gnomes is a standard neoliberal tenet, precisely such independence precipitated a debilitating currency crisis in Russia in 1993, and, more importantly, it precluded the extremely successful directed credit programmes characteristic of tightly reined East Asian central banks.

Yet Tito Mboweni of the ANC Department of Economic Planning (DEP) waited only a few hours after Pillay delivered the Oliver Tambo Memorial Lecture at Wits University on Friday night, 5 November, to rebuke the Merg recommendation. The next Monday, *Business Day* editor Jim Jones latched on to the ANC's unnecessary display of punch-drunkenness, arguing that Pillay does not rank highly in the ANC ... That the ANC's DEP unambiguously rejected Pillay's suggestion, indicates that members of the organisation who count are aware of economic policies necessary if the economy is to grow and create jobs ... Presumably Pillay realised that the tide was turning against Merg. And that prompted him to reinforce his case by reaching into the ANC's panoply of saints and claiming wholehearted but previously unpublicised support for Merg by Oliver Tambo – just as Stalin and other Soviet demagogues once did by claiming authentic insights into a dead Lenin's mind. After the ANC rebuttal we need not ascribe too much significance to Merg.

In the short term *Business Day* was wrong (though independence was confirmed in 1995 during a parliamentary debate over the final constitution). The ANC's National Executive Committee took up the issue a few days later, and the DEP decision was overturned. The ANC would seek to make the Reserve Bank 'subject to the powers of parliament', which the government promptly accepted at Kempton Park to the 'great disappointment' of the Democratic Party (the party of English-speaking capital).

It was a minor skirmish, but unveiled the trajectory of economic policy-making. The ANC DEP had begun shifting unequivocally into the neoliberal camp once Manuel took over from Max Sisulu in 1990. Sisulu then took responsibility for Merg, which later became the National Institute for Economic Policy. Given the internal power shift, at no point did the ANC's progressive economists dare venture into socialist discourse. And while at most congresses Cosatu regularly made more militant statements in favour of nationalisation and worker control of the means of production, these were watered down substantially by its leading strategists, particularly the group of post-Fordist intellectuals who were close to key decision-makers like Jay Naidoo and Erwin.

Meanwhile, the late apartheid state's econocrat agenda was finally taking on a programmatic character, which was nicely summarised in the *Normative Economic Model*[27] in early 1993, wherein the Finance Department's Professor Lombard conjured the following 'Vision': 'a process of structural adjustment in the developed market economy and a reconstruction of its less developed socio-economic framework, in particular the equitable access of all South Africans to all opportunities in the economy'. The Finance Minister, Derek Keys, explained this as 'classical supply-side with a human face'.[28]

To address SA's lack of competitiveness, *NEM* suggested some orthodox remedies: export processing zones, differential pricing of inputs for the export market, removal of import surcharges and continued export subsidies. In addition, *NEM*, perhaps fatally, over-estimated other economic inputs: anticipated increases in business confidence and investment, and prospects for ending capital flight through encouraging an investor-friendly environment.

What was left was a tired, predictable piece of homegrown structural adjustment – emblematised by *NEM*'s intemperate hostility to centralised bargaining and its call for the phasing out of exchange controls and 'innovation and deregulation in the private financial sector' – which only in the conclusion entered into the rhetorical spirit of the times: 'Finally, constructive co-operation within the so-called "golden triangle" of Labour, Enterprise and Government, is a further necessary condition for the return to prosperity along the road indicated in the model.'

But behind the scenes, even mainstream economists were worried. A University of Cape Town economist involved in *NEM*'s drafting, Terrence Moll, publicly condemned the official 24-page report as too shallow. Notwithstanding public requests by Pillay and Stephen Gelb of Merg, *NEM*'s underlying assumptions and equations were never aired.

Normative means what *should be* (as opposed to 'positive', what *is*), so it was natural to contrast the situation at the time *NEM* was built with scenario projections for 1997 (the main target year). In 1992, GDP growth was –2 per cent, employment growth was also –2 per cent, inflation was 14 per cent, and as a percentage of GDP gross private investment was 11.4 per cent, total (public and private) investment was 15.1 per cent, and government borrowing to finance consumption spending was 5.8 per cent. Within five years, *NEM* promised 4.5 per cent GDP growth, 3 per cent employment growth, just 5 per cent inflation, private investment of 15.3 per cent of GDP and total investment of 25.6 per cent of GDP. (In reality, these all missed the mark by 50 per cent or more.)

The *NEM* projections were widely recognised as fantasy. As *Finance Week* commented at the time, 'On the conclusions of the Stellenbosch Bureau of Economic Research, neither the model's scenario nor that of the IMF have any hope whatever of being achieved.' The

Stellenbosch economists 'effectively tossed the model out of the window' on the grounds that *NEM*'s 3.6 per cent 1990s GDP growth rate (3.2 per cent in the IMF forecast) was over-optimistic by a factor of 70 per cent. (Interestingly, Stellenbosch's Ben Smit made the mistake of participating in a *NEM* update just over three years later, and its reincarnation as *Gear* was even more optimistic.)

NEM was not completely spurious, for the Finance Ministry moved slightly towards the middle ground with its auto-critique of the 'functional imbalances' of apartheid, in particular siege era 'inward industrialisation' economics undergirded by protection of SA's local luxury goods producers. (The erratic Professor Lombard could claim credit for having led both sides in the inward versus outward debate.) But *NEM* cemented state thinking about the economy in a manner that became exceedingly hard to unstick.

*GEAR*ING DOWN

In mid-1996, similar mistakes were made by a new set of conservative econocrats in the Finance Ministry. *Growth, Employment and Redistribution* was also based on the Reserve Bank's apparently unaltered model, along with models of the Development Bank of Southern Africa, World Bank and Stellenbosch.[29] All were extremely orthodox, with biases that favoured neoliberal policies and that treated markets as reliable, well-functioning institutions. Finance Minister Trevor Manuel – quickly nicknamed 'Trevor Thatcher' by the *Mail and Guardian* newspaper – immediately commented that the strategy was 'non-negotiable' in its broad outlines.[30]

The models collectively predicted that if the desired policies were adopted, South Africa would reach 6 per cent sustainable growth and create 400,000 new jobs a year by the turn of the century. But both left-wing and right-wing economists questioned assumptions in the model – particularly the exchange rate, level of government revenues, willingness of workers to accept wage cuts and extremely high levels of job creation in the wake of three years of 'jobless growth'.

Gear began by labelling government spending – particularly 'consumption' expenditure on wages and services – as excessive. The overall deficit (the amount government borrows beyond what it raises in revenue) would be halved by 1999, with the social wage most likely to fall victim to cuts. Corporate and personal tax rates were also regarded as excessive, and future revenues would be enhanced through economic growth, increased efficiency in tax collection, taxation of retirement funds and higher excise tax rates for tobacco products. This meant that the potential for progressive income tax policies (workers pay lower rates and the upper and middle classes pay higher rates) would shrink. With further income taxes cuts for the rich, the Finance Ministry would face pressure to raise more money instead from Value Added Tax, a regressive tax on consumption, which leaves poorer people shouldering more of a burden for supporting government.

The Reserve Bank's control of the money supply and interest rates would continue unchanged. The Finance Ministry projected that the bank rate – which was 16 per cent in mid-1996 (10 per cent in real, after-inflation, terms) – would fall to 7 per cent in real terms within six months, to 5 per cent in 1997 and 4 per cent by 1998. But even if the projections had been accurate, 7 or 5 or 4 per cent rates were still extremely high in historical terms (in reality the true bank rate soared to nearly 15 per cent at its peak in mid-1998).

The Finance Ministry was so confident of the macroeconomic strategy's success that it stepped up liberalisation of exchange controls as applied to both foreign investors and South Africans. Foreign companies were now able to borrow locally much more easily and local institutional investors were granted much more scope to expand their international portfolios by exporting funds to foreign stock markets. Full exchange control liberalisation continued to be the Finance Ministry's objective, and the IMF's managing director, Michel Camdessus, took special pains to endorse the phased approach. Manuel continued to confirm that all remaining controls would be dismantled as soon as circumstances were favourable, notwith-standing what was sure to be a flood of money out of the country.

The Finance Ministry also anticipated the exchange rate (the value of the rand) to strengthen rapidly in the second half of 1996 and to stabilise at levels equivalent to the currencies of South Africa's main trading partners over the subsequent five years, a prediction that proved seriously flawed. Trying to offset more costly imports to some degree, the Ministry of Trade and Industry continued lowering tariffs to encourage competition from imports.

But even with cheaper imports due to trade liberalisation, the overall effect of economic dynamics would, *Gear* predicted, lead to slightly higher inflation (from around 6 per cent in June to 8 per cent by December 1996). Hence the Finance Ministry asked labour and business for support in maintaining stability of wage and price levels. Private sector employees were expected to lose 0.5 per cent of their after-inflation salary in the first year. Wage and price stability would, it was claimed, also be pursued through a broad national social agreement (although this never came anywhere close to being negotiated).

In addition, rising productivity of workers and of capital required greater labour-absorbing investment and enhanced human resource development. Compared to South Africa's competitors, local firms scored poorly, and government claimed it would consider the feasibility of applying a mandatory payroll levy in order to increase the effective investment in training. Overall, though, such strategies were often much more a matter of rhetoric than reality. *Gear* contained none of the details necessary to determine whether assumptions about the benefits of human resource development for labour productivity were realistic.

There were other provisions in the strategy aimed at enhancing domestic fixed investment. New tax incentives for new manufacturing investments were part of a broader set of supply-side measures aimed at promoting investment and stronger export competitiveness. Others included a six-year tax holiday for pre-approved projects that met job-creation and other criteria; the promotion of twelve sectoral clusters considered of high priority in industrial policy; reform of industrial finance; and special arrangements for better access to international markets. Small and medium-sized enterprises would also receive added support.

Would such policies spur investment? They didn't, because the conditions for expanding the domestic market were not in place, and indeed the rate of GDP growth slowed markedly for the next several years, moving into recession in late 1998. Labour-saving investment continued to be the rule, with 1990s multi-billion rand projects – Columbus, Alusaf, Iscor retooling, Coega – characterised as extremely capital-intensive.

Restructuring of state assets – government's pseudonym for privatisation – was a high priority, again with the objective of increasing efficiency and attracting new investment. The government–labour National Framework Agreement – won by Cosatu after a December 1995 stayaway – remained the basis for government and organised labour to air their differences. But notwithstanding the Agreement's non-operational status, in 1996, the government announced forthcoming privatisation and joint ventures in telecommunications, minerals and energy, agriculture, forestry, leisure and transport over the next nine months. The sale of six major regional radio stations had already been approved by cabinet. Concern was repeatedly expressed by workers in such industries that their wages and jobs would come under enormous pressure, while consumers who had hoped for access to cross-subsidies for increased access to electricity, telephones or recreation would be disappointed as commercial values predominated in parastatals, leading to increased price competition for the accounts of the major users and less interest in the low end of the various markets. Delaying the privatisation of Telkom slightly, for instance, Jay Naidoo attempted to retain cross-subsidies so that large phone users would subsidise small (administratively expensive) rural and township accounts, but new managers – thanks to a 30 per cent shareholding – from Texas and Malaysia fought this trend effectively.

The Finance Ministry also anticipated greater public sector investment, including better education and health services, housing, land reform and infrastructure for businesses and households. But as shown in Chapters 3–5, these investment hopes were based on the false premise that (market-oriented) policies would deliver the goods.

Gear had signalled that, in the wake of the currency crash, government would pursue a 'National Social Agreement' whose 'immediate objective' would be to ensure that 'the recent depreciation of the currency does not translate into a vicious circle of wage and price increases leading to instability in the financial markets and a decline in competitive advantage. For this reason it is important that wage and salary increases do not rise more than productivity growth.' But this was too much to ask, and an all-encompassing social contract was never seriously pursued.

Interestingly, the Finance Ministry claimed to have considered the opposite fiscal option, a more expansionary approach, but it was rejected immediately, because 'even under the most favourable circumstances, this would only give a short term boost to growth since it would reproduce the historical pattern of cyclical growth and decline'. Such a comment implied that the new strategy had outlawed the business cycle. 'More importantly', warned the Finance Ministry, 'in the present climate of instability a fiscal expansion would precipitate a balance of payments crisis.' But the strategy did not even consider other means of addressing the pressure on the country's foreign reserves, such as higher import tariffs on luxury goods, repudiating (or at least renegotiating) the apartheid debt, and tighter exchange controls (see Chapter 6).

This may have been because most of the 15 economists who devised the strategy were from institutions such as the Development Bank of Southern Africa, World Bank, Reserve Bank and Stellenbosch Bureau of Economic Research. Just one, Stephen Gelb, had solid roots in the Democratic Movement (which he severed through this consultancy); and only one black economist was said to have participated. In reality, though, the Labour Department's chief director for policy, Guy Mhone (whose name was misspelled Mahone), attended just one session of the group before quitting. But the econocrats were fortunate to have ample political cover from Erwin, particularly in the SACP, where controversy immediately arose over untenable endorsements of *Gear* by Jeremy Cronin and Philip Dexter (Box 2.2).

Yet having won what looked like a social contract on macroeconomic policy, there were still serious problems for conservative forces within the Finance Ministry and business. Big capital had shown the capacity to cajole, threaten and simply go on 'investment strike', but not to deliver the goods. Even with the lifting of further exchange controls in mid-1996 – meant to soothe foreign and local investors – capital flight intensified and the rand kept crashing, leading business leaders to call for still further, faster liberalisation. The Finance Ministry could pursue what were widely recognised by orthodox commentators as 'sound economic policies', yet it was mainly hot money that erratically flooded in and out of South Africa. And notwithstanding the arm-twisting of a few SACP intellectuals by Erwin, as workers and community residents – and women and disabled people, who were barely mentioned in the strategy – learned more (and as, Chapter 6 shows, virtually all of *Gear*'s macroeconomic targets fell far short of the model's projections), they wondered what was in it for them.

Box 2.2: Spin-control in Gear

The scenario was not rosy for big business in the wake of the 1996 currency crash. In May, an official of the International Institute of Finance – a Washington, DC banking think-tank – projected that foreign money then parked in South Africa could expect only eight months of safety. 'The three-year perspective is terrible and the five-year perspective is impossible.'

June brought relief to those worried about a pre-revolutionary situation. Nick Barnardt, an economist at BOE NatWest Securities (a major financial institution), accurately explained the politics of *Gear*: 'It is a clear choice for the market-related way of doing things and a defeat for the ANC left-wing.' At the press conference announcing *Gear*, Thabo Mbeki seemed to agree: 'Just call me a Thatcherite.'

Responding graciously, the South African Chamber of Business termed the strategy 'a major step in the right direction' and the South Africa Foundation considered it 'a creative and decisive response which speaks of courage and conviction'.

Others were more optimistic about its implications for workers, however, including even the SA Communist Party: 'The most important contribution of the strategy is its consistent endeavour to integrate different elements of policy and in particular, it provides a clear framework within which monetary and interest rate policy must work.' In reality, though, the Reconstruction and Development Office had tried earlier – in the February 1996 'National Growth and Development Strategy', which was never released for public debate (see Chapter 4) – to integrate six policy 'pillars', whereas *Gear* focused nearly entirely on one of these: macroeconomics. Left largely unstrategised in *Gear* were other earlier pillars such as social development, human resource development, transformation of the public sector, crime prevention and infrastructure investments.

As for monetary and interest rate policy, these were among the most Thatcherite elements of the entire policy; it was surprising to see the SACP taking a supportive position, particularly – given the Party's excellent track record in criticising 'neoliberalism' – with such a fundamental error of interpretation. But *Gear* opponents within the SACP – for example, the Political Education Secretariat, led by Langa Zita, Vishwas Satgar and Dale Mckinley – insisted that *Gear* was extremely dangerous.[31]

Cosatu also reacted critically to *Gear*: 'We have serious reservations over conservative fiscal policies that the document intends to implement.' After a month, Mbhazima Shilowa commented, simply, 'Something has gone terribly wrong.' Only a year later, in June 1997, did the SACP formally offer its condemnation of *Gear*, and by June 1998 Mandela and Mbeki were berating Cosatu and especially the SACP for disloyalty (notably, at the SACP congress, during another currency crisis, when the two ANC leaders were understood to be addressing the financial markets more so than the Party).[32]

CONCLUSION: THE SCENARIOS' SUCCESS IN COERCING COMPROMISE

Some significant material damage to the interests of poor and working-class people was done in all of this scenario posturing and econocrat-led pacting. With coerced harmony reaching new levels of ideological authority, social compacts became virtual prerequisites for development projects, even to the point at which subsidy applications for true community-driven housing plans were rejected for state subsidies for not having a liberal capitalist, local neo-apartheid government agency or non-governmental organisation (no matter how dubious its background) on board. The Labour Relations Act was passed a little later, with its post-Fordist insistence on workplace social contract vehicles which appeared very likely to reduce the practical power of trade unions, in the name of draining that unhealthy swamp of class conflict.

But such bandages on society's gaping political and economic wounds were not durable. The compromises were reached, while the deeper contradictions remained and, with globalisation quickening, intensified. What was most enlightening about the ensuing period, perhaps, was how little the corporatist deals seemed to matter to ordinary workers and residents, as neoliberal development strategies were cemented around them. Their endemic economic suffering, the threat of job losses due to globalisation, the housing and land hunger, the ongoing deprivations associated with life in townships and rural areas, all added up to a popular rejection of South Africa's macro-economic compromise and growing alienation.

This would be reflected in so many different forms of organic protest witnessed during the mid- and late 1990s, including land invasions, building occupations, ongoing rent and bond boycotts, urban rioting over municipal services, wildcat strikes, student demonstrations and protest ranging from the anarchic to the highly organised. Most of these eruptions were the inevitable result of successful macroeconomic compromise amongst policy elites, a compromise that could offer so little to the vast majority of South Africans. What remained for the Democratic Movement was to move away more decisively from the corporatism of policy-making into a mode of activist remobilisation, so as to resist the neoliberal agenda from a position of strength, in order one day to regroup local and global allies for a more substantive assault on macroeconomic policy. One basis for doing so was to revisit the *Reconstruction and Development Programme* and reassert the democratic, often radical features of the 'Meeting Basic Needs' chapter. As described next, however, the *RDP* lay in ruins by the time of the 1999 election.

PART II

The Ascendancy of Neoliberal Social Policy

3

Rumours, Dreams and Promises

The argument: The RDP *– contradiction-ridden as it was – did not 'fail', as conventional wisdom would have it; instead, its progressive sections simply were not adopted as government policy, and indeed were actually contradicted in large measure, beginning with the* RDP White Paper *and continuing through all the major intersectoral policy documents, as well as through most of the new government's social policies.*

CONFLICTING INTERPRETATIONS

The *RDP* became official ANC policy in January 1994 due in large part to the initiative of Cosatu (led by Jay Naidoo), supported by key figures of the SACP, the broad ANC Left and ANC-oriented social movements and NGOs – the Mass Democratic Movement (MDM). To illustrate: in a deal brokered between Nelson Mandela and Moses Mayekiso in November 1993, Sanco endorsed the ANC for the 1994 election in exchange for the integration of the Sanco housing and economic development policy into the *RDP*.[1] The final draft of the *RDP* booklet appeared in early March, and as a result of having no other articulated set of policies, the ANC unreservedly adopted the document as its most substantive set of campaign promises.

Immediately after the April 1994 election, the *RDP* took on a mythical tone, as Mandela himself – at the ANC election victory celebration on 2 May – elevated the document to a lofty status:

We have emerged as the majority party on the basis of the programme which is contained in the Reconstruction and Development book. That is going to be the cornerstone, the foundation, upon which the Government of National Unity is going to be based. I appeal to all leaders who are going to serve in this government to honour this programme.[2]

Some two years later, with the *RDP* evidently ditched in favour of neoliberal policies, the residue of those progressive forces – a group known as the 'RDP Council' which met regularly from 1994 to 1996 but which faded in 1997 – endorsed a Working Group paper entitled 'Rebuilding the MDM for a People-Driven *RDP*': 'Through the *RDP* we provided the only viable vision for change in our country. It is a vision based on meeting the needs of the impoverished majority of our population, through a people-centred, people-driven developmental process. This is a vision that our opponents do not dare to challenge openly.'[3]

Yet even if the 'people-driven' character of the *RDP*[4] was not challenged openly, it was, by all accounts, fatally undermined by timid politicians, hostile bureaucrats and unreliable private sector partners. It is useful to explore in some detail the causes and effects of the new *RDP* moniker: Rumours, Dreams and Promises. The reconstructed acronym represented the wit of Gatsha Buthelezi (whose own commitment to reconstruction, development or central government programmes was ambiguous),[5] but there was no denying that a degree of doublespeak also characterised the *RDP* base document. The policy framework was beset by enough fragmented voices, multiple identities and competing discourses to leave even postmodern analysts confounded.

Who could make sense of the following, all within a few weeks of the 1994 election?

- In his first post-election interview, Mandela remarked that the *RDP* document contained 'not a word about nationalisation' – but apparently neither he nor the interviewer, Ken Owen, had read as far as page 80, where the *RDP* cited the need for 'increasing the public sector in strategic areas through, for example, nationalisation'.[6]
- A month into his new job (June 1994), the Defence Minister, Joe Modise, advanced the extraordinary claim that Armscor had

'the capability to participate meaningfully in the *Reconstruction and Development Programme*'.[7] The next day, Housing Minister Joe Slovo announced, 'Government cannot condone squatting', possibly having mistaken the *RDP* promise of squatters' rights legislation for advocacy on behalf of the rights of upper middle-class property-owners and mining companies.[8]

- In the wake of the election, the hawkish National Party Western Cape Premier, former Law and Order Minister Hernus Kriel, and KwaZulu-Natal Inkatha Premier Frank Mdlalose, both endorsed the *RDP*. So did a variety of ministers and parliamentarians at national and provincial levels, who never actually opened the *RDP* book, much less ever considered the logistical difficulties of meeting the nation's basic needs.

- Similarly, Eskom chief executive Allan Morgan pointed out his desire to support the *RDP* in a *Mail and Guardian* interview, yet ruled out the cross-subsidisation from rich to poor customers which is explicitly recommended by the *RDP* (interviewer Reg Rumney was, predictably, silent on the discrepancy), and soon announced his intention to raise foreign loans for one third of Eskom's electrification projects, a financing route explicitly prohibited in the *RDP*.[9]

- Labour minister Tito Mboweni had already, in February 1994, 'declared triumphantly' to *The Economist* that minimum wages and nationalisation got no mention in the *RDP*, while the magazine presumed financing would occur through 'drawing on World Bank loans' (wrong on all counts).[10]

Whether blame for the early stages of mystification should be levelled at pliant politicians or gullible journalists was beside the point. So much murkiness characterised the elites' interpretation of the *RDP* that our first objective must be to identify the deeper political channels through which the ideologically motivated commentary swirled.

There are at least three ways to read the *RDP*: from Left (or 'socialist'), Centre ('corporatist') and Right ('neoliberal') perspectives – the latter two of which are summarised in Box 3.1. After we consider aspects of the *RDP* which coincide with progressive values, it is useful, on the one hand, to review the role of the *RDP* as a populist symbol, but on the other, to document its abandonment – at national and local levels, in city and countryside, and in a variety of socio-economic sectors – within the ANC government's initial term.

Box 3.1: The *RDP* of the Right and Centre

There was no denying that the *RDP* document was influenced in part by right-wing ideas, such as maintaining excessively strict limits on state expenditure generally (with a projected stagnation in the education budget in particular), the promotion of international competitiveness and the endorsement of an independent Reserve Bank insulated from democratic policy inputs.

Moreover, what was not in the *RDP* was also revealing. There was a profound failure to grapple with challenges posed by private property rights within the Constitution, especially with respect to land reform and evictions. And the complete lack of attention to monetary policy and the failure to protest the scheduled onerous repayment of the $20 billion-plus apartheid foreign debt all implied that anti-social, sado-monetarist Reserve Bank policies were acceptable. *RDP* fiscal, monetary and trade policy were all welcomed by neoliberal watchdogs. Even industrial policy was peppered with visions of post-Fordist competitiveness that neoliberals also endorsed. In sum, in key areas of economic management, conservative principles prevailed in the drafting of the *RDP*.

Yet the *RDP* was much more centrist that conservative, when all was said and done. The broad presumption was that when the market failed, as it so often did in South Africa, the state would step in both to force capital to follow a long-term rational, non-racial capitalist logic, and also to facilitate access to basic goods and services, to environmental and consumer protection, or to industrial and technological development. This was ultimately no profound challenge to the market, but rather an affirmation of its hegemonic role in the ordering of society.

Corporatism in this spirit pervaded the document. Writing in the *South African Labour Bulletin* in early 1994, the main *RDP* author, Alec Erwin, explained the approach using surprisingly orthodox, 'modernisation theory' language: 'The programme to meet basic needs will in fact open new opportunities for the private sector to take up a wide range of economic activities, and for market forces to come into play in areas where they never operated.'[11] The primary problem here was that the private sector was already playing a very substantial role in many basic needs markets (housing rental/bond payments and taxi transport were easily the two most significant, consuming more than a quarter of the average township household budget), and the result was disastrous. Indeed, it was the need to transcend the limits of the market – for example, in housing and local economic development – that led to *RDP* commitments of new state subsidies (in the case of housing, the 5 per cent of the budget promised was nearly four times late apartheid levels).

Also of concern was that the socio-economic forums in which the centrist *RDP* placed excessive faith (notwithstanding a call for their restructuring) would remain the domain of the think-tanks of capital (the Urban Foundation's early 1990s colonisation of the National Housing Forum was emblematic). Ultimately, though, it was for another reason that what would otherwise appear an ideal moment to forge social contracts was spurned by big capital: the broader crisis of capitalism, which continued through the post-1993 recovery and beyond, and worsened as the international law of value bore down on South Africa. In the process, the capitalist class lost a chance at developing an expansive 'class interest', as practically every firm fought for its own sectional interests.

LEFT DEFENCE OF THE *RDP*

Before the ink was dry on the *RDP*, leading activists of the SACP began defending the document as consistent with the longer-term socialist project. Although such a defence remained relatively superficial in public debates (and never once breached mainstream media coverage), the central argument certainly had merit. There were mutually supportive means within the *RDP* to 'decommodify' (remove from the market) and 'destratify' (make universal) basic needs goods, in addition to other radical reforms.

To begin, the words decommodification and destratification were complex and perhaps excessive as descriptions, but they represented themes that had deep roots within most of South Africa's social struggles. One SACP leader, Phil Dexter, argued that by 'gradually infusing the *RDP* with socialist ideals and practices a socialist programme for South Africa can be developed'.[12] He pointed in a concrete direction – 'We need to find ways to ensure alternatives to capitalist markets; for example, by decommodifying certain resources and services' – and he promoted 'communal access to economic resources. Housing, for instance, could be provided through associations, and be offered as non-sellable property rather than rented or privately-owned units.'

As observed in the next chapter, the *RDP* specified precisely this: 'Mechanisms (such as time limits on resale, or compulsory repayment of subsidies upon transfer of property) must be introduced to prevent speculation and downward raiding.' Indeed, such a decommodifica-tion process was viewed by socialist housing experts as a necessary component not only of a new mode of production, but of even a social democratic-style solution to the low-income housing crisis.[13]

Joining Dexter, SACP intellectual Jeremy Cronin also advanced an embryonic appeal for 'recasting our theoretical approach [to] help us to understand how we should engage, *as socialists*, in the *RDP*'.[14] Such recasting Cronin also attributed to Langa Zita, who regularly insisted on imposing 'a working-class political economy upon the political economy of capital'. As Cronin pointed out, Marx referred to co-operatives and the Ten Hours' Bill to shorten the length of the working day in such terms. Likewise, the leader of the National Union of Metalworkers – and later a quite conservative Eastern Cape provincial Finance Minister – Enoch Godongwana argued that industrial 'restructuring' must be 'informed by a socialist perspective characterised by working-class politics and democratic practice and accountability of leadership'.[15]

Such was the character of debates over what sorts of 'structural reforms' – to borrow from John Saul's useful contribution to the debate (in his book *Recolonization and Resistance in Southern Africa*) – were appropriate. Naturally, every reform to these ends merits analysis on its own terms, in order to gauge the impact of the specific demand and struggle on the workings of the capitalist system, as well as to forge alliances and develop campaigns with such knowledge and to put this in the context of the struggle for new relations of production more generally. There were what could also be considered socialist reforms embedded within the *RDP*.

For example, progressives initially took satisfaction from the *RDP*'s central commitment to meet the basic needs of all South Africans. In nearly every sector, some of the best technical experts of the ANC and Democratic Movement debated the merits of detailed *RDP* policy directives. In most cases the more visionary, ambitious arguments about how to meet basic needs won the day. The five-year targets were quite feasible: a million new low-cost houses available to even the poorest South Africans, electrification of 2.5 million houses, hundreds of thousands of new jobs, redistribution of 30 per cent of good agricultural land, clean water and sanitation for all, a cleaner environment, full reproductive rights for women, universal primary health care and social welfare, a massive educational initiative, and more.

The motor force behind such expansive – but feasible, none the less – promises was the legacy of concrete struggles which were waged over several decades to win basic needs demands. Progressives also recognised that such struggles could never relax, and for this reason the *RDP* also gave high priority to maintaining the fighting capacity of civil society. Here, Cronin's own role in the *RDP* was substantial, and his contributions to the 'Democratising State and Society' chapter included assuring mass organisations would gain increased access to resources. The *RDP* promised:

> Social movements and Community-Based Organisations are a major asset in the effort to democratise and develop our society. Attention must be given to enhancing the capacity of such formations to adapt to partially changed roles. Attention must also be given to extending social-movement and CBO structures into areas and sectors where they are weak or non-existent.[16]

Second, the Left could build upon several specific foundations which might one day form the basis for deeper socio-economic transformation. These included a new Housing Bank to blend state subsidies with workers' pension funds (protected against repayment risk) so as to ensure loans were affordable (in addition to permitting the blended subsidies to be 'socialised' through social housing mechanisms); a call to change (by law) the directors of the major mutually-owned insurance companies, Old Mutual and Sanlam; the decisive commitment to reproductive rights (the *RDP* was generally very strong in pointing out women's existing oppression, and fair-to-middling on proposed solutions); potential anti-trust attacks on corporate power; and other challenges to the commanding heights of capitalism, racism and patriarchy.

And the Left could relax, ever so slightly, that the World Bank (the maximum enemy of the progressive *RDP*) would be kept at bay, at least with regard to lending (see Chapter 5). In areas where social policy did not directly contribute to foreign exchange earnings – such as infrastructure, housing, health, welfare, education, land reform and the like – the *RDP* prohibited foreign loans.

Finally, progressives looked forward to a strong but slim state which would continually empower civil society through not only capacity-building but also opportunities to input into major decisions. In the *RDP* chapter on 'Democratising State and Society', that over-used phrase 'deepening democracy' took on more substantive content through explicit endorsement of direct democracy ('people-driven development,' 'community control,' etc.). The *RDP*'s discussion of bourgeois democracy, in which a semi-representative parliamentary system speaks (and acts and controls) in the name of the people, paled in significance.

But that all such talk might contribute to a vapid populist ideology (Box 3.2) was not sufficiently recognised. Nor was it sufficiently understood that the *RDP* mandate would be rapidly replaced by sectoral deals and ministerial patronage networks, or that a series of train-wrecks would pulverise progressive aspirations.

Box 3.2: Populist developmentalism

Any hope for hegemonising a progressive reading of the *RDP* was very quickly snuffed. 'Reconstruction and development' soon became code words for patriotism, as society's traditional economic elite (egged on by the ANC's *comprador* class) won back the ability to demarcate the national project. The charade of exalting the *RDP* while doing precisely the opposite of what it instructed became increasingly popular within government too.

All of this compels us to interpret the usage of the words reconstruction and development with a high degree of scepticism. Here, progressive exiles from nationalist regimes north of the Limpopo had much to contribute, as periodic victims of a populist-developmentalist ideology against which the Left – with its enthusiasm for the occasional wildcat strike or land invasion – becomes as much an enemy as are status quo forces of neocolonialism.

Under such conditions the practical arguments mobilised by the state or development agencies to justify particular interventions – the 'development discourse', in short – could be contrasted with the conditions and processes that in reality determine access to goods and services at grassroots level. Academic analysis of development had taken any number of twists and turns over the previous couple of decades, but critique of development discourse was surely one of the more fruitful directions.[17]

Most case studies demonstrated how the construction of a development discourse was about the definition of socio-economic problems in such a way as to offer those in charge of the definitions the opportunity to propose 'technical' (rarely political) solutions. In turn, those solutions were often more geared to reproduction of a state's or international development agency's *bureaucracy*, and reinforcement of the economic power structure, than to addressing local issues in a sensible way.

RDP TRAIN-WRECK 1: THE *WHITE PAPER*

The MDM's lead *RDP* strategists had met frequently in early 1994 to consider how to operationalise the programme. Optimal, perhaps, would have been a combination of the *RDP* coordination function with the Ministry of State Expenditure, under the presumption that s/he who has the gold makes the rules. This was vetoed when it came time to allocate ministries in early May, and Finance captured state expenditure.

Second prize was to have the *RDP* coordinator located within the Office of the President, so as to gain from the proximity of the prestige. This was accomplished, but the new minister, Naidoo, found that notwithstanding his high-ranking (No. 6) position on the ANC parliamentary list, he still did not have the respect of his colleagues required to cross ministerial boundaries and discipline errant policy-makers.

Nor did he and Mandela necessarily think alike. A report by a *Business Day* journalist in May, following a speech by the President, is revealing: 'Mandela clearly promised a lower deficit and tried to dispel fears that the *RDP* would lead to rampant government spending. It seems the *RDP* is more a state of mind – a philosophy – rather than an actual programme. One wonders what the "comrades" on the left who helped write the *RDP* will think of the way in which it is implemented.'[18]

The comrades were less than impressed, in part because many of the new Cabinet appointments were seen to be deeply conservative. But did Naidoo himself try hard enough? This was not clear, for in June, the first responsibility he appeared to launch into wholeheartedly was translating the *RDP* into a formal *White Paper*, to be the new government's first. This presaged the first train-wreck, as Naidoo initially derailed by allocating the drafting of what was then called the *RDP Green Paper* to two technocrats (André Roux and Ishmail Momomiat) closely associated with the ANC's neoliberal wing, based at the Development Bank of Southern Africa. Heart-felt critiques by progressive Democratic Movement strategists – Cronin in particular – gave Naidoo an opportunity to revise the strategy. But there was not as much space as the minister probably needed.

For Naidoo had other constituents now: 'the markets', as they were impersonally known. His mandate from the ANC leadership – to 'send the right signals to the markets' – turned out to be a simple matter of running the newly drafted *RDP White Paper* past big capital's two leading organic intellectuals (Bobby Godsell of Anglo and Rudolf Gouws of Rand Merchant Bank) and getting good reviews from Jim Jones, Alan Fine and Greta Steyn at *Business Day*.[19] Only then did Cabinet get a look, and only minor amendments were made to the document that was released in November.[20]

What signals, precisely, were demanded by the markets in September 1994? Simply the amplification of Box 3.1: an independent Reserve Bank to continue setting ridiculously high interest rates; fiscal discipline to become more extreme; currency controls to be lifted at the earliest opportunity; an already export-biased trade policy to grow more obsequious to global corporations and to bankrupt more uncompetitive firms – through tariff cuts – than required by even the General Agreement on Tariffs and Trade; and industrial policy to 'pick the winners' and deindustrialise those sectors (like clothing, textiles and autos) which would not stand the heat of international trade. And though the markets may have been pleased, that did not solve the more durable economic problems of the day.

Perhaps predictably, more durable problems were barely mentioned, and certainly not tackled, in the *White Paper*: the vast excess capacity in many industrial sectors; insufficient consumer buying power amongst the black majority; inadequate global competitiveness (due to bad and expensive corporate management, debilitating lack of international *savoir faire*, relatively high wages compared to Third/Fourth World competitors, high costs of production due to apartheid planning, etc.); the structural bias of production towards luxury (not basic) goods and away from capital goods (machinery); inefficiencies caused by enduring racial and gender imbalances; and the drain of capital abroad or into speculative investment pools controlled by a small crew of unpatriotic financiers.

But with neoliberal signals sent and well received, the rest of the *White Paper* could begin to provide some semblance of a counter-balance. The document claimed to develop 'a policy-making methodology and outline government implementation strategies within the framework provided by the Base Document' (the original *RDP*). The danger, though, was obvious to all: the 'framework' would be kept intact, but the *RDP*'s details – especially those where the Left made a strong stand – would get lost in the process. For while the *White Paper* did not actually contradict the original *RDP*, its emphasis was on government implementation as opposed to reaffirming the original policies and programmes – aside, notably, from those in the economic sphere.

What this meant was a potentially tasty menu for governance, but considered as a whole the serving satisfied the appetite of big business for conservative economic policy, added a bit more meat to centrist bones, and saved only some rather sparing side-dishes for the Left (such as a generous chapter on civil society capacity-building). Naidoo immediately won glowing praise as a 'hard-nosed ANC pragmatist' in *The Economist*, and *Business Day* lauded the chefs: 'Minister Jay Naidoo's technocrats want to foster new, business-like attitudes towards the management of government- and state-backed projects ... The central government has realised that a business-like approach is needed at all levels of the *RDP* if the private sector is to play its willing part.'[21]

'Business-like'? According to Cosatu, 'The *RDP White Paper* will reduce the *RDP* to no more than a social net to cushion the impact of job losses and poverty.' And the National Institute for Economic Policy worried that, as a result of the *White Paper*, the original *RDP* had become 'fairly worthless'.[22]

Yet the answer was still not definitive at that stage, for Naidoo insisted that a progressive reading of the *White Paper* strategy was also possible, namely that smashing many of the most objectionable features of the apartheid state could only truly be accomplished using the variety of tools now celebrated by *Business Day* and big capital. These tools include zero-based budgeting, a restructured and rationalised civil service, new intergovernmental fiscal relations to force lower tiers of government to function more responsibly, new planning frameworks and business plans for all levels of government, Presidential Projects to highlight new priority areas, and the *RDP* Fund as a carrot to draw resources and personnel into new areas.

Even that siren-song of neoliberalism, 'fiscal discipline', could be re-engineered, Naidoo reckoned, as he warned left critics not to be

> too simplistic so as to reduce the need for fiscal discipline to a neo-liberal agenda. Fiscal discipline is an instrument – it's a tool for either pursuing a neo-liberal agenda, which is antagonistic to the interests of the majority of people, or for pursuing a radical agenda, which addresses the needs of the majority of people, and addresses growth and development as interdependent issues. It does not belong to Margaret Thatcher or to the IMF, and that is the assumption that some of our comrades are making.

There were certainly apartheid era departments and programmes worth defunding: state subsidies like Mossgas or the monies going to incompetent white farmers, defence spending and new privileges aboard the gravy train including well-publicised conspicuous consumption by Mandela and Mbeki (a first-floor elevator, English-crafted silver, etc.).

Hence the best spin that could be put on the *White Paper* was that the RDP Office was using these unfamiliar tools of governance as 'wedges' to crack open the apartheid state and as 'hammers' to panel-beat Old SA politicians and bureaucrats into shape. And indeed some progressives breathed a faint sigh of relief that the overall political objective of governance was not to pad the bureaucracy with a new petit-bourgeois class of civil servants.

On the other hand, the existing bureaucrats were already doing very well to frustrate Naidoo's roving bands of hammer-wielding technocrats. Indeed the bureaucrats caught on as quickly to lean, mean *White Paper* rhetoric as did big business to the *RDP*'s basic needs arguments, and learned how to make right noises and avoid threats to their survival.

The *White Paper* promised policy and programme delivery from government that fell far behind schedule due to bureaucratic lethargy and failure of political will – sometimes disguised as an excess of 'consultation' – as well as a second *RDP White Paper* in 1995 that in fact was never written. The orthodox economic policy promises were religiously adhered to, as discussed in Chapter 1, while the most crucial *White Paper* commitment for progressives was practically ignored:

> A vibrant and independent civil society is essential to the democratisation of our society which is envisaged by the *RDP*. Mass-based organisations will exercise essential checks and balances on the power of Government to act unilaterally, without transparency, corruptly, or inefficiently. The *RDP* envisages a social partnership and Government should therefore provide services and support to all sectors, especially organised labour, the civics, business, women's groups and the churches ... Government has a duty in terms of the *RDP* to encourage independent organisation where it does not exist, such as rural areas ... Strong consumer and environmental movements are essential in a modern industrial society and should be facilitated by Government.[23]

Attempts by the civic movement to access funds – R20 million was bandied about by Naidoo's office, in exchange for supporting Operation Masakhane (see Box 3.3) – were decisively rebuffed by the then NP Minister of Constitutional Development, Roelf Meyer, who had responsibility for local government. Meyer was the guru of elite-pacting – Cyril Ramaphosa famously pulled a hook from his finger during a fly-fishing session at a crucial stage in the negotiations[24] – but this was a highly circumscribed process, limited to several hundred leaders who participated in the constitutional negotiations.

At the provincial level, the deficit of elite-pacting required national government to delay transferring powers set out in the Interim Constitution until sufficient capacity-building had occurred within provincial portfolios, a process that took many months in most cases. But the fact that local elites were nearly entirely unschooled in fly-fishing was considered a problem, possibly – this was certainly the impression with which some of us working extensively at local level in 1993–94 were left – because the national negotiators (including some ANC leaders) were wary of grassroots democratic (hence populist and confrontational) instincts. 'Building trust' was the code phrase for justifying the highly circumscribed character of elite municipal transition.

The municipal election deal in the Interim Constitution and the Local Government Transition Act was thus designed to force together powerbrokers from white conservative and black radical camps, straitjacketed for five years into unsatisfying compromises. The deal effectively sabotaged attempts to redistribute local income, or even redevelop buffer zones (which separated races under apartheid) for low-income housing (see Box 3.4). But Meyer wanted nothing to do with the potentially militant actors in civil society who could upset the balance of power, instead giving the R20 million to Saatchi and Saatchi to run 'Masakhane' advertisements to persuade township residents to pay their municipal bills. Community organisations and NGOs were then promised millions by Naidoo through the interim Transitional National Development Trust. Though the Trust received more than R100 million from the European Union and the *RDP* Fund, it was soon the recipient of the same old complaints of inefficiency and political bias that had been levelled at the previous NGO funding clearinghouse, Kagiso Trust. In aggregate, NGOs reportedly ran a 33 per cent deficit in 1995, leading to notable shutdowns.[25]

Box 3.3: Masakhane mistake

Residents of South African townships during the 1980s and early 1990s had any number of compelling rationales – related (but not exclusive) to the legacy of undemocratic local government and the 1985 ANC campaign to 'Make the Townships Ungovernable' – for not paying the monthly bill for rental or service charges.[26] Poverty and mass unemployment were the simplest and most durable reasons – and if because the charges were not paid individual supplies were cut off, electricity or water could simply be stolen (with the help of informal electricians and plumbers) or mass action by street committees would halt eviction.

But aside from resistance politics, the waning household budget and poor quality homes and services, there were – and in many cases remained for years – other important structural contradictions that contributed to the success of the rent and service boycotts. It was not surprising if these added, in many residents' minds, to their personal justifications for ignoring Operation Masakhane:

- Apartheid spatial location and the high cost of (extremely dangerous) transport – the single largest component of the urban black household budget – meant that the average township resident paid far more of the household budget on commuting than did whites (and most new black housing developments were sited in even worse locations on the urban periphery due to the cheaper land costs).

- Not by choice, blacks historically subsidised white residents' rates, due to the fact that blacks worked and bought goods in white towns while those firms and retail outlets paid their rates to white town councils, thus generously supplementing residential rates (while black townships had only the beer hall for revenues). This reverse-Robin Hood phenomenon was well understood in the townships, and was the basis for the 'One City, One Tax Base' demand; it also justified a historic reparation for cross-subsidies to finally flow in the other direction.

- Due to the effectiveness of earlier boycotts, many local authorities simply neglected even to send township residents their accounts (published reports suggest billing rates in many large townships remained at well below 50 per cent). This changed only gradually, because although it was a high priority for the new government, billing required accurate township residents' rolls and the identification of street addresses in informal settlements – neither of which was particularly feasible.

- Those townships residents who received electricity accounts from the parastatal Eskom – which had simply left black townships powerless until the 1980s – often felt justified in boycotting, meter-tampering and hooking up power supply illegally, due to the regressive pricing (typically a 20 per cent per unit hour surcharge) associated with the pre-paid meters installed in townships (not traditionally white areas).[27]

- Schools, clinics, crèches, libraries, recreation and other publicly funded facilities were of very low quality in townships, if they existed at all, and the physical environment (air, water, hygiene, etc.) was lamentable.

- Police were far worse at combatting crime in townships – which was in any case far more extensive and violent – than in well-fortified suburbs.

- Perceptions of racial, class and gender injustices run very deep. Reports and perceptions of increasing inequality between low-income blacks and upper-income whites (and a small but potent group of upper-income blacks) contributed,

feeding a general social alienation that was entirely under-
standable considering what hell it was to live in a township.

Box 3.4: Hands and feet of the *RDP*?

The RDP Office made a terrible error when thinking through the
division of labour for implementation. For according to the *White
Paper*, 'local authorities are key institutions for delivering basic
services, extending local control, managing local economic
development, and redistributing public resources'.

Why, in reality, were most municipalities so miserable at delivery
during the first years of liberation? First, there were practically no
serious local-level deals between ANC/civic forces and the apartheid
government from 1990 to 1994. Second, the Local Government
Transition Act (LGTA) was cobbled together hurriedly in the closing
minutes of the December 1993 constitutional negotiations.[28] In
1994–95, nearly every municipality failed to meet deadlines for
achieving interim councils, largely because of residual power
maintained in the hands of Old Guard councilors and officials.

But the compromises went deeper, to the point where, in late
1993, even the Democratic Party – later to run a 1999 campaign
that attracted many of the hardest-core racists away from the
National Party and Freedom Front – was up in arms over the Act's
'racist provisions'.[29] Complaints quickly surfaced about

- the greater voting weight accorded to whites in the first local
  government election (30 per cent of municipal seats were
  granted to formerly white residential areas, on top of the
  proportion of their total vote), though this effect was reversed
  in the Western Cape (where coloured voters outnumbered
  Africans);
- the extraordinary veto power that white councilors enjoyed
  (with just a third of the local council seats, they could prevent
  passage of local budgets and town planning bills);
- the persistence of white bureaucrats at many interfaces with
  the public;
- the treatment of working-class coloured and Indian people
  as whites, thus neglecting to write off their rental arrears
  (which were often based either on limited affordability or on

the ungovernability strategy aimed at crippling local apartheid) and thereby setting the stage for extremely divisive protests in Johannesburg's southern suburbs and the East Rand in 1995;

- intensifying local budget constraints, accompanied by neoliberal cost recovery principles and municipal privatisation programmes; and
- the sometimes undemocratic process by which local candidates were chosen, which led to enormous acrimony and numerous independent candidacies (some by progressive local Sanco leaders).

For such reasons, local elections in November 1995 failed to enthuse township residents. Voter registration and turnout were less than reassuring, as no more than a third of potential voters bothered to vote. From the standpoint of mobilisation, the other real danger was that leading cadres from local ANC and SACP branches and from Sanco, Cosatu and other local organisations were tempted by salaries and benefits to move, *en masse*, from the movement into the local state. There they largely toiled in vain, highly circumscribed as a result of the constitutional compromises. Notwithstanding heroic work in many locales, the balance of forces at municipal level was stacked against progress.

Later, most local governments were targeted for closure; of 843 municipalities, fewer than half were considered financially solvent (in the Eastern Cape, only 30 out of 190 municipalities were expected to survive). But this in turn reflected another phenomenon: top-down fiscal strangulation. The core central-to-local government funding transfer required for municipalities to pay staff and subsidise low-income residents (the 'Inter-Governmental Grant') declined by 85 per cent in real terms from 1991 to 1998.

Because of fiscal strangulation, the pressure to cut water and power services became formidable. To illustrate from a not atypical Eastern Cape town, Mount Ayliffe (whose finances were overseen by a small, unelected Umtata agency), the *Daily Dispatch* (26 April 1999) reported that local citizens were up in arms in 1999 because of service cuts due to 'excessively high, disputed tariffs'. The local civic association:

called on the Umtata-based Presidential Project Team (PPT) to 'go' or to stop 'interfering' in the town ...

A memo to the town clerk, received last month, from PPT's Kayaletu Gashi ... suggested several courses of action to make the water cuts 'hurt most' for defaulting ratepayers. Gashi's memo suggested defaulters without waterborne sewerage facilities in their homes should have night-soil buckets removed from their toilets. Where septic tanks were used, the memo suggested the Transitional Local Council suspend sucking services until defaulters paid in full.

Naidoo once explained that municipalities would be the 'hands and feet of the *RDP*', to which local government advocates (like Mark Swilling) replied, 'Why can't we also have eyes, ears, a brain and a voice?' (and maybe a chequebook would help). It wasn't the local cadres' fault, of course, that they found themselves maimed by a small group of elite deal-makers in the (renamed) Department of Provincial and Local Government whose disregard for local democracy would lead to the closure of half South Africa's municipalities early in the twenty-first century.

RDP TRAIN-WRECK 2:
THE DEVELOPMENT OF URBAN AND RURAL UNDERDEVELOPMENT

There were three other major documents generated by the RDP Office that aimed to integrate government policies in the spirit of the *RDP*: the draft *Urban and Rural Development Strategies*, both gazetted in October 1995; and the stillborn *National Growth and Development Strategy* (*NGDS*) of February 1996 which followed the deputy vice-president's 'National Strategic Vision' of November 1995.[30] Despite trying to pull all government departments into some coherent form, the RDP Office was itself no liberated zone; by late 1994, World Bank staff (led by Junaid Ahmed) claimed successful penetration thanks to the invitation of a chief director (Chippy Olver) responsible for most of the department's policies. Thus three of the four authors of the urban and rural strategies were from neoliberal institutions.[31] By early 1996, as Naidoo's progressive flank (led by Neva Makgetla) attempted to make a comeback through the *NGDS*, competition emerged with the core team drawing up the Finance Department's neoliberal economic strategy (led by André Roux, who had made such a mess of the *RDP Green Paper*). The RDP Office's demise soon followed, in March 1996.

The competition over policy drafting in these three instances reflected some of the most important debates over the nature of the *RDP*. Was it a populist symbol whose details were to be ignored, or a set of policy directives to be taken seriously? Was there any reason to believe that the draft *Urban Development Strategy (UDS)* was 'underpinned by the principles of the *Reconstruction and Development Programme*', as claimed by its authors?[32] The neoliberal strategist Anne Bernstein provided a more daring appraisal:

> The overall direction and ideals contained within the document stem from a large body of work produced by the old Urban Foundation and the Private Sector Council on Urbanisation, and now carried forward by the Centre for Development and Enterprise. This is a heartening development for the private sector (which sponsored all this work) and for the country as a whole.[33]

A careful examination of this document thus made it hard to see how the *UDS* could claim to be following *RDP* principles.[34] But it was not just in the drafting of policy that the RDP Office ignored its mandate. As shown in Box 3.3, Operation Masakhane was illustrative of poor planning more generally. In early 1995, at the same time the first steps towards the *UDS* were being taken, Naidoo, Mandela and the ministries of Constitutional Development and Housing launched the doomed Masakhane, 'Let's Build Together'. The campaign was aimed at both improving services (though only R700 million was initially allocated, a drop in the bucket) and goading larger percentages of residents into paying the rent/service bills – in the process, atomising residents as consumers and deradicalising township organisations.

But it was not to be. In August 1995, Tokyo Sexwale, the leader of Gauteng (Johannesburg-Pretoria-Vaal) province, proclaimed, 'The people of Gauteng have rallied behind the call to implement the Masakhane campaign as a vital step in the reconstruction and development process.' In reality, official statistics released a month later showed that Gauteng townships from Mamelodi outside Pretoria, to Ivory Park in northern Johannesburg, to Daveyton in eastern

Johannesburg, to Sebokeng and Sharpeville in the Vaal Triangle, were all recording payment rates of less than 5 per cent.

Masakhane actually seemed to be having the opposite effect, for in most townships the millions of rands spent on publicity coincided with a 15 per cent drop in rate payments. Following a crisis meeting in January 1996, Department of Housing director-general Billy Cobbett commented, 'The campaign and the ideas behind it are correct but it needs to be politically reinvigorated. It's not just about getting people to pay for services but a social contract between government and the people in terms of rights and responsibilities on both sides.'[35] But it was evident then that Cobbett in particular had no intention of fulfilling his responsibility for delivering ANC housing campaign promises, as the next chapter documents.

No amount of multi-million rand Masakhane advertising campaigns (featuring the likes of Archbishop Desmond Tutu and former Sanco leader Moses Mayekiso) changed the material realities and the psychological aversion that many township residents had to spending declining take home pay on inferior services and rented matchbox homes. To reverse these causes would require far more serious policy and financial commitments by the government and by society at large than appeared possible in the near term. A tough first question often posed by my own township sources was this: in a middle-income country like South Africa, why should anyone pay anything to live in a typical township? Reviewing a list of reasons for the legacy and durability of rent boycotts (Box 3.3) – or merely having a close look at one of South Africa's open township sores – made it difficult to argue.

As for rural policy, the main question asked – and answered in the negative – was, would the *RDP*'s promised 30 per cent redistribution of good farmland ever occur (given that, as described in Chapter 5, the World Bank designed the willing-seller, willing-buyer policy)? (The 30 per cent figure was not unreasonable, given that the land market itself witnessed roughly 6 per cent turnover each year, even before a post-apartheid withdrawal of crony-based subsidies to white farmers and other anticipated state interventions.) Notwithstanding the rave reviews that Agriculture and Land Minister Derek Hanekom received for an unpretentious attitude and (inconsistent) fearlessness when taking on white farmers, and for his May 1996 appointment of a progressive land affairs director-general, conservative structural forces and earlier bouts of bad policy-making were overwhelming.

For example, Hanekom announced in mid-1996 that the bargain-basement price of R15 billion in state subsidies would pay for land reform over the subsequent five years. It was not clear how the figure was arrived at, because his staff reckoned that 1.7 million families required land (itself a conservative estimate). Given the standard grant of R15,000 (a figure chosen because it was equivalent to the housing subsidy) and inflation of 10 per cent each year, just over 900,000 families would be served. Indeed, Land Affairs conceded privately in some early 1996 studies that it was aiming to redistribute not 30 per cent but 6 per cent of the country's good land before the turn of the century. That too was ambitious (by a factor of more than ten), in view of the glacial speed of redistribution up until then.

This was not the only problem in Hanekom's ministry. Land restitution for victims of forced removals was far behind schedule – nearly 30,000 claims were filed by the end of 1998 but only two dozen had been resolved – due to bureaucratic inertia, and realistically would never catch up before many would-be beneficiaries gave up hope, or died. Labour tenants (sharecroppers) faced a bum deal, for many thousands were ousted in the year following the 1994 election – a new law provided for labour tenants' security of tenure only if they were living on farms beginning in July 1995 (and there were severe problems in enforcing the law, with regular reports of police siding with white farmers in illegal evictions). Farmworkers were off the map entirely, it seemed, for they were not even mentioned in the draft *Rural Development Strategy (RDS)*.[36]

And although within the Agriculture Department Hanekom found a rich source of rural credit – the Land Bank, that bastion of Afrikaner rural profligacy (and foreclosure potential, given how many white farmers were technically in default) – he also inherited a paradigmatic problem: for whatever tragic reason, agricultural credit policy was drafted by a commercial banker with conflicts of interest galore (in his own agriculture loan portfolio), Conrad Strauss of South Africa's largest and most profitable bank, the Standard.[37]

In addition to Strauss, other bankers became policy-makers under Hanekom, again assisted by Naidoo's RDP Office. The Development Bank of Southern Africa (DBSA) – which had allegedly 'transformed' itself during the late 1980s from designer of bantustans to self-styled World Bank junior partner and vanguard – managed to place its leading policy expert on the *RDS* drafting team (as final editor), along with a staffperson of the Land and Agriculture Policy Centre (itself an institution of neoliberal ideological orientation).[38] The process of editing the *RDS* emasculated the most important parts of the document – land reform, rural housing, health care – and, according to one reliable source, was done with much haste and waste merely so that the *RDS* document would match the page length of the *UDS* (they were printed back to front in the *Government Gazette*). Hence some of the major problems that arise in comparing the *RDS* with the *RDP* concern omissions: no discussion of land reform, for instance.

There were also neoliberal provisions as well as sharp deviations from (and ambiguous comments regarding) the *RDP*. For instance, the *RDS* argued that public works programmes 'must offer a fairly low wage that ensures that only the poorest benefit'; in contrast, such a philosophy was rejected in the *RDP*, which insisted instead that 'Such programmes must not abuse labour standards nor create unfair competition within sectors of the economy.' This was already a problem in practice, with reports of large construction firms firing union workers and replacing them with rural women earning R7 per day in relabelled 'community-based public works projects'.

Most disturbingly, like the *UDS*, the *RDS* continued the neoliberal tradition of rolling back basic infrastructural rights won in the *RDP* (such as access to water, sanitation and energy) by linking the scope of services provided to buyer affordability, rather than providing an acceptable level of services and charging an affordable amount. A typical paragraph, inspired by the December 1994 World Bank report on municipal infrastructure, reveals the nature of the argument:

> Affordability must be evaluated at the macro or national level, at the level of local government, and of the household. At the national level, too much investment will lead to inflation. The national government therefore requires mechanisms to manage the economy, and also to ensure affordable foreign borrowing. Central government must therefore set limits on overall investment.

A more objectionable – or vapid – formulation could hardly be imagined. First, the *RDS* failed to 'evaluate' affordability at national level (or any other level) with any degree of specificity (for example, even simply assessing the amounts of funds available in the budget). Second, raising the spectre of inflation as a deterrent to satisfying local needs – in the context of the continuing low national levels of fixed investment and the clear multiplier effects of such investment – was a red herring. Third, the reference to foreign borrowing completely refuted the *RDP*'s insistence that 'The *RDP* must use foreign debt financing only for those elements of the programme that can potentially increase our capacity for earning foreign exchange', of which basic rural infrastructural services would not qualify.

In fairness, some areas of the document were extremely strong, such as the attention to gender and occasional arguments that emphasised

> the need for rural people to set the agenda, through taking active steps to involve themselves in local decision-making through, or with, local government, and the accountability of those who draw up proposals for government spending, in service delivery and in infrastructure development, to ensure that funding is well spent through consideration of sustainability, through capacity building of local government and CBOs and through drawing up and monitoring business plans based on good information.

But this latter sentiment appeared little more than lip-service, for it was spoiled by the otherwise lukewarm attitude to organised civil society: 'There is great need for caution in assuming that local [community] structures are representative or competent.' Furthermore, the *RDS* complained, 'Some departments have also found communities demanding payment for attendance at meetings, even though the end result is supposed to be a community-owned asset such as a water system. Thus many government departments are having to learn caution and patience.'

There was an obvious disjuncture here with the *RDP*'s commitment to providing capacity-building resources so as to achieve local control of development, and the *RDS* made no effort to unravel the bureaucratic layers of government that existed between communities and funding for essential projects. Given the slow speed at which delivery occurred and the time wasted complying with social contract provisions in many government programmes, it was probably not unreasonable for communities to insist upon payment merely as an incentive for the civil servants finally to act seriously.

Nor was the institutional base of rural development well considered. The crisis in rural local government was extreme, more so than was recognised in the original *RDP*. Entrenched racism followed from the fact that the Local Government Transition Act nearly entirely neglected rural government, effectively legitimising two-tier systems in which white farmers exercised disproportionate power. In addition, high levels of tensions between local community organisations and traditional African leaders (and between traditional leaders) made headlines in 1994 and 1995. RDS proposals regarding the 'role of traditional authorities in rural development' were extremely vague, with no concrete mechanisms to resolve such tensions. The profound imperfections of rural local government were considered simply 'a reality'.

Ironically, the RDS ended with the following statement, which it should have begun with and taken seriously throughout:

> The two RDP processes that are constantly emphasised in this strategy are the need for rural people to set the agenda, through taking active steps to involve themselves in local decision-making through, or with, local government; and the accountability of those who draw up proposals for government spending, in service delivery and in infrastructure development, to ensure that funding is well spent through consideration of sustainability, through capacity building of local government and CBOs, and through drawing up and monitoring business plans, based on good information.

RDP TRAIN-WRECK 3: MARKET-DRIVEN SOCIAL POLICIES

It was now clear, in part through the UDS and RDS, that the RDP was being systematically distorted. More evidence can be found when comparing each of several hundreds of policy directives in the RDP's 157 pages with the corresponding White Papers, Green Papers, policy documents, Constitution and other relevant government statements that were put into place between mid-1994 and late 1998. Such an exercise – An RDP Policy Audit[39] – was mandated by ANC President Mbeki in 1998, when he claimed to the SACP that there had in fact been no departure from the RDP:

> At a recent meeting of the National Executive Committee of the ANC, we made the suggestion that the ANC should prepare and publish a booklet reporting on what our Government has done to implement the perspectives spelt out in the RDP. This will be done. We made this suggestion because we were confident that we have,

in fact, not departed from those perspectives. We say this without fear of contradiction that the assertion that we have abandoned the RDP is false and completely without foundation. All that any honest person needs to do is to look at the RDP document and analyse what the government has done in the short period of four years in which we have been in power.[40]

Mbeki then pointed with smug satisfaction to direct links between the *RDP* and *Gear*. Before considering these, it should be clearly understood that there were indeed several major *progressive* policy directives that were achieved – or at the least promised as a matter of government policy – during the ANC's first term (in the order they appeared in the *RDP*):

- There should be a strong commitment to affirmative action in the civil service (notwithstanding the job guarantees assured in a negotiations compromise).
- Community structures should be involved in water delivery projects (though without funding to assure project sustainability).
- There should be sliding tariff scales for water, whereby larger consumers pay more per unit than 'lifeline' (free) consumers (this occurred at national though not, typically, at local level).
- There should be universal access to telecommunications in the short term and universal service in the long term (though local phone call rates soared in price, while long-distance calls dropped, as a function of the reduced cross-subsidy which in turn made telephone access far more expensive for newly installed black consumers than it had been for poor whites).
- There should be community participation in environment policy and decision-making processes.
- There should be a strong commitment to meet basic nutritional needs (though budget cuts made this commitment hollow in many areas).
- There should be free health care at primary health care facilities, and community participation in health care (though construction of clinics was a very slow process).
- There should be reproductive rights for women.
- There should be new legislation for school governance.

- There should be a National Qualifications Framework and legislation.
- There should be transformation of publicly funded arts structures (though funds were cut).
- There should be multi-purpose community arts centres pilot projects.
- The convention on the Rights of the Child should be ratified.
- Most minerals should be taken back into formal state ownership (though compromises with mining houses made this a relatively weak measure).
- Mine safety and health should be affirmed in legislation (except, notably, relating to nuclear safety).
- Responsible tourism should be promoted.
- Workers' rights (and no lock-out clause for employers) should be affirmed in Constitution.
- Labour market policy should be reviewed.
- There should be prohibition of sexual harassment.
- International labour conventions should be ratified.
- Socio-economic rights and gender equality should be affirmed in Constitution.
- There should be limitations on property rights in Constitution.
- There should be human rights for prisoners in Constitution.
- There should be participation in policy-making by civil society.

For progressives, perhaps most notable in the list are promises kept regarding free primary health care (initially for pregnant women and children under six years of age, but in future – if provincial departments gained sufficient financial resources – for all) and reproductive rights, legislated workers' rights (such as mine safety) and the lack of a lock-out clause in the Constitution.

For conservatives, a high point of any *RDP* audit was the way in which very conservative economic policies – fiscal restraint, an independent Reserve Bank (hence inoculation from democratic inputs), trade liberalisation and co-optive labour policies were all endorsed in Chapter 4 (reflecting the Left's lost battles on these issues by late 1993) – were not only adopted but amplified. As Mbeki told the SACP gathering in 1998:

> I would like to invite the delegates to Congress to study these pre-
> scriptions contained in the RDP and inform both themselves and the

Alliance in what ways we have departed from them, and therefore replaced the *RDP* with *Gear*. In clear and straight forward language, the *RDP* identified a high deficit, a high level of borrowing and the general taxation level as, to quote the RDP again, 'part of our macro-economic problem'. ... It is because our movement as a whole understood clearly the economic challenges we face, that it refused, as it worked on the RDP, to fall victim to a subjective and populist approach to the economy and therefore insisted at various points in the RDP document that 'particular attention (must) be paid to these (macroeconomic) ratios'. Comrades also appear to have forgotten that, having noted the fiscal crisis, characterised in part by a large budget deficit, and having called for new macro-economic ratios, the RDP did not then go on to say what these ratios should be. For some strange reason, when work is then done to translate the perspective contained in the *RDP* into actual figures, this is then interpreted as a replacement of the *RDP* by *Gear*. The ANC has been very concerned by the seeming ease with which comrades within our broad movement for national liberation have levelled a charge of treachery against specifically the ANC, basing themselves on allegations that we have abandoned the *RDP*, which in reality, they cannot prove because they are false.[41]

But the charge by the Left that the ANC had abandoned the *RDP* was indeed true in most crucial areas of social policy (with the exception of health and a few others noted above). Directives that were apparently distorted, contradicted or simply ignored in subsequent government policies included the following (again, in the order they appeared in the *RDP*):

- Instead of being paid market-related wages prevailing in the construction sector (R60 per day), as promised in the *RDP*, extremely low public works payments for workers (typically amounting to below R20 per day) were linked to discrete tasks (not wages).
- The promised land redistribution target of 30 per cent within five years was scaled down dramatically (less than 1 per cent of land was redistributed), and substantial funding for land redistribution was not forthcoming.
- The promised minimum standards for housing were replaced by 'incremental' process and inadequate 'basic services', and a

strong state role in housing was negated in favour of market-driven approach (see Chapter 4).

- The promised municipal supply of 'lifeline' water (based on cross-subsidies) was rejected in favour of insistence on virtually full payment of operating and maintenance costs (plus an erratic local 'equitable share' grant that only became effective in mid-1998, and only in a few areas).
- There was a lack of commitment to promised cross-subsidisation within the electricity sector (hence the rate of rural electrification slowed to a crawl).
- Publicly owned passenger transport – mandated to increase in the *RDP* – was instead replaced by tendered contracts and permits for rail, bus and taxi operations, with privately controlled passenger transport (even the chaotic kombi-taxi sector) deemed to be 'self-regulating', at a time transportation subsidies were reduced.
- Workers' environmental rights were not addressed.
- There was a shift from state to individual responsibility for retirement resources.
- There were dramatic cuts in social assistance grants to impoverished, dependent children (in the course of broadening the programme, slowly, to all children, not just apartheid-era grant recipients).
- There was a lack of commitment to adult basic education and training.
- The special educational needs of the disabled were not aggressively addressed.
- The reception year of compulsory education was not mandatory.
- There was a reduced commitment to funding of senior secondary education.
- There remained a lack of clarity on funding for arts and culture.
- There was a focus on sports excellence rather than accessible, affordable sport and recreation.
- Youth needs were not adequately addressed by government departments.
- Children's rights and needs were not coherently addressed.
- References to nationalisation were ignored in the *RDP White Paper* and *Gear*.
- There were no subsidies available, as promised, for local economic development.

- Community/worker input on decentralisation subsidies was completely ignored.
- Conversion of defence technology to civilian use was contradicted.
- Commerce policy directives were ignored.
- There was virtually no policy on financial sector reform (non-discrimination, community-based banking, democratisation of pension funds, and combating capital flight).
- Provisions for minimum wages were subject to lengthy process.
- There were few changes in company taxes, laws and subsidies to promote workers' rights.
- Southern Africa commitments were not taken seriously.
- There was not much worker participation in public services.
- Civil society participation in parastatal governance was largely ignored.
- Provisions for the role of women in local government were also ignored.

This list includes many of the key expectations of progressives, and subsequently dashed: widescale land reform, massive employment creation through public works, housing and municipal services, enhanced social welfare, community development, shake-up of the financial sector commanding heights, Southern African integration, and youth programmes.

How to explain the dramatic deviations? Was the original *RDP* insufficiently clear in its policy directives? Did the *RDP* fail to define state-centredness and people-drivenness? Did it raise expectations, unrealistically, by virtue of its function as a populist campaign platform? Did the Base Document contain technical flaws? Conservatives answered in the affirmative to such questions, though they would have a long and arduous argument with defenders of the *RDP* from the Left.

In contrast, progressives might have posed a different set of leading problems regarding the *RDP*. Was its role always meant – by those at the helm of government – to be a nation-building signifier rather than a detailed policy guidebook? Hence, were business and right-wing political endorsements of the *RDP* a systematic hindrance, rather than a help, to realising the progressive vision? Was the role of the RDP Ministry intrinsically flawed given the lack of control of resources? Was the RDP Parliamentary Portfolio Committee similarly flawed by virtue of its symbolic rather than meaningful watchdog role? Did leading left forces within civil society – in particular, Cosatu and the Nedlac Community Constituency, which both issued policy documents in 1996 begging for a return to *RDP* values – have unrealistic expectations of their erstwhile comrades' power and inclinations in government? Did the RDP Council itself fail to coordinate the MDM around the accountability of government, instead spending excessive time and energy on the non-starter Masakhane campaign?

CONCLUSION: THE USE AND ABUSE OF DEVELOPMENT DISCOURSE

One of the biggest problems for the *Reconstruction and Development Programme*, from its outset, was that it faced the ignominy of suffocating love from newfound friends. Big business hacks thumped it like a bible, an army of yuppie and ageing consultants joined the bandwagon, while old-guard bureaucrats and sundry technocrats across government were naively given responsibility for establishing *RDP* implementing policies and programmes.

Disaster subsequently befell the *RDP*. Government failed to abide by much of the policy mandate and to deliver on most basic election promises. There was a discursive degeneration into developmental slang ('Jay-talking', as the *Mail and Guardian* meanly suggested on several occasions). There was partial disintegration of the social movements which wrote the document. And the decay of development was confirmed not only by the variety of neoliberal policy documents subsequently produced, but by the sudden, ill-considered and undebated closure of the RDP Ministry in the Office of the President in March 1996 (and the redeployment of Naidoo to what some unionists described as a political Siberia: forced to sell postal and telecommunications workers on the idea of privatisation).

But the *RDP* lived on. It lived on rhetorically, because President Mandela took the decision to close Naidoo's office on the explicit grounds that the *RDP* had become successfully embedded in the line departments. This was at best wishful thinking, as noted above. Yet the political rhetoric continued, for example in the ANC's 1999 re-election campaign *Manifesto*, which – because it lacked any detail of its own about government's second-term strategic orientation – called the *RDP* 'the only relevant detailed programme to carry SA to freedom and social justice'.[42]

It also lived on in attempts – by no means off target – by the Department of Finance (in a December 1997 *Business Day* article)[43] and by Mbeki to draw direct links between *Gear* and the *RDP*'s Chapter 4 (along the lines pointed out above). Mbeki continued to rely upon a telling elision of the government's core deviations from *RDP* Chapters 2, 3 and 5 (as well as many of the progressive aspects of Chapter 4). Moreover, while citing only those aspects of the *RDP* of the Right which the government implemented, in the process he claimed the moral high ground. At the 1998 SACP Congress, his defence of government's *RDP* record effectively equated his leftist critics, even within the ANC Alliance, to 'right-wing opposition party' pundits:

> One of the issues which the right-wing parties in our country are very fond of repeating is that our movement has abandoned the *RDP*. By this means, they hope to turn the masses of our people who voted for us in 1994 against our movement by seeking to project the notion that we have betrayed the trust that the people placed in the ANC. We must, of course, expect that these opposition parties will play this role, in their interest, as part of their strategic objective to weaken and defeat our movement to bring to a halt the process of the fundamental transformation of our country. What is however surprising is that we also find this same message about the *RDP* repeated by people who claim to represent the Left.[44]

Hearing Mbeki's description, in the same speech, of the *RDP* as 'the combat orders of our movement as we continue the struggle for the genuine liberation of our people', it is easy to be cynical about the use and abuse of developmental rhetoric.

On the other hand, realists might rebut, why should such systematic dishonesty not be expected? Mbeki's wordplay was, after all, nothing compared to the often painful fading within ANC power-circuits of potential competitors and critics from 1995 to 1999: Bantu Holomisa, Pallo Jordan, Patrick Lekota, Winnie Madikizela-Mandela, Mac Maharaj, Mathole Motshekga, Jay Naidoo, Matthews Phosa, Cyril Ramaphosa, Tokyo Sexwale, Max Sisulu. Though by no means were any consistently left-leaning (save Jordan and perhaps Sisulu, who in any case gracefully accepted redeployment to the arms manufacturer Denel), and although at least two (Lekota and

Madikizela-Mandela) were accepted back into the ANC leadership fold, Mbeki earned himself a durable level of mistrust by movement activists. The most extensive biography of Mbeki to date (by conservative *Star* reporters Adrian Hadland and Jovial Rantau) is blunt about

> an aspect of Thabo's style that has persistently caused him problems: an uncomfortable sense among colleagues and opponents alike that behind the suave facade lurks a Machiavellian and ruthless manipulator ... Holomisa said the following shortly after his expulsion from the party: 'He is a manipulator and he uses the media and manipulates to get to the top. He used [Mandela's] stature to climb the ladder to the top of the ANC leadership. He always crushes opposition as he did with me' ... As one senior ANC member has described, 'You don't know that Thabo has stabbed you in the back until you feel the blade against your sternum.'[45]

Yet in the case of the *RDP*, prior to his 1998 endorsement of its *Gear*-like phrases, Mbeki was explicit about his ambivalence regarding the 1994 campaign platform's implementation (according to Hadland and Rantao):

> A cabinet minister at the time (1994–96) recalls how the growing animosity between Thabo and Naidoo became a common feature of cabinet meetings. 'Thabo gave off strong indications that he hated Jay Naidoo,' says the minister. 'He used to refer to Jay in the most aggressive and frustrated terms. It got so aggressive at times, I couldn't believe it. But Jay was trying to coordinate all the activities of the cabinet for the *RDP* ... Jay, in the Office of the President, a minister without portfolio, this was too much for Thabo.'[46]

Mandela's successor was not to be underestimated, for in his brazen appropriation of *RDP* developmental discourse arises the warning that, as in 1980s Zimbabwe (where Robert Mugabe regularly labelled his left critics 'counter-revolutionaries'), the populist-autocratic tendency within the ANC leadership would 'talk left, act right', as the saying went.

But it was not only in the role of unifying emblem of the liberation movement's contradictory socio-economic agenda that the *RDP* would remain a useful discursive device. As we shall see in Chapter 6, the *RDP* also lived on in the unmet demands of its authors in the social movements (and in periodic critiques of particular ministers for rejecting *RDP* mandates).

Progressive forces of South African civil society and the more committed of their Alliance partners once regularly met in the RDP Council to contemplate their relative impotence, prior to that body's gradual demise during 1997. Later, however, in the early twenty-first century, can the same social forces potentially be drawn towards a much more productive campaign defending and amplifying the *RDP* of the Left? One ripe area in which such campaigning should have emerged, but did not in any organised way prior to the 1999 election, was housing policy.

4

The Housing Question

The argument: What with South Africa's formidable legacy of social struggles over urban shelter issues, more was expected of the first democratic government's housing policy, and less was delivered, than in practically any other area of social policy – largely because neoliberal assumptions and housing delivery mechanisms were adopted during the carefully managed transition process.

MATERIAL INTERESTS, IDEOLOGICAL CONFLICTS

Whether looking at housing from bottom up or top down, this is perhaps the most important component of social policy to get right.[1] The employment potential, substantial macroeconomic multipliers and relatively low import cost together mean that housing is well suited to play a central role in any progressive economic development strategy. From the standpoint of the household – particularly women caregivers – decent housing improves family health and hygiene, provides privacy and a chance to raise children, and ensures the psychological security that comes from 'tenure' (the ability to stay in a house without fear of being displaced). Finally, secure, well-integrated housing developments can enhance community and mutual aid activities within a given neighbourhood.

But housing represents a rather different set of costs and benefits to individual capitalists. As the single most substantial expense in most household budgets, it represents the main financial cost in what is often termed 'the reproduction of labour power'.[2] Housing costs in turn drive up wages higher than they would be if either substantial state-provided housing existed for workers, or some form of 'self-help' system lowered the cost of shelter (a self-built shack entails only a fraction of the carrying costs of a formal house with a bond, although as we shall see, there are social and health costs which get passed back to women and the family). In the past, industrial firms often offered housing on or near factory premises to employees at no cost, in order to directly lower such costs while at the same time assuring tighter control of the workforce; for millions of South African mineworkers, farmworkers and domestic workers, this is still the case.[3]

From this standpoint, the incentive for capital in general is to lower the costs of reproduction of labour power, which has meant a shift from grudging acceptance of major public housing programmes for workers (common when the townships were built in the mid-twentieth century) to the site-and-service model of the late 1980s. And yet the opposite incentive exists for other firms engaged in the act of supplying housing: the provision of building materials, acquisition of (and speculation on) suitable land, construction, financing and management of housing.[4] The construction industry ultimately proved weaker than the interests of capital-in-general, and particularly than the deficit hawks in the financial sector.

Indeed, as in most fields of socio-economic development in transitional South Africa, the struggle over housing boiled down to a classic conflict over resource allocation. When debates over the direction of post-apartheid housing policy began in earnest during the late 1980s, a series of housing questions emerged:

- Would the rulers of the changing society permit a substantial portion of the social surplus – particularly the government budget – to be directed into housing and related services?
- Would those resources be allocated in a non-sexist, non-racial manner which broke from old practices?
- Would housing and services be linked to the restructuring of other development programmes (health, education, childcare, urban planning, environmental protection, recreation, etc.)?
- Would a housing construction programme support macroeconomic growth and micro-socio-economic objectives?
- Would public resources be used in a manner which could maximise the contribution of funds from private financial sources?

- Would state subsidy funds be delinked from the nuclear family model of black petit-bourgeoisification which characterised late apartheid policy?
- Would they be delinked from market forces, which in turn might undergird the demands for permanent affordability and community solidarity which were the basis of so many popular struggles?
- Would hostels be transformed into family units as the inhumane migrant labour system was phased out?

The answer to all these questions – not only during the early 1990s transition but in the years immediately following the 1994 election – was no. To understand why, and to establish the basis for a different approach in future, requires us to delve deeply into the policy-making process, or more precisely, into the construction of policy discourses which evolved from the late 1980s through the early 1990s.

No was a surprising answer, for no one defended the existing quagmire of state and private corruption, incompetence, collapse of public services, ingrained official racial and gender discrimination, and market failure (such as 'red-lining', 'negative equity' and the utter inability of low-income to enter the formal housing market). Indeed, these state and market failures were often met by fierce community resistance. Yet a fundamental break with past housing policy appeared impossible under conditions set by multi-'stakeholder' negotiations (the National Housing Forum), recalcitrant bureaucrats, the spectre of neoliberal fiscal constraints and, ultimately, a lack of political will and imagination. Not even the appointment of Housing Minister Joe Slovo in May 1994 (who served until his death in January 1995), concurrently the chair of the SA Communist Party, made a substantive difference in many of the key areas.

The missed opportunities here were substantial, given that the prospects for an alternative economic development model based on a housing 'kick-start' were well recognised by progressives (and had been used, in previous eras, to great effect in developing countries with such divergent macroeconomic strategies as Singapore and Colombia). The moral imperative was also clear, as there emerged realistic estimates of 3 million homeless families in South Africa's cities and countryside (and more conservative figures such as 1.3 million, cited by Slovo in his inaugural parliamentary speech, a figure which ignored the need to provide replacement housing for hundreds of thousands of inhumane hostel beds, for urban shacks that were on deeded properties, and for rural huts).[5]

In any humane society this degree of backlog would have generated an immediate consensus for a massive housing construction programme, subsidised by the state, tapping private financial resources, using the dramatic overcapacity of the building materials and construction industries, and with the participation – and ultimately under the control – of community-based organisations. In the New South Africa, however, it was not to be.

The profound failure of transition politics in the housing field can mainly be traced to very hard ideological positions taken by late apartheid state agencies and liberal capitalists, exacerbated by inadequate and inconsistent ANC staff attention, and cemented through the 'coerced harmony' of the kind of bogus social contract formation described in Chapter 2. By the time the ANC took power, there was a bizarre consensus in place in the housing policy-making field which recognised all players – no matter their track records, their intentions, or their relation to the democratic forces – as equally viable, credible and necessary components of the grand pact.

This is not to say that the democratic forces did not initially adopt (and maintain) equally hard principles: the traditional Freedom Charter promise that decent, affordable housing is a human right, a promise translated into a tough-talking 1994 *Reconstruction and Development Programme* housing pledge and even into a hard-fought constitutional 'right to housing' provision in the Bill of Rights, adopted in 1996. But it is then to acknowledge the gradual demise of those principles as processes of coercive harmony set in.

We can set the stage for understanding the elite transition in housing policy in this chapter by considering the old regime's 'deracialised urbanisation' strategy gradually to evolve apartheid racial segregation into class-based segregation. As we shall see, this was done in a manner that also invoked a new political strategy: a form of corporatism based on the definitive mediation of the market.

The agents most responsible for introducing the late apartheid regime's neoliberal housing policy were a group of academics, advocates and deal-makers located within and around the Urban Foundation (UF), the privately funded think-tank and housing developer set up by the Anglo American Corporation in the immediate wake of the 1976 Soweto riots. The UF was untiring first in its search for minor palliatives for apartheid – for example, drafting the despised

Black Local Authorities Act of 1983, and always falling just short of endorsing one-person, one-vote during the 1980s – and then as lead stormtrooper for neoliberal social policy from the late 1980s until its closure in 1995.

Thus we begin the chapter by considering how the UF was indirectly responsible for the plight of community organisations which found their hands tied by the diminishing options for solving concrete problems. At the same time, Democratic Movement politicians were hoodwinked by Establishment promises during this turbulent period of 'paradigm shift', much like the broader social contract elite-pacting exercises described earlier.

The UF's success was based in some measure upon an earlier sell-out by a coterie of formerly radical scholars who drifted rapidly into consultancy mode. Intellectual struggles are rather minor in the whole scheme of things, but they do occasionally foretell trends in broader societal discourses, as academics scramble to claim relevance and legitimacy in the sphere of popular politics. For that reason it is also interesting to note the ideological journey travelled by some of South Africa's most respected urban scholars, who played a crucial role in what became a non-stop barrage of conservative policy argumentation and politicking. This attack found progressives either wilting under the pressure or falling into oblivion outside the harmony model.

The neoliberal barrage continued from the early days of UF site-and-service policy (adopted by the Independent Development Trust in 1990); to a series of World Bank studies beginning in 1991 which mainly served to highlight the distance between Washington, DC and Johannesburg; to the econocrat-influenced De Loor Task Force on housing in 1992; to the demands of banks to recoup their questionable township investments in 1993; to the meanderings of the National Housing Forum (practically a subsidiary of the UF) in 1993–94; to the status quo policies of both new and residual bureaucrats who appeared to wield so much power over transitional housing policy in 1994; to the mild amendments made to a failing policy in 1995–98, amendments which (until Cosatu finally intervened in the October 1998 Jobs Summit with a more expansive plan) propped up the most destructive techniques of housing policy with yet more badly directed subsidies favouring banks and developers, not real people.

Nevertheless, as we shall see in the concluding chapter, ultimately it was the conceptual strength of South Africa's urban social movements during the late apartheid era when neoliberal housing policy became generalised – as witnessed in a 1993 Sanco housing policy document subsequently adopted by the ANC within the 1994 *RDP* – that kept hope for a real housing policy alive until (and perhaps beyond) the bitter end. For even if the transition from late apartheid housing policy was barely discernible, thanks to the fact that civics and other community radicals were forced to swallow and to regurgitate the conservative line at key junctures, this offers no basis for the maintenance of status quo policies in future.

As the failure to accomplish anything like the expected delivery of mass housing continues, resurgent social movements will denounce the growing crisis, look back at the *RDP*, and ask a new version of the timeless housing question: how was it that the visionary *RDP* pages on housing became loo paper in the hands of the new government's bureaucrats? This chapter offers one interpretation of the astonishing advent, in an ANC-led South Africa, of a scaled-down, market-oriented approach which earned the epithet 'toilets-in-the-veld' policy – from no less than Slovo's successor as Housing Minister – instead of the policy anticipated by the Democratic Movement.

STORMTROOPERS OF MARKET-CENTRED HOUSING POLICY

Notwithstanding the peculiarities associated with formal racial segregation, many of the same problems that characterise housing in fully-fledged capitalist societies – displacement of the poor, homelessness, rampant slums, sterile land and ghastly suburban strips, side by side with excessive urban and suburban affluence translated into overconsumptive, atomistic housing – were exacerbated in the years immediately preceding and following the 1994 election. To understand why shelter in transitional South Africa may actually be worse for more people than during the harshest years of apartheid oppression requires an explanation of the process by which racial segregation degenerated into a combination of residential class segregation and housing market failure, overlaid by neoliberal fiscal policies which slowly but surely strangled the potential for realising the benefits of proper shelter.

This was not accidental, and in an accompanying box (4.1), we consider how the UF came to be the main vehicle for imposition of neoliberal policy in South Africa's cities. Thanks in part to UF lobbying efforts, blacks were allowed to live permanently in urban townships by the late 1970s (on 99-year leases), and then during the early 1980s were gradually permitted to take out bonds on new houses, and then on improving those township matchbox houses that were in the process of being privatised. During the mid- and late 1980s, townships were inundated by private capital, ranging from huge financial institutions to shoddy small developers out for a quick killing.[6]

Yet black township resistance to the UF – often as intense at the ideological level due to the UF's big business sponsorship as it was at the practical level due to substandard development projects[7] – generated a range of responses. One measure after another was taken from the late 1980s to improve the UF corporate image, including gradually reaching out to influential leftist intellectuals (see Box 4.2), until finally in 1995 the institution was considered a lost cause and shut down.

Box 4.1: Housing's shaky foundation

What the UF was trying to accomplish was the development of a black middle class through massive increases in personal debt. In this manner, the militancy of trade unionists or civic association leaders would be tempered by the responsibility of repaying a housing bond. As expressed by Zach de Beer, South Africa's lead capitalist politician, in 1988, 'When people are housed – more especially when they are homeowners – they are not only less likely to be troublesome. They are also likely to feel they have a stake in the society and an interest in its stability.'[8] One leading UF strategist, Jeff McCarthy (formerly the leading urban Marxist scholar in South Africa) had hoped that local alliances between local civic associations and developers/financiers would 'hasten the prospect of alliances on broader political questions of "vision"'.[9]

The UF's own vision was often disguised, rhetorically, as 'social-democratic', consistent with a (German-style) 'social market economy'. But even in cases where the UF promoted some role for the state, the market would set the parameters. Thus the UF lobbied hard for policies which promoted investment competition between towns and cities, although this denied outlying areas and regions access to 'decentralisation subsidies' (no matter how well or poorly they were used) and reduced urban areas to mere export platforms.

In generating these policies, UF strategists were inspired by the World Bank, especially during the late 1980s/early 1990s drafting of the UF *Urban Futures* policy series. One direct result of UF lobbying was a R750 million site-and-service programme – which quickly became known as toilets-in-the-veld – implemented by the Independent Development Trust (IDT). The IDT was a parastatal-cum-NGO itself founded in early 1990 (by de Klerk, who turned it over to the then UF chairperson, Jan Steyn). The IDT was given R2 billion to foster local social contracts in townships and rural areas, concomitant with the rapid political liberalisation then underway. It was, quite explicitly, a fund for buying out or at least deflecting militant grassroots opposition, an update of the Botha regime's mid–late 1980s 'oil spot' strategy of pouring oil on troubled water.

Aside from playing unpopular guinea pig by implementing frugal UF policies – which won the agency's acronym a new popular tag: 'I Do Toilets' – other side-benefits of Steyn's IDT early 1990s reign included temporarily rescuing a failing UF housing loan guarantee initiative; channelling millions of rands into a questionable UF Cape Town 'group lending' operation which ineffectually relied on peer pressure for small loan repayment; and lending tens of millions of rands to a UF subsidiary (the Land Investment Trust) at 5 per cent interest which – because the loans were then repaid by poor people as bridging finance at 18 per cent – bailed the UF out of its disastrous mid-1980s land acquisition strategy. That earlier strategy of Steyn's had resulted in the UF's development subsidiaries declaring an impressive R17 million loss in 1991, on a R12 million turnover that year.[10] But soon the various under-the-table IDT donations kicked in and the UF was back in the black.

Box 4.2: Retreat of the urban scholars

During the late 1980s, the UF forged important relationships with an ageing clique of white radical men who at that stage began acquiring new homes, cars and the like, finally discovering their logical class location after a decade or more of anti-apartheid rebelliousness. A variety of academics allied to the Democratic Movement[11] were given lucrative consulting gigs to produce highly confidential UF papers on urbanisation. Barring the odd exception, in the process they not only sold out their earlier radical beliefs, but also showed a surprising disdain for the emerging societal demand for transparency.[12]

Most of these consultancies were mediated by the former radical geographer, McCarthy. In 1989, McCarthy and his collaborator Dan Smit moved to the UF from the University of Natal, where both had previously criticised capital's agenda with undisguised venom. But faster even than apartheid bureaucrats changed their stripes, McCarthy and Smit rapidly transmogrified into the UF's leading guides to the Left and its most insipid apologists.[13] Amusing in retrospect, this, but quite disheartening at the time, considering that some of the white radical urbanists had served a generation of students and activists as role models for both non-racialism and academic-based involvement in the Democratic Movement. In a 1986 article characteristic of the earlier spirit, for example, McCarthy (and his far more reliable co-author Michele Friedman) condemned his soon-to-be employer the UF for

> the way in which the ideology of 'community self-improvement' was harnessed by the bourgeoisie and petit bourgeoisie: an ideology that served both to mystify the sources of class oppression, and to alleviate some of the objective causes of dissatisfaction (and hence class action) amongst the urban poor ... It is no secret of ... the Urban Foundation, of course, that the 'social responsibility' of big business in South Africa was and still is identified as being in the areas of the rapid creation of a black petit bourgeoisie, and the promotion of the philosophy and practice of 'self-help' in areas such as housing and the provision of community facilities.[14]

More ironically yet, McCarthy unerringly noted the 'real danger' that researchers would,

> once more, be caught up within a momentum of the social construction of urban problems, the complex nature of which is seldom the subject of scrutiny or critical self-reflection. We now find, in urban geography and planning, for instance, erstwhile liberal intellectuals marching hand-in-glove with progressive elements of the State and capital in a veritable orgy of work on 'informal sector solutions to black housing problems'. These 'solutions', however, are inevitably slanted towards the

principles of homeownership, 'self help' and 'local control', the profoundly ideological nature of which has been alluded to in this chapter.

Given the UF's shaky practical foundation and eclectic local intellectual heritage – not to mention the enormous social control challenges and economic interests represented in the housing debate – the ideological position of liberal capital required continual fortification. The World Bank seemed to understand this; its 'Urban Reconnaissance Missions' produced *Urban Sector Aides Mémoire* in May and December 1991 which were important markers in the Bank's fervent – ultimately successful – campaign to elevate the township housing market to the role of central pillar in the subsequent government policy (see Chapter 5). Michael Cohen, the Bank's main urban strategist, explained: 'We are trying to enter the debate in South Africa with a full awareness that virtually anything that we do will have an unhappy outcome for one side or the other. There are some important ways of demonstrating that reform and changes are to be to everyone's advantage, but politically this is going to be difficult. I do not have any difficulty in being regarded with suspicion – that's the way it goes.'[15]

Locating itself between the 'extremes' of Democratic Movement housing-for-all discourses and residual apartheid, homegrown Bank-think prospered in South Africa's liberal capitalist and econocrat subcultures. One bastard product of Bank neoliberalism and Afrikaans statism was the 1992 De Loor Report.

LATE APARTHEID POLICY PUZZLES

Given the orthodox composition of the authors and its philosophical origins – 'Deregulation, commercialisation and the employment of sound policies which strengthen market forces and provide access to opportunities are all strategies which need strong promotion and high priority' – progressive critics generally ignored the report of Joop de Loor's Task Group on National Housing Policy and Strategy, a document touted as the official transitional policy.[16] Upon its release in mid-1992, the De Loor Report got barely a few days' press coverage from the corps of mainstream journalists who ordinarily fawned at official studies. And although De Loor the individual was promoted to chair of the National Housing Board in 1994, his personal ideological influence, based as it was on incoherent muddling through, remained marginal.

Nevertheless, the De Loor Report is interesting for illustrative purposes, combining as it did some of the worst features of neo-apartheid practice with neoliberal principles. Consider first how the voluminous study posed the central problems. De Loor condemned 'economic inefficiency brought about by the spatial structure of SA cities, a dualistic financial system with regard to housing, and a socio-political mindset that will be difficult to change'. Bigger issues – the biased structure of the economy, the worst unemployment rate in the industrialised world, black workers' low incomes, the rural crisis, etc. – were already off the agenda.[17]

Early on, De Loor asked why the per centage of the SA economy devoted to housing had dropped to a puny 2.6 per cent (in contrast, for example, to Tunisia's 7.4 per cent). He answered, with no supporting data whatsoever, that 'the real problem over the last number of years has been the lack of available capital'. (If so, one wondered how the Johannesburg Stock Exchange become the fastest growing of any major stock market in the world from early 1989 through to mid-1992, and how bank credit creation rates topped 30 per cent per year in the late 1980s.) 'Capital shortage' was a standard refrain of the neoliberal, evoked to lower the state's responsibility for providing a decent standard of shelter to all South Africans. De Loor was wrong: the capital existed, but was simply not making its way from the hyper-speculative financial markets down to the ground. At one point he claimed that township bond boycotts and unrest were 'primarily responsible' for the red-lining practices of banks and building societies; nowhere did he acknowledge that shoddy construction (with no recourse to the builders and developers) was the main reason for the boycotts.

Following directly from the way he asked and answered what was wrong with the existing system, De Loor spent inordinate energy constructing from the rubble of housing finance a new institution and policy.[18] But when it came to a mandate to implement new housing finance policies, De Loor revealed both a curious loyalty to the Development Bank of Southern Africa – main supporter of apartheid homelands and illegitimate Black Local Authorities – and a propensity to criticise DBSA competitors.[19]

As a synthesis defending status quo institutions and promoting neoliberal mean-spiritedness, the report was a washout in intellectual and policy terms. While De Loor's specific recommendations came to naught, his mendacious neo-apartheid/neoliberal synthesis proved persistent in the forced marriage of transitional housing minister Louis Shill and the newly formed National Housing Forum.

In August 1992, as chaos was erupting across the political landscape in the wake of the Codesa negotiations crash, the National Housing Forum was initiated to great fanfare. It encompassed a range of stakeholders including civics, the ANC and other political parties, trade unions, NGOs, developers, suppliers of building materials, bankers and parastatal agencies (although there was no formal government representation). By far the greatest power within the NHF was a bloc dominated by the UF, whose conservative technical experts controlled most of the proceedings and whose policy advice was warmed-over neoliberalism.[20] (There was also a strong – if somewhat irregular – input from the ANC representative, Cobbett, subsequently director-general of housing.)

Yet ironically, as if to highlight the limits of coerced harmony at this early stage, the NHF also experienced numerous conflicts with Minister Louis Shill, which are worth recounting. In May 1993, then-President de Klerk searched to fill a new cabinet post so as to win big-business confidence, as well as to begin to assure audiences that the securocrat era was indeed past (a previous Housing Minister was Adriaan Vlok, formerly the hated Law and Order Minister).[21]

Innocent perhaps of Shill's incompetence in the field of real estate, and perhaps also of the political implications of a forthcoming election campaign, NHF leaders had high expectations of their man in the ministry. So they too gambled wildly, in effect handing back a R500 million commitment to NHF programmes from the February 1993 budget to the NP government in an attempt to gain consultation and cooperation on a far larger amount of anticipated housing expenditures. But that gamble also soured, as Shill subsequently ignored interim arrangements he had forged with the NHF and then in October 1993 announced – in a move widely seen as political posturing influenced by the forthcoming April 1994 vote – that the government would spend R2 billion on grants to help mainly 'Indian' and 'coloured' residents to buy their state-owned houses. NHF leader Matthew Nell (a former UF bureaucrat where he designed the failed Home Loan Guarantee Company) quite rightly complained that this simply added to 'the confused web of inequitable and mostly inexplicable state subsidies for housing'.

Notwithstanding more political confusion when Sanco president Moses Mayekiso briefly – and, admittedly, opportunistically – appeared to endorse Shill's privatisation plan, the NHF was sufficiently miffed by the lack of consultation to temporarily break off negotiations with Shill in late 1993, and to send him an extremely critical letter (endorsed by even the staid Association of Mortgage Lenders) accusing him of being 'deliberately provocative'. Shill responded with counter-accusations and declined to rule out further unilateral restructuring of housing policy. He was backed by De Klerk, who said his minister was on 'firm ground'.[22]

It was difficult to understand the underlying political conflict at this stage, for Shill's philosophy remained generally in line with that of the hegemonic conservative bloc in the NHF, namely that the 'state should, as far as possible, limit its role to facilitating the housing process by creating an environment conducive to participation by private and financial sectors'. Thus the NHF generated only five wishy-washy demands upon which negotiations would reopen and future trust between itself and Shill would be rebuilt: public participation, no unilateral restructuring, consensus-based policy-making, no unilateral disposal of state houses, and speedy implementation of the interim arrangements. Typical of elite posturing during the transition, all in all, this remained a fight between the hostile brothers, Shill and Nell (the latter regularly pulled to the right by the NHF's banking, business and parastatal groupings). For such turf struggles and political tiffs were relatively superficial in comparison to the massacre of progressive positions within the NHF.

THE NATIONAL TOILET FORUM

The NHF was formed at the time a threat emerged from Sanco to jump scale with its bond boycott tactic from approximately a dozen local campaigns (against poorly built housing) to the country as a whole, a veritable 'nuclear weapon' against the banks, as was often remarked.[23] The efficacy of this tactic must be understood against the backdrop of militant township strategies which continued into the early 1990s. During the previous decade, the civic movement had used the philosophy of 'ungovernability' to cripple, politically and financially, illegitimate black local governments. Residents' refusal to pay rent on township houses also conformed to local grievances and waning household economics. Such struggles played a large role in forcing the Botha and De Klerk regimes to contemplate power-sharing, and by 1991 had resulted in the resignation of most of the apartheid township councils. Then in mid-1992, attempts by Sanco to channel the bond boycott threat into national political gains – by demanding banks cease funding homeland dictators, in much the same spirit as the ANC's financial sanctions campaign – met with firm opposition from ANC moderates, including a poorly briefed Mandela (who condemned the tactic when reading a speech, prepared by his Department of Economic Policy, upon returning from the Barcelona Olympics in July 1992).

It was at this stage that the collapse of the progressive agenda in concrete housing policy negotiations was perhaps most decisive. With Sanco now trying to sort out a separate deal with the banks, the Democratic Movement caucus within the NHF was often incoherent, awaiting guidelines from the ANC. Yet its representative, Cobbett, often left the ANC unrepresented at key moments due to a myriad of other duties (such as doing a deal on the wretched Local Government Transition Act and serving in the Transitional Executive Council). Meanwhile, second-tier representatives of Sanco and Cosatu were rarely firm enough on their organisations' 'Affordable Housing for All' principles, and Sanco representatives proved miserable at upholding grassroots interests, particularly demands for support to the emerging social housing movement.

Indeed, characteristic of most such forums, failure by Democratic Movement representatives to report back to their mass constituencies was the norm, and the speed of manoeuvres within the NHF outpaced the ability of most participants to respond with any degree of democratic integrity. Thus, the NHF was soon reduced to a hollow shell of Democratic Movement participants, as a handful of white males from big business, development agencies and consultancy firms took control. As a result, the NHF's conservative wing – egged on especially by IDT and UF technical advisers – demanded that a new housing subsidy policy be adopted for 1994–95 so as to utilise leftover National Housing Department funds. Notwithstanding fairly solid progressive opposition, there was no way to stop the juggernaut.

Thus just weeks prior to the 1994 election, with momentary harmony achieved between the NHF and the campaigning Shill, a compromise on an 'interim housing subsidy' was announced. Immediately heralded by Shill, De Klerk and uncritical journalists as the NP's R90 billion, ten-year housing plan – again, leaving naive ANC technocrats furious at being outmanoeuvred, and hence compelling Cyril Ramaphosa to demand (fruitlessly) Shill's resignation – the deal was little more than the developer-led, site-and-service policy which had failed so miserably in past years (instead of R7,500 as a capital grant, the new inflation-adjusted figure was R12,500, which added a small pile of bricks to the basic site and toilet).

The NHF–Shill deal failed to address a number of aspects earlier raised in the *RDP*: no explicit commitment to eliminating gender bias; no support for squatters' rights; no commitment on linking subsidies to ending bank loan discrimination; no assurance of end-user and bridging finance availability to complement the meagre subsidies; no protection against downward-raiding of subsidies; no possibility of land banking for future development (so as to lower land prices and make subsidies go further); no means of applying subsidies to higher cost inner-city areas; no attention to linking subsidies to the pricing of building materials or to private sector anti-trust considerations; and so on. The NHF–Shill deal effectively limited the tenure form to individually owned sites, at a time the *RDP* was explicitly advocating a variety of tenure forms (such as co-operative housing, social housing and public rental housing).

The main problem, however, continued to be the size of the NHF–Shill subsidy itself.[24] For those earning in the lowest income brackets, the state provided a maximum R12,500 capital grant applied only to individually titled sites. (This contrasted with what was actually required: below-market rate loans of approximately R25,000–30,000 for fully-fledged dwelling units, with payment levels set at no more than 20 per cent of income.) Moreover, in the name of sustainability, transparency and efficiency, i.e., not interfering in market determinations of interest rates and hence avoiding financial market distortions, the distribution of the subsidy was to be through a one-off capital subsidy (rather than a larger, low-interest loan through blending of public and private funds, as advocated by the *RDP*, or than an affordable rental programme, as past apartheid governments had provided to low-income white, coloured and Indian residents).

This approach, which would result either in more serviced sites for the poor or lower-cost houses for the upper echelons of the working class but not housing for the poor, filled various desires of the corporate lobbyists, not least of which was limiting government spending on housing subsidies. In addition, the one-off capital grants – as opposed to long-term loan commitments – would also reduce popular pressure on subsequent government budgets to sustain a sufficient housing budget. In sum, NHF–Shill's application of the notion of 'sustainability' mainly meant that a subsidy had to be maximally market-oriented and minimally threatening to the government budget.

'It is a major scam', ex-Sanco president Moses Mayekiso surmised during an interview shortly before the 1994 elections (and prior to his own late 1994 U-turn on housing policy):

> There are other problems with the interim scheme. We don't want those subsidies to encourage speculation and immediate sale of the plot. Our country must not be left bankrupt by people selling their plots to the middle-class, leaving us with a low-income housing crisis. The subsidy should not be meant to enrich individuals, but to solve the homelessness crisis ... But we feel this is a temporary arrangement, until we have a humane government policy in place.[25]

Indeed Mayekiso and Sanco (and this author) appeared to believe, naively, that in light of the more progressive housing policy adopted as the official *RDP* housing programme in early 1994, it was merely the existence of Shill and the conservative NHF that prevented progress in the interim. Mayekiso concluded of Shill:

> He was outdated, a real NP hack, with top-down schemes that don't work. He was inexperienced, because he came from a big insurance company with no record of housing delivery. And he caused an enormous crisis. His government and parastatals like the Independent Development Trust simply pursued the idea of 'toilets-in-the-veld' for blacks. This legacy shows the cold-heartedness of the NP. The NP had bad advisors, including the Urban Foundation, a big business think-tank. The Urban Foundation in turn got these ideas from the World Bank. This shows the extent to which this philosophy is in fact a global problem. Sanco has launched a Commission on Development Finance to look into all of this.[26]

That Sanco Commission raised plenty of hackles, as principal author Joe Hanlon produced an important, exceptionally progressive document in March 1994, consistent with the *RDP*, arguing in favour of a National Housing Bank, a larger subsidy, and scaled-back roles for the big parastatal agencies and for international aid (courageously ignoring the fact that the US Agency for International Development was Sanco's main funder).[27] So progressives had transcended the normal problem of offering merely critique, and indeed were probably as proactive in the fields of housing and housing finance as in any arena of social conflict, with both policy recommendations (the *RDP*) and concrete project design (several pilot schemes illustrated the benefits of progressive principles).

THE ELITE TRANSITION IN HOUSING POLICY

But the legacy of NP politicking and the influence of the NHF proved surprisingly durable. For while Shill retreated into oblivion at Sage following the election, his men in Pretoria stayed in place thanks to the 'sunset apartheid' concession in late 1992 – ironically, made by then-negotiator Joe Slovo – which guaranteed bureaucrats their jobs until at least 1999.[28]

Worse, the new Department of Housing relied nearly entirely on conservative NHF and DBSA consultants and on its own discredited internal policy-makers, leaving out in the cold the progressive technocrats of the NGO world (such as Planact, which with Sanco had played a strong role in formulating the *RDP* housing programme).[29] A prime example was the consultant (and Cobbett confidant) who emerged as the premier policy adviser in the housing field, Johan de Ridder, a man widely touted within the NHF as an expert deal-maker and link into the state bureaucracy, but whose record as a top-tier SA Housing Trust official was miserable.[30] Yet De Ridder was granted official ANC authority to suggest reallocations in the 1994–95 budget and later went on to run the National Housing Finance Corporation (though he was fired in a 1998 controversy with its chair, Eric Molobi).

But it was not only a problem that due to Cobbett's increasingly small circle of advisers or Slovo's sunset apartheid legacy, only a tiny crew of ANC comrades were permitted access to the new Department of Housing (where they would have watched the Old Guard settling comfortably into the quick-drying transitional cement).[31] More importantly, progressive forces remained fragmented and ineffectual during the period immediately following the 1994 election. Sanco was quiescent at this stage and soon there was a stunning back-down on the *RDP* and Sanco housing policy from even Mayekiso.[32]

Ironically, this was a time when people on the ground were invading land and vacant housing (such as boarded-up inner-city buildings) at a record pace, reflecting the immensely powerful confidence boost from the ANC electoral victory. Yet Democratic Movement leadership and most formal organisations (with the exception of the Homeless People's Federation) were twiddling their thumbs. The NHF, meanwhile, had accomplished such a high degree of coerced harmony and acquired sufficient legitimacy within powerful centrist and media circles that the struggle for an entirely new and more progressive approach to housing – the *RDP*, for instance – proved impossible to talk about, much less win. Means of implementing the *RDP* housing programme was never even considered within the NHF.

In this false consciousness void of meaningful consensus towards an effective housing policy, it was perhaps only logical that politicians would exhibit enormous confusion in the ranks. Just one reflection of this, in the days immediately following the election, was the endorsement granted by Gauteng provincial Premier Tokyo Sexwale and his Housing Minister Dan Mofokeng of the fantastic claims of mega-developer Stocks & Stocks that in Gauteng alone, 150,000 houses could be built each year for the homeless, on the sole basis that Stocks & Stocks had constructed the lavishly opulent R1 billion Sun City 'Lost City' resort in a mere 18 months. Nationally, just 90,000 low-cost houses were projected in the first year of ANC rule by Minister Slovo, which was also wildly optimistic in view of the essentially status quo policies adopted.[33]

Perhaps predictably, in this context, the populist politicians and then the mass movement began to receive 'blame the victim' treatment for the continuing housing delivery quagmire, even from Slovo. Witness the minister's first recorded remarks in May 1994, as the wave of land invasions began: 'Government cannot condone squatting.'[34] But this was nothing compared to Slovo's next bit of demagoguery, shocking to most progressives, in a missive delivered during an October 1994 conference in Botshabelo township, which generated the *Housing Accord*:

Yesterday's targets are clear. The boycott damaged the enemy and ultimately played an important role in bringing down the system. But who is the enemy today? Who is being hurt by rent and bond and service charge boycott today if not the very people who are most dependent on the resources being withheld by the boycotters? It's clear who the boycotters are knocking: Nelson Mandela, our first democratically elected president.[35]

There were enormous flaws in the logic, for the fewer than two dozen bond boycotts were directed entirely against shoddy developers and the bankers that failed to bring them to the table to negotiate repairs. What Slovo's comment represented, however, was a dangerous intensification of coerced harmony strategy; progressive forces in civil society were being warned that principled opposition entailing mass action tactics would be met with political charges equivalent to high treason.

And yet it was only mass action that forced Slovo, Cobbett and others to wake up to their earlier constituents' needs and demands, and understand the sabotage of even their toilet policy (the Shill–NHF deal) occurring in the various housing bureaucracies. A good example was in Gauteng's Provincial Housing Board, which was dominated by extremely conservative elements hand-chosen by Shill and the NHF. At its first opportunity in July 1994, the board rejected outright a subsidy application from the country's oldest, largest housing co-operative project – the Seven Buildings Project in inner-city Johannesburg – on the extraordinary grounds that the Project's collective ownership form of tenure made it ineligible for government funds.[36]

Then the more than 2,000 Seven Buildings tenants received eviction notices from their landlord. More than 500 engaged in a sit-in at housing board offices, which won them a meeting with Slovo. Yet even after Slovo promised the Project that it would become the government pilot for 'social housing' (the term for co-operatives and housing associations), the housing board once again rejected the Seven Buildings' tenants subsidy application on even more spurious grounds. After more protest the tenants finally won access to the subsidies in February 1996, conclusively proving that mass action was the only way to break through the quagmire.

Yet mass action became Slovo's primary nemesis. That is the only way to interpret his ministry's first attempt to address the chronic problem of bank red-lining. Rather than tackle the issue head-on by promoting a tougher version of the widely anticipated Community Reinvestment Act (which would prohibit red-lining), Slovo and Cobbett negotiated a 'Record of Understanding' with the banks in October 1994. Under the guise of generating incentives for 50,000 loans (in amounts as low as R10,000 each) to low-income borrowers in the first year, the agreement denuded the civic movement of its most powerful negotiating weapon: the physical power to prevent banks from following through foreclosure action on a township house with removal of occupiers.

With this deal, the state would now guarantee that once a default was registered (in the wake of a retrenchment or period of illness, for instance), there would be no basis for a community organisation negotiating a revised repayment schedule. Slovo thus consciously disempowered the grassroots, achieving only a vague commitment to lend from bankers whose interest rates remained obnoxiously high (at a record level above their cost of funds), whose branches remained far away from borrowers, whose commercial practices and employees were often racist and sexist, and whose deplorable track record in the low-cost housing finance field should have disqualified them from future contact with innocent consumers. Suffice to say, Slovo bent over backwards to please the banks and reduce their risk, and did so in the most despicable way possible, by reducing community power. This gave the impression of momentum, and so at the Botshabelo conference, the *Housing Accord* was generated and signed by practically all major stakeholders.

The *Housing Accord* was arrived at in a manner, one front-row observer confided, that was 'amazing but also limited. I think most of the consensus was face-saving rather than actual agreement. The battles continue behind closed doors. For instance, the NHF is now going to review this banks/government compact – initial reports say it's totally immoral.'[37] A key tactic of the *Accord* was its refusal to confront the issues fairly and squarely, resorting instead to evasive language and – in the case of Slovo's speech – to extremely shoddy analysis. The final document formally defined the housing problem in a way that, to a large extent, let the private sector off the hook: 'In a series of twists and turns which mirrored the inefficiencies, irra- tionalities, and injustices of apartheid, housing in South Africa became increasingly fragmented. For black people, urban housing development virtually stopped three decades ago.'[38]

This crucial statement revealed amnesia on the part of the *Accord's* authors, with respect to the *roaring* urban housing development for the top 10 per cent of black households from 1986 to 1990, when nearly 200,000 units were built and bonded by the private sector. The *Accord* problem statement thus differed markedly from the *RDP*, which noted 'the housing problems created by apartheid and by the limited range of the capitalist housing markets'. By ignoring the latter, namely that developers and banks were in fact very active in the market, it was exceedingly easy for the bureaucrats to forget why there were bond boycotts in the first place: because the product delivered by the private sector was so inferior, and consumers had no recourse to the builder but only, through bond payments, to the bank. Instead, the *Accord* attributed bond boycotts to purely political strategies: 'As a popular expression of defiance and a weapon in the battle to bring down apartheid's local government structures, rent and bond boycotts played a fundamental role in effecting the changes which have led to democracy in South Africa.'

A couple of corrections are in order. Although Sanco's mid-1992 national bond boycott *threat* (never carried out) was aimed at effecting national change, it was snuffed so quickly by ANC conservatives that no fundamental change was achieved or even influenced. In point of fact, bond boycotts were never, in any instance, suggested as weapons aimed at *local* government structures; all of them have been aimed at getting banks to fix cracked houses. In any case, local authorities were never particularly bothered by bond boycotts (and hence were never involved in negotiations over their resolution), since their revenue stream was derived mostly from rental income.

Was this line from the *Accord* merely, then, sloppy analysis and wording, or was it the deliberate stretching of the truth by increasingly panicky bureaucrats? Probably the latter, because mythologising conflictual politics is a favourite device employed in South Africa by individuals and groups across the political spectrum, with only rare corrections from the media (for the sake of selling newspapers, reporters highlighted and indeed encouraged threatening rhetoric, never questioning why only a tiny fraction of the threats were ever carried out). The *Accord*'s language has a particular function: to make it appear that with a new ANC-led Government of National Unity in place, all grievances relating to government had now evaporated.

To do so required specifically ignoring the fact that there were many local grievances not about apartheid but about *the markets* in housing and consumer finance. For Slovo to acknowledge these, however, would have been to acknowledge that he was going to do nothing material about these problems, and hence to admit that there was instead a logic for continuing mass action strategies and tactics on the part of grassroots housing activists. That kind of honesty was apparently unacceptable. Much the same spirit permeated the writing of the *Housing White Paper* two months later.[39]

The *Accord* recorded the following broad objective:

> Our goal is to see housing's share of the total state budget increased to five per cent and to increase housing delivery on a sustainable basis to a peak level of 300,000 units per annum within a five year period ... We commit ourselves to the development of viable alternatives to the site and service approach of the past. Every family, no matter how poor, has the right with commensurate responsibilities to a basic structure with water, electricity, and waste water disposal, which is both capable of protecting them from the elements and of being extended as resources become available.

At least here the *Accord* remained true to the *RDP* (though the *RDP* aimed for 'over' – not 'a peak of' – 300,000 houses per annum). Yet what was most remarkable about this strong commitment to fight for budget funds was that if the 5 per cent figure had truly become national policy (as indeed the *RDP* was meant to be), then there existed no fiscal constraint to a more generous housing policy (i.e. not just a site-and-service capital subsidy, but a full Housing for All commitment).[40] Indeed, when approving the *RDP* housing section as official ANC policy in early 1994, Cobbett acknowledged that it was indeed within the realm of possibility to win the 5 per cent commitment.[41] Since Slovo had announced that only 90,000 houses would be supported by the state in the first year of ANC rule, gradually increasing to 300,000+ within five years, housing would not have to reach 5 per cent until the fifth year (in 1998–99, this would have been R10 billion of government's R200 billion expenditure).

Yet suddenly, 'fiscal constraint' rhetoric was taken from dry Finance Department and Reserve Bank economists and adopted, albeit quite uncomfortably and unconvincingly, by populist politicians. Initially two provincial Housing Ministers – Mofokeng and Vax Mayekiso of the Free State (a cousin of Moses) – had strongly opposed Slovo's adoption of the Shill–NHF 'incremental' housing policy, saying it reeked of the old order.[42] Later, following Slovo's death in January 1995, his replacement, Sankie Mthembi-Mahanyele, labelled the policy she had inherited 'toilets-in-the-veld',[43] thus raising – but soon dashing – hopes that the policy could be overturned.

With the formal adoption of the *Housing White Paper* (*HWP*) and two subsequent amendments by a Ministerial Task Team in December 1995 and October 1996,[44] and an extremely weak response by the parliamentary committee with oversight responsibilities in April 1996, internal opposition to the decidedly market-centred policy was squelched. Only Cosatu, the National Homeless People's Federation and a few other dissident voices defied the coerced harmony. Indeed, the most telling reflection of the degeneration of the mainstream debate was well-publicised pseudo-research in November 1995 – by McCarthy and the rump of the Urban Foundation which was renamed the National Business Initiative – claiming that blacks actually liked living in shacks.[45]

POST-APARTHEID NEOLIBERALISM IN THE *HOUSING WHITE PAPER*

The *HWP*'s Preamble stated, arrogantly, 'The time for policy debate is now past', which was confirmed by the first report of the Ministerial Task Team on Short-term Delivery: 'No review of the fundamental position of government in respect of [minimum standards and levels of housing subsidies] is on the table and will be on the table for some time to come.'

What policy debates there were never occurred in a context of true public consultation and entailed little or no participation on the part of those forces within society which were opposed to the market-centred policy. In particular, key issues – the role of the state, the nature of rental policy, housing standards, worker and community participation and control, and the alleged 'fiscal constraint' to higher subsidies – were never convincingly addressed by officials, leaving constituents and progressive organisations within civil society nearly uniformly angry and alienated. Neither could the stubborn commitment to an ineffectual policy prevent land invasions, occupations of vacant buildings, rent strikes or other forms of popular resistance. Yet because of the firm commitment by Cobbett, his consultants and the much more powerful interests they were ultimately serving, such protest was typically met with repression; there was no budging from the core neoliberal premises.

The *HWP* and its amendments by the Task Team can be considered neoliberal because they celebrated 'the fundamental pre-condition for attracting [private] investment, which is that housing must be provided within a normalised market'.[46] The Ministerial Task Team confirmed in October 1996 that the state's 'gradual withdrawal' from housing provision was a fundamental principle.

In contrast, the *RDP* critique of housing markets was based on the dismal recent experience in private sector township housing, namely, the unsustainable, disastrously implemented investments by developers and banks during the late 1980s. Hence the *RDP* concluded that a housing policy far beyond the realm of the market should be urgently implemented, including two crucial non-market mechanisms: a national housing bank,[47] and mechanisms that ensure state expenditures on housing take the form of 'non-speculative' subsidies.[48] Neither was given serious consideration in the neoliberal policy.

Indeed, in contrast to the *RDP* mandate, each major facet of housing policy relied upon or rewarded the market: the broad policy objectives (specifically, 'to contribute to the certainty required by the market'); the role of communities (none, effectively); the size of the housing backlog (the 'present housing backlog' was considered to be merely the 1.5 million urban informal units such as shacks, not hostel beds or rural huts); housing standards (extremely low); the (unsubsidised) interest rate on bonds; housing finance guarantees that favour lenders not borrowers; an insistence upon full cost recovery for services; (self-)regulation of the construction industry; building materials price inflation (ignored); emerging construction firms ('not seen as a primary housing responsibility and therefore does not justify the allocation of housing funds'); housing tenure (no rental and very little support for co-ops); and a variety of other *RDP* policy provisions that were disregarded.[49]

The effect of the neoliberal policy was to transfer state resources that should have gone into public or social housing, into the private sector, with little to show for it in return. Massive incentives found their way to banks and developers (Box 4.3). The results were appalling.

For example, incentives enjoyed by banks did not succeed in fostering low-income housing delivery. Indeed, the Record of Understanding social contract in which banks committed to providing

50,000 bonds in their first year of activity using the incentives resulted in fewer than 20,000 bonds granted in applicable areas in the intended price range. Without any 'stick', the hope that providing 'carrots' would dramatically raise the level of bank low-cost home financing was unrealistic.[50] Moreover, the policy was based on the assumption that most people eligible for subsidies would be able to secure bond finance or other forms of credit to top up the R15,000 housing subsidy. However, the poor could seldom afford bank loans or meet bank lending conditions (such as having secure regular employment), particularly at the prevailing rate of interest. Other forms of less formal credit simply failed to materialise on the scale expected. Thus despite the financial incentives directed at retail banks, fewer than 20 per cent of houses built under the subsidy scheme were linked to credit.[51]

Box 4.3: Subsidies to bankers and developers

In implementing the neoliberal policy, the Department of Housing rewarded financiers in at least four specific ways – with total funding allocated from 1994–96 of more than R650 million – in exchange for delivery promises that were never fulfilled. When these measures failed, the Ministerial Task Team's second report subsequently shifted financial support and incentives to developers.

To consider the transfer of resources to banks first, the Mortgage Indemnity Scheme announced in October 1994 guaranteed banks against politically related non-payment of new housing bonds in those areas covered by the scheme, up to 80 per cent of the value of the bond. By September 1996, 113 areas of South Africa had been either denied cover by the scheme (i.e. formally red-lined) or 'deferred', leaving 437 areas covered.[52] Second, a new joint venture agency between government and commercial banks ('Servcon') – developed in late 1994 in order to 'rehabilitate' non-paying bonds and ultimately to 'right-size' households to properties they could more easily afford – received R50 million.[53] Third, the National Housing Finance Corporation was established in early 1996 to provide wholesale funding to retail banks, to encourage banks to increase their low-income loan portfolios. The Corporation was meant ultimately to finance 700,000 houses, a goal seen as extremely unrealistic, especially in the wake of fatal problems experienced by one of the prime vehicles for the Corporation's funds, the Community Bank. Fourth, the National Urban Reconstruction and Housing Agency guaranteed bank-originated bridging finance for developers. The agency aimed to make available R2 billion in low-cost housing finance by the year 2000.[54]

In addition to these schemes, one of the most generous incentives that government granted banks was to permit their mid-1995 imposition of a 4–5 per cent interest rate premium on housing bonds to low-income borrowers. In view of the banks' 1 per cent (and greater) discounts to many higher-income borrowers, this represented a substantial mode of redistributing income from the poor to the rich. Further, government failed to promulgate legislation or policies aimed at reform of the financial sector (especially prohibitions on discrimination) called for in the *RDP*. Central government also took unusual steps – not even attempted by the apartheid government – to support banks in their default proceedings against borrowers, even where non-payment was due to temporary involuntary unemployment or other conditions beyond the borrowers' control. Moreover, government's market-centred housing policy was echoed by a variety of other incentives and sometimes hidden subsidies offered by different tiers of government (e.g. the Inner City Housing Upgrading Trust in Johannesburg) and international agencies (e.g. US AID guarantee and financing schemes).

Moreover, incentives for private sector developers and managers recommended in the 1996 Task Team report were also generous. The amended policy provided R100 million of central government funds for joint venture housing projects between provincial/local state housing departments and developers. Another R400 million in guaranteed housing sales financing would be provided to underwrite the bulk purchase of joint venture products. Further subsidies were targeted to support 'professional' expertise related to management of rental housing (but not, apparently, to community- or tenant-managed housing corporations).

The Ministerial Task Team's December 1995 report did acknowledge profound practical limitations to carrying out the market-centred housing finance policies, including 'projects being delayed due to excuses put forward by banks ... the Mortgage

Indemnity Fund being positioned as a red-lining process ... inadequate or inappropriate pressure being applied to banks to lend in areas where lending is most needed ... [and] additional (more onerous) barriers being perceived to be erected by banks to historically disadvantaged borrowers'.[55] Yet neither that report nor the subsequent report of October 1996 provided any remedies. Instead, through the absence of strong countervailing policies or programmes, these Task Team reports effectively endorsed the status quo. The second report insisted upon principles that included: 'The state's involvement should be structured to enable gradual withdrawal without disruption ... Measures introduced should not constitute an additional subsidy and the principle of full cost recovery should apply ... Measures introduced should entrench savings as the primary mechanism for prioritisation of access to housing opportunities created.'[56]

Eventually in 1998, Mthembi-Mahanyele herself conceded:

Some contractors and developers have taken advantage of the unre-strictive and loose definition of norms and standards, coupled with the fact that these were left to the discretion of the operatives on the ground. The rationale behind this was mainly to produce a groundswell of innovation and creativity in encouraging people to produce units of good value. This has led to unscrupulous developers skimming off and producing units that are substandard in terms of providing adequate living spaces for families.[57]

The consequences of a market-centred approach to low-income housing delivery were disastrous, judging by the record of the ANC government's first term of office:

- Far fewer than a million homes were built (definitions vary, but although claims of 600,000 were made in the 1999 election, it is generally acknowledged that fewer than 100,000 subsidy recipients were lent sufficient 'top-up' bank credit to construct houses even equivalent to matchboxes, and another 300,000 rooms constructed with R15,000 subsidies were defectively built).
- Yet vast state funding – 80 per cent of money allocated in 1994–96 – went unspent, followed in 1997–98 by vast over-commitments to developers (and cancelled construction contracts) due to insufficient budget allocations (5 per cent of the

state budget was anticipated for housing by 1998–99, but just
1.5 per cent was forthcoming, a lower percentage than during
the apartheid era).

- The geographic locations of new projects were in far *worse*
locations than apartheid era townships (further from the city
and job opportunities, with no hint of community, school, clinic
or shopping facilities in most new housing projects).
- Dissatisfied subsidy recipients sometimes refused to move into
tiny new homes, terming them 'kennels' and 'bus shelters'.
- Existing housing construction capacity was destroyed due to
the failure to recognise contradictions within the market and
provide a state-driven counter-cyclical construction boost.[58]
- State capacity withered in fields as diverse as construction,
building materials management, public works delivery, retail
financing and management.
- There was an inequitable allocation of funding between different
low-income groups (favouring those with higher incomes
because they had the capacity to gain access to credit and hence
were the target of private sector developers' projects).
- Most communities were disempowered in the course of project
planning as well as in the more general need for capacity (given
that many local leaders moved into government), which led to
an increasing gap between developers' promises and community
expectations (often resulting in intense conflict).
- There was great reluctance on the part of the private sector
developers to build within conflict-ridden townships where the
need for housing was often the greatest.
- There was widespread abuse of the policy by local authorities
and developers (according to even Cobbett in September 1996),
leading to a reduction in value of the subsidy by 50 per cent in
some cases.[59]
- A worrying element of housing-related corruption surfaced
elsewhere (especially in Mpumalanga and Gauteng Provinces,
with unproven allegations against the national minister
ultimately responsible for the extremely embarrassing 1997
departure of director-general Cobbett).
- The Mortgage Indemnity Scheme continued to indirectly act as
a redlining instrument for several years, and Servcon had
virtually no available low-cost properties for households to right-
size into.

- Apartheid-style ghettos were reproduced, although these in future would not be segregated along racial lines but in class terms, specifically where the new slum settlements excluded – as a matter of public policy (see Chapter 5) – sewage systems, electricity lines, stormwater drains and metalled roads.

CONCLUSION: AN ANSWER TO THE HOUSING QUESTION?

Marx's collaborator Friedrich Engels remarked in 1872: 'The essence of both the big bourgeois and petit-bourgeois solutions of the "housing question" is that the worker should own his [*sic*] own dwelling.' This doctrine was easily observed in the policies of big capital and the late apartheid regime during the 1980s and early 1990s, and of the first democratic government after power-sharing began in May 1994. We observed, too, that this approach was not the only one available and that each step along the road to a market-centred housing policy was fraught with contradictions and opposition by progressive forces (though ultimately not sufficient opposition to force changes).

And this compels us to return to Engels' broader argument:

In reality the bourgeoisie has only one method of solving the housing question after *its* fashion – that is to say, of solving it in such a way that the solution continually reproduces the question anew ... No matter how different the reasons may be, the result is everywhere the same; the scandalous alleys disappear to the accompaniment of lavish self-praise from the bourgeoisie on account of this tremendous success, but they appear again immediately somewhere else and often in the immediate neighbourhood! ... The breeding places of disease, the infamous holes and cellars in which the capitalist mode of production confines our workers night after night, are not abolished; they are merely *shifted elsewhere*! The same economic necessity which produced them in the first place, produces them in the next place also.[60]

In a neoliberal, post-apartheid South Africa, these breeding places of disease – the mass shantytowns and squatter villages, the hostels, the decaying inner-city areas, the nooks and crannies where the homeless congregate – are all to be found growing, not shrinking. What would soon have to be asked was whether indeed there was an 'economic necessity' of producing them. Would there thus be any opportunity to break conclusively with the neoliberal approach, without challenging the larger capitalist power relationship itself?

Housing was not the only policy arena in which such questions could be asked. Conflicts over policy issues became more regular across the spectrum, what with so much backtracking from the *RDP* mandate, more popular leaders succumbing to coerced harmony, more popular movements disillusioned with the results of the social contracts, and more alienated individuals and small groups taking matters into their own hands with land invasions, housing occupations and other means of influencing housing policy through popular struggle. The spirit of resistance remained the greatest strength of the grassroots forces and, too, their best hope of achieving decent housing in the face of powerful neoliberal influences which had reached deep into their own movements.

But to make lasting progress, the atomistic and sectorally discrete struggles would have to confront a double barrier, not just a state–capital nexus within South Africa, but exceptionally powerful (though contradiction-ridden) international neoliberal forces led in many respects by the World Bank.

PART III

International Lessons

5

The World Bank as 'Knowledge Bank' (*sic*)

The argument: Conventional progressive critiques of the near-mythical importance of the Bretton Woods Institutions require amendment in South Africa, where the World Bank barely established a loan portfolio during the ANC's first term; instead, the damage done was in the ideological and policy spheres, where Bank staff were prolific in their support for essentially status quo arrangements even where clear, redistributive alternatives had been mandated by the Democratic Movement.

THE POWER OF GLOBAL NEOLIBERALISM

The contradictions between expectations and reality, in relation to democratic South Africa's relations with the World Bank, were unveiled in this 1992 *Business Day* report:

> A questioner from the floor of the World Bank's final function at the annual meetings asked Bank president Lewis Preston whether this year's meetings had been any different because of the absence of socialists following the collapse of the command economies. 'There are still some socialists here,' Preston replied. 'There are still even some communists around. But they are talking in very low voices, and they are mostly South Africans.'[1]

Offhand wit aside, the reason Lewis Preston – and four years later Michel Camdessus, and in between a stream of World Bank staff –

identified a threat from the South African Left was because progressive forces managed, as few others around the world did, to keep the two major international neoliberal institutions at arm's length with respect, at least, to lending. The history of the Bank and the International Monetary Fund in South and Southern Africa was embarrassing, to put it mildly, and it was not particularly difficult for labour and social movements openly to criticise the Bank and IMF at the same time a half dozen or so ANC leaders sought cosiness. That those leaders (e.g. Thabo Mbeki, Trevor Manuel and Alec Erwin) turned occasionally to a kind of leftist rhetoric in defending their 'engagements' with the Bank, as we see below, should not confuse matters (presumably *their* purpose).

Where the progressive social forces were not as careful – in permitting World Bank advisory teams to make a huge impact on social and economic policy, and in international trade relationships (as shown in Chapter 1) – the combined logic of neoliberalism and uneven development had a devastating effect. This chapter documents the damage done by the IMF (through policy advice and in informal conditionality on a December 1993 loan) and by the Bank's advisory role in several key areas of social policy. Nevertheless, building on some degree of local resistance to the Bank, the next chapter discusses the strategic orientation of principled opposition to global neoliberalism during a late 1990s context of widespread delegitimisation of what came to be termed the 'Washington Consensus', reflecting just how much rigidly homogeneous power emanated from a few institutions and ideologues in the US capital city.

(The Washington Consensus refers to the 1980s–1990s ideology of the World Bank, International Monetary Fund, US Treasury Department, Federal Reserve Board and assorted Washington think-tanks funded by large corporations and banks, as well as institutions outside Washington like the World Trade Organisation and sundry conservative university economics departments modelled on the Chicago School.)

In short, there are slim but important roots of resistance in South Africa that may help a new internationalism to prosper. Those roots were seeded not only during the heroic solidarity struggles of the anti-apartheid era, but during the 1990s when the World Bank, IMF and their allies claimed, with the utmost conviction and self-confidence, 'There Is No Alternative' – TINA (the slogan made famous by Margaret Thatcher) – to neoliberal globalisation. South African activists, especially in the Campaign Against Neoliberalism, soon understood the implications of TINA, and learned a rejoinder: 'There Must Be an Alternative' – THEMBA, the Zulu word for 'hope'.

A LEGACY OF FINANCIAL INDISCRETION

There are numerous examples of the Bretton Woods Institutions' historical support for oppressive systems in the Southern African subcontinent. By the 1950s, the Bank had become the largest foreign financier to several regional colonies then still under minority rule. The Bank provided loans to the then 'Rhodesias and Nyasaland', to South Africa, and to Portuguese-ruled Angola and Mozambique to build white-controlled infrastructures for the benefit of white economic interests and relatively rich white consumers.

The then largest Bank project was the huge Kariba hydroelectric dam on the Zambezi River, between what are now Zambia and Zimbabwe. The dam summarily displaced tens of thousands of Batonga people from their ancestral lands and livelihoods without compensation (leading to many deaths due to degraded resettlement conditions), primarily to serve South African, British and US multi-national copper-mining corporations' interests. The Bank did not direct its 'development' programmes to the needs of indigenous majority populations – except by attempting in then-Southern Rhodesia to promote – through a loan aimed at implementing the hated Native Land Husbandry Act – alien individual-ownership title systems on African communal lands (thus generating sufficient peasant protest to halt the process).

Despite a belated formal endorsement of the need for democracy and development, the IMF and Bank continued to collude with oppressive regimes – black neocolonial as well as white racist – in conformity with the Cold War geopolitical designs of their chief sponsors (as well as their own institutional financial interests). Despite blatant corruption and human rights abuses, Mobuto's notorious dictatorial regime in Zaire continued for decades to receive IMF and Bank funding. Even during the late 1980s, when foreign donors finally imposed financial sanctions against the authoritarian regime of Hastings Banda in Malawi, the Bank, none the less, approved loans to his widely discredited government.

As Southern African nations struggled to undo the negative political, social and economic effects of long years of colonial domination and exploitation, they found themselves saddled with 'odious debts' (as international legal doctrine terms illegitimate loans) built up by previous oppressors. For example, while conducting a war against Zimbabwean liberation forces, the illegal UDI Rhodesian regime of Ian Smith defaulted on its World Bank loan repayments. Yet, at the end of that war, the government and people of newly independent Zimbabwe were obliged to repay the Rhodesian debt. Such debts should have been annulled with the elimination of the illegitimate regimes that had created them.

As the Third World debt crisis mounted in the early 1980s, the Bank and IMF stepped in to 'manage' the external debts – and government policies – of countries in Southern Africa, as they did elsewhere in the world. However, this did not solve – but instead deepened – the debt. The Bank and the IMF continued to squeeze whatever they could from our countries. Even Mozambique, plunged into deep economic crisis by a decade of devastating war sponsored by apartheid South Africa, faced an official debt service obligation to its international creditors of more than 93 per cent of its export earnings in 1991 (though it typically paid around a fifth, which was still more than the health and education budgets combined).

Utilising such indebtedness as a weapon, the IMF, the Bank and other Northern creditors compelled country after country in Southern Africa to implement structural adjustment programmes under their aegis. Others which did not agree to structural adjustment (war-torn Angola, relatively prosperous Botswana, and South Africa) still had to give the IMF 'policy undertakings' – under the threat of losing international 'creditworthiness' without the IMF's stamp of approval.

In South Africa, the World Bank's history was just as questionable, in light of its mandate to promote development projects that reduced poverty. Its role began just two years after apartheid was formally introduced in 1948, and its first loans – $30 million to Eskom and $20 million for South African railways/harbours – were granted in 1951 and repaid at the end of 1953. Follow-up loans of $162 million for both projects continued through 1968. Indeed, even in the wake of the 1960 Sharpeville massacre, the Bank granted loans worth $45 million, including $20 million in 1966 (even after then ANC president Albert Luthuli and Rev. Martin Luther King, Jr. had already called for financial sanctions against Pretoria). There was no direct benefit for black consumers, who because of apartheid were denied Eskom power financed by the Bank and whose rail transport prospects were mainly linked to their employment – if they possessed a pass book – in urban centres. The Bank discontinued lending to South Africa when the last Eskom loan (for a coal-fired power station) was repaid, because per capita GDP rose to levels that disqualified access by Pretoria.[2]

However, the Bank still contributed to apartheid coffers, via the $8 billion first phase of the Lesotho Highlands Water Project, which dammed rivers and tunnelled through mountains to supply a voraciously thirsty Johannesburg – mainly white households, white-owned farms and white-owned mines – with water notwithstanding huge social and environmental costs. In October 1986, following a coup in which Prime Minister Leabua Jonathan was ousted with Pretoria's support, and at a time of harsh repression in South Africa after the foreign debt repayment 'standstill' of September 1985, there was little chance of South Africa getting access to fresh foreign funds. The Bank chose that moment to begin the project, and lent Lesotho – with its $600 per capita income, and reliance upon foreign aid for 20 per cent of its GDP – $110 million, solely because of South Africa's ability to stand surety (indeed, the only financial risk analysis in the Bank's initial report concerned whether Pretoria would default).[3]

The IMF, meanwhile, had snubbed international condemnations of apartheid and the financial sanctions campaign during the late 1970s and early 1980s, in the wake of the Soweto uprising, in order to channel $2 billion to Pretoria for vitally needed balance of payments support. The IMF credits raised all manner of social and economic controversies, including mainstream criticism of South Africa's unrestrained government budget (especially for defence), of the Reserve Bank's inadequate monetary control, and of economic distortions and artificial barriers created by apartheid. Loans were pushed through anyway. Only in 1983, after it was forbidden to continue bailing out the South African regime – through pressure by social movements exerted upon the US Congress – did the IMF change its policy.

The IMF ceased lending, but during the 1980s sent in advisory teams each year to help the apartheid government switch to neoliberal economic policies. In 1991, IMF experts designed the regressive Value Added Tax, which led to a two-day strike by 3.5 million workers in November that year. In 1992, the IMF took another swipe at South African blacks with its pronouncement that 'real wage growth must be contained'.[4] Given this sort of history, the IMF had no real prospect of winning hearts and minds. And the Bank was forced to bend over twice as far as anywhere else in the world to even have a fighting chance against South Africa's mass movements.

CONTEMPORARY WORLD BANK WOES

In May 1990, when the World Bank made its first substantial appearance in South Africa in more than two decades, a war of position began that finally resulted, nearly seven years later, in a minor face-saving victory for the Bank's Johannesburg staff. The first World Bank loan to democratic South Africa – worth R 340 million – was only granted in 1997, for the supposed purpose of making small and medium enterprises more globally competitive. The Bank had tiptoed into South Africa's development maelstrom with exceptional sensitivity. For on the one side it faced a strong left rump of the Democratic Movement (as well as other radical forces), well aware of the Bank's reputation as the most powerful oppressive force in the Third World since the days of colonialism. Many within the ANC who had lived in Tanzania, Zambia, Uganda and elsewhere on the African continent shared a gut feeling that a democratic South Africa must avoid the World Bank like the plague.

On the other side – inviting the Bank and International Monetary Fund (IMF) with indecent haste – were powerful bourgeois forces. Business ideologues and civil servant scoundrels of the late apartheid era, including leading strategists of the Development Bank of Southern Africa (DBSA), were ever more anxious to show that Pretoria's control of bantustans was dependent not merely upon securocrat muscle power, but also upon homeland 'structural adjustment programmes' (the DBSA did, clumsily, actually use that name). Such econocrats were drawn from both old guard government and big business cliques, and harboured firm ambitions not only of surviving the transition process but indeed of actually thriving in whatever environment lay ahead. At the vanguard was the Urban Foundation, which tried to position itself as the favoured World Bank junior partner (ahead of its rivals the DBSA and Independent Development Trust). Using increasingly strident but nevertheless quite effective policy advocacy, the UF invariably cited free-market conventional wisdom from

Washington DC as the gospel. As Chapters 3 and 4 show, the UF's vision of cities was decisive.

But as an unintended consequence, the econocrats' arrogance gave many Bank opponents in South Africa experience in understanding the logic and codewords of neoliberalism, critiquing these based on their emergence in the late apartheid state's development practice, and also gradually coming to know Bank personnel. For example, during that first Bank visit in 1990, several key ANC leaders were visited by Geoffrey Lamb, a former SACP intellectual who had spent time in jail during the 1960s before escaping to East Africa and then to England. There he had completed his doctorate and acted as supervisor to South Africa's emerging cadre of Marxist sociologists, prior to migrating to Washington where during the 1980s he focused on the crafty goal of making neoliberal African economic policies appear to be 'homegrown':

> Building an independent technocratic policy capacity within member countries is therefore important to encourage domestic political accountability for policy decisions over the longer run and for improving the credibility of economic advice to countries' political leaderships – provided that support for technocratic 'policy elites' does not too drastically compromise the recipients' influence.[5]

Indeed, being too close to the Bank was a danger that would emerge later. But in the early days, Lamb broke the ice effectively with his old friend from Sussex, Thabo Mbeki (also a tough young Communist Party ideologue during the 1960s). The two proceeded to assign specialist teams to analyse conditions and generate policy options in macroeconomics, industry, health, education, housing and land reform. The Bank agreed, apparently reluctantly, that there would be no loans to the De Klerk government, which it too came to label 'illegitimate'.

Lamb's colleague Jeff Racki – scion of a wealthy liberal family from Cape Town, who was responsible for extremely low-quality urban programmes in neighbouring Zimbabwe – received formal endorsements for research, along with chaperons (drawn even from the SACP) for several 'urban missions'. The Bank also funded handsome consultancies to bring aboard a few influential left-leaning intellectuals and researchers who had previously devoted nearly all their energies to the Democratic Movement, including the trade union movement.

Yet notwithstanding a well-lubricated entry to South Africa, the early 1990s were also extremely difficult years for the Bank and IMF, in part because their international reputation was plummeting to unprecedented depths. Bank ideology had, under the influence of the 1980s Reagan Administration, DC, gone over the top towards neoliberalism. By 1990, Bank economist Manuel Hinds, for example, felt comfortable openly arguing that

> the overall model chosen to integrate the economy into the international markets ... should aim at avoiding the appropriation of rents by suppliers of nontradables and workers. That is, they should maintain the real wage low, so that excess profits accrue to capital ... In carrying out all these activities, a close alliance between Government and private agents must be developed.[6]

Such vulgar propaganda for big business was apparently the norm for Bank staff at the height of the Washington Consensus era. Scandal emerged, however, when the Bank's chief economist, Lawrence Summers (who in 1999 was named US Treasury Secretary), wrote some infamous lines in a December 1991 internal memo (leaked to *The Economist* magazine): 'I think the economic logic of dumping a load of toxic waste in the lowest wage country is impeccable and we should face up to that ... Underpopulated countries in Africa are vastly under polluted.'[7] Apologies and retractions followed, but the Bank again made unwanted headlines in 1992 when senior staff suppressed a United Nations report critical of their role in the disastrous Sardar Sarovar dam in India. Shortly thereafter, Summers' predecessor, South African-raised Stanley Fischer (later the deputy managing director of the IMF), conceded to the *Financial Times* that the Bank/IMF 'culture of secrecy' had been characterised by 'few checks and balances'. Next came the October 1992 'Wapenhans Task Force' internal Bank report on portfolio performance, which concluded that 37 per cent of Bank projects were completed 'unsatisfactorily' in 1991, and more than 40 per cent of Water Supply and Sanitation projects (especially in Africa) had 'major problems'. Wapenhans also conceded a variety of valid borrower complaints (mainly from Third World Finance Ministries):

- 'Bank staff know what they want from the outset and aren't interested in hearing what the country has to say.'
- 'After all the documents are signed, the Bank can change philosophy again.'
- 'The Bank overpowers borrowers, and the country negotiating team often doesn't have the strength to resist.'
- 'The staff rigidly insists on as many conditions as possible, some of which reflect insensitivity about the political realities in the borrower country.'

Indeed, in a 1993 speech, Bank Africa chief Kim Jaycox admitted that 'The donors and African governments together have, in effect, undermined capacity building in Africa. They are undermining it faster than they are building it, or at least as fast.'[8] Jaycox had made much the same concession in private discussions with his opponents in Johannesburg the previous year. To stay in business, the Bank was apparently learning how to concede *past* mistakes, and claimed to be 'learning by doing'.

Sensing that their critiques were hitting home, the world's more advanced social and environmental advocacy movements began to have a field day. A '50 Years is Enough!' campaign of NGOs gathered momentum following protests at Bank–IMF Annual Meetings during the late 1980s and early 1990s in Washington DC, Berlin, Bangkok and Madrid. There was a growing move within the campaign to stop transcend the objective of reforming the Bank, as a limited degree of success had been achieved, after years of Bank-bashing, around gender awareness, environmental considerations, community participation and transparency (though enormous damage to women, ecology and communities continued through Bank structural adjustment policies, especially budget cuts). Instead, using the divestment tactic learned in the anti-apartheid movement, groups associated with the Ralph Nader Washington DC networks and with Global Exchange proposed defunding and boycotting the Bank and IMF.[9]

At the same time, a right-wing populist resurgence in the United States was adding to the Bank's sense of fragility, particularly because future 'recapitalisation' (new infusions of funding) came to depend upon the approval of the proto-fascist senator Jesse Helms (chair of the Foreign Relations Committee after the 1994 Republican congressional victory). Helms and his allies considered the Bank to be a statist if not socialist one-worlder agency intent upon throwing his constituents' money down the black hole of cheeky Third World bureaucracies, with Pat Buchanan's right-wing populist legions adding the charge that this was done largely for the benefit of stateless, soulless corporations. Because of the tiny degree of overlap between right and left critiques, there was occasional congressional cooperation – such as the near-successful refusal, in 1998, of the IMF's $90 billion bail-out fund.

It was no surprise, then, that as early as 1992, Bank president Lewis Preston wrote a memo complaining of his institution's 'increasingly negative external image', concluding that the Bank should be 'actively reaching out to under-exploited constituencies in developed countries, such as private sector industrialists or major academic centres; taking a more pro-active role in defining the agenda for debate with Bank critics; and using modern communications techniques, such as mass media advertising'.[10] With Preston's death in 1995 and his replacement by James Wolfensohn (a charmer), such efforts were undertaken (such as in a major 1995 newspaper advertising campaign showing how Bank loans helped US corporations) and gradually began to bear fruit (Box 5.1).

Box 5.1: Wolfensohn to the rescue?

The Clinton Administration's February 1995 nomination of James Wolfensohn – 'Wolfie', as he was called within the Bank – to lead the World Bank was passionately endorsed by bankers, politicians and mainstream press reports. He became the Bank's 'renaissance man' both because of the hoped-for resurgence of the problem-ridden institution and for his talents in athletics (fencing) and music (cello).[11]

Originally an Australian, the US-naturalised Wolfensohn was formerly an executive of Salomon Brothers investment bank (when it was owned, during the apartheid era, by Anglo American Corporation) and started his own private New York advisory firm in 1981, which was subsequently chaired by former US Federal Reserve chairman Paul Volcker.

Wolfensohn had two other notable career highlights. He spent nearly a decade near the helm of the controversial J. Henry Schroeder banking group (in London and New York, from 1968 to 1977). The Schroeders bank was founded by the offspring of a

Hamburg baron, and was closely tied to Hitler. Later, it also served as a base for Allen Dulles, who became head of the CIA. Schroeders was involved, as a functionary of the CIA, in financing the 1953 coup in Iran, the 1954 coup in Guatemala, the Cuban Bay of Pigs invasion in 1961, and the Chilean destabilisation and coup from 1970 to 1973. Though passed over for chair of Schroeders (which led to the Salomon Brothers position from 1977 to 1981), Wolfensohn held executive positions with the bank beginning in 1968, including running the New York office while the CIA connections were intact.

Wolfensohn was also treasurer of the 'American Friends of Bilderberg'. The Bilderbergers had emerged as a US cheering section from the important 1954 conference in Holland's Bilderberg Hotel, a crucial meeting of North Atlantic rulers from across the political spectrum. The Bilderberg group was concerned, first, with combating communism and second, with 'dependent regions and overseas peoples'. It was co-sponsored by the Dutch firm Unilever and by the CIA, and subsequently served as a top secret, intellectual and ideological 'testing grounds for new initiatives for Atlantic unity', according to historian Kees van der Pijl.

Wolfensohn was not merely a hyper-successful individual, one capable of lobbying the prized job away from the one other serious candidate (former Bank chief economist Summers, a difficult sales job due both to his infamous 1991 memo and – as a US Treasury official in early 1995 – his dismal handling of the Mexican currency crisis). As shown in Chapter 6, he would also be crucial, along with senior vice-president and chief economist Joseph Stiglitz, to the task of reorienting the Bank's image into something more distinct from – and indeed occasionally critical of – the IMF.

As early as 1995, ordinarily more sensible NGOs like Oxfam and the Development Group for Alternative Policies succumbed to 'inside-the-Washington-Beltway' (i.e. power-crazed) tendencies, endorsing co-operative activities with Wolfensohn (such as a Structural Adjustment Participatory Review Initiative highly biased towards technocratic Bank analysis, and even an endorsement, in Oxfam/Washington's case, of Bank recapitalisation and the much derided Highly Indebted Poor Countries conditional debt relief initiative) which more militant NGOs and social movements considered a cheap form of co-optation. Matters were not so easy for Wolfensohn in much of the Third World, however, including South Africa.

Box 5.2: The pit latrine controversy

In designing urban infrastructure, several Bank economists led by deputy resident representative Junaid Ahmed revealed shoddy intellectual work and uncaring professional ethics. Ahmed's 'Urban Infrastructure Investment Framework' team (which included several neoliberal South African consultants) envisaged supplying 'communal standpipes (water), on-site sanitation, graded roads with gravel and open stormwater drains and streetlights (electricity). These services will be targeted at households with an income of less than R800 per month and charged for at between R35 and R50 per month.'[12] The Bank hoped to fund the programme through a $750 million loan which was often discussed in 1995, although only brought to fruition in late 1998 indirectly, via the Development Bank of Southern Africa and African Development Bank.

The standards were appallingly low, and the target population – assumed to be 20 per cent of urban residents in 2005 – would in fact be a much larger proportion given the failure of the macro-economic policy to raise incomes. Perhaps most shocking was that Ahmed neglected to follow – or even acknowledge – RDP directives relating to cross-subsidies for universal access to water, sewage or electricity. Nor did the Bank team factor in important environmental, public health, educational and gender-time benefits of full services that would have swayed the cost-benefit analyses away from pit latrines and communal water taps, back towards RDP promises.

Such failures gave Bank opponents plenty of ammunition to challenge policy and demand a major rethink. The Bank had argued for the low standards on the grounds that the recurrent (operating and maintenance) costs of supplying water and electricity were too high for poor people to afford on a cost-recovery basis. Therefore the urban poor should not have access to the services,[13] and, by implication, should live in segregated income ghettoes. If their income improved and an indoor tap and flush toilet and electrical outlet were desired, they would have to move to another area where the neighbourhood infrastructure for the services was in place (since it would be impossible to upgrade the low-standard areas on a piecemeal basis).

The only real solution to the affordability problem – a national tariff structure consistent with the cross-subsidisation and 'lifeline tariff' provisions mandated in the *RDP* – had not even been considered by the Bank as a funding option. In the case of water, consumption by domestic households amounted to just 12 per cent of total use (and most of that was for watering white suburban gardens). In the case of electricity, just 15 per cent was household consumption; it would have been easy to add a small surcharge to the big users to fund the rest (large corporate consumers paid as little 2c per kWh in 1996, compared to 22c for most households and 48c for those in rural areas using pre-paid electricity meters).

Political pressure gradually mounted.[14] By December 1996, Chippy Olver, the government's chief infrastructure bureaucrat, wrote to the *Mail and Guardian* to distance himself emphatically from the earlier work – 'Not one of the people working on the current municipal infrastructure policy is from the World Bank' – yet most of the low standards (especially pit latrines) and cost-recovery principles remained intact. By late 1996, Olver was quoted as explaining why he had acquired, as he put it, the reputation of 'a mean neoliberal bastard'. He and other Department of Finance econocrats would simply not consider widescale redistributive national tariffs through *RDP*-style cross-subsidies, because of globalisation: 'If we increase the price of electricity to users like Alusaf, their products will become uncompetitive and that will affect our balance of payments ... It's a fact that international capital holds sway as we come to the end of the 20th century.'[15]

URBAN MISSIONAIRIES

Following their colleagues' lead, the Bank's South Africa teams also began suffering self-inflicted wounds during the early 1990s. Many of these occurred in the realm of housing policy debates and urban reform, as shown in Chapter 4. Gaffes were quickly picked up by Bank opponents who were by then well trained, thanks to ideological battles with the Urban Foundation, at spotting neoliberalism.

For example, in 1992, when Bank local economic development expert Kew Sik Lee advised that 'low income housing development in the "available land" between the central city and townships should be avoided', he was met with bitter criticism by Civic Associations of Johannesburg, who were demanding that Johannesburg free buffer-strip land for new low-cost housing. Lee went so far as to suggest 'densification should take place within the existing townships' instead of through a more compact city – a conclusion that could only rest on assumptions such as that Johannesburg's Alexandra had just 134,000 residents (a figure only half right, which Racki inserted into his own 1992 study of Johannesburg infrastructure requirements). This argument also left leafy white suburbs free from demands for restructuring.[16]

Lee also praised Soweto because it maintained some informal sector vitality and thus offered hope for retrenched workers. No mention was made of widespread black small business crises. And by ignoring township income levels and nearby corporate retailing power (e.g. Southgate Mall), Lee offered only meagre reforms ('African-style marketplaces') for township small businesses. Indeed, this reflected Bank staff's methodological limits. Apartheid (not racial *capitalism*) always received the blame for South Africa's urban problems. Where market forces were the clear culprit – for example, Johannesburg inner-city decay resulting from (among other factors) enforced tenant overcrowding due to unduly high rents, landlord refusal to maintain buildings which were already fully paid off, and bank red-lining – the Bank had little or nothing to say, notwithstanding major policy debates then underway. Nevertheless, persistence and enormous expenditure of resources on the urban missions meant that by late 1994 the Bank had established a stronghold in the RDP Office, which ultimately set in train a furious debate over the obligations of the state to meeting social needs (Box 5.2).

In fact, it was not just in South Africa, but internationally, that contestation of the city became central to the struggle against neoliberal development.[17] That struggle became increasingly difficult for people of Third World cities as a result of what seemed to be a shift in the scalar strategy of international capital and aid agencies. Instead of the nation-state attracting all the attention of neoliberal institutions – though it was still crucial, as the prime borrowing agent – the mega-city emerged more and more as a unit of analysis, control and implementation for the purpose of more efficiently imposing structural adjustment policies (especially in the wake of the destruction of many nation-state capacities).

To illustrate, one senior adviser to the United Nations Conference on Human Settlements, Shlomo Angel, argued that the 1996 Habitat conference in Istanbul was about 'creating a level playing field for competition among cities, particularly across national borders; on understanding how cities get ahead in this competition; on global capital transfers, the new economic order and the weakening of the nation-state'. Angel continued, 'The city is not a community, but a conglomerate of firms, institutions, organisations and individuals with contractual agreements among them.'[18]

From such atomistic foundations – so reminiscent of Margaret Thatcher's denial of the concept of 'society' – an entire neoliberal edifice was constructed. The World Bank's efforts to do so took on far greater energy beginning with the 1986 launch of the 'New Urban Management Programme', which was further articulated in an important 1991 policy paper that received wide circulation in South Africa through the Urban Foundation.[19] Meanwhile, the US Agency for International Development, the European Union, British, Canadian, German, Japanese and other official donor agencies began to reinforce urban neoliberalism through cross-conditionality on grants and loans. The overall orientation was nearly identical to the austerity policies at the macroeconomic scale, which also had the effect of splitting the urban working class into a small fraction of 'insiders' served by the market, and masses of peri-urban, slum-dwelling 'outsiders'. US Agency for International Development consultant George Peterson explained just such a linkage between cities and macroeconomic policy to a 1991 conference in Johannesburg:

It aims to eliminate or reduce urban food subsidies and price controls, abolish requirements that part of export food production be diverted into the domestic market, reduce the urban wage structure in cases where government pays or mandates above-market wage levels, and reallocate government capital investment away from subsidies for urban industrial production and public service provision.

This philosophy went entirely against the grain of South Africa's progressive movement, yet Peterson and his colleagues went on to argue on behalf of an important change in policy thinking in the developing world closely linked to the acceptance of market-oriented economies: the growing acceptance of rapid urbanisation ... An emphasis on national economic growth and export-led development will usually mean that new investment resources must be directed to already successful regions and cities ... Governments have considerable control over the entire cost structure of urban areas. Public policy should be directed to lowering these costs.[20]

This, perhaps, came closest to the point. Lowering these costs, especially by lowering the social wage, is integral to a more direct insertion of competitive cities into the world economy. The focus here was not merely on limiting public financing of social services to those deemed to add value, though this is one of the more obvious effects of structural adjustment and the catalyst for many an 'IMF Riot'. Just as importantly, the New Urban Management Programme also highlighted the productivity of urban capital as it flows through urban land markets (now enhanced by titles and registration), through housing finance systems (featuring solely private sector delivery and an end to state subsidies), through the much celebrated (but extremely exploitative) informal economy, through (often newly privatised) urban services such as transport, sewage, water and even primary health care services (via intensified cost recovery), and the like.

IMF riots were the main form of resistance to the intensification of uneven capitalist development in the world's mega-cities. But these reactions were usually defensive, ephemeral and quite destructive. Peru, Bolivia, Brazil and Argentina each witnessed a dozen major anti-austerity urban protests during the 1980s; repeated uprisings were experienced in the cities of Chile, Ecuador, the Philippines, Zaire, Jamaica, Morocco, Sudan and the Dominican Republic; in Venezuela in 1989, security forces killed more than 600 people involved in a single IMF riot; and there were isolated incidents in dozens of other countries. In the early 1990s, these countries were joined by India, Albania, Nepal, Iran, Ivory Coast, Niger and Zimbabwe, where large-scale IMF riots broke out, with even more intense protest during the late 1990s emerging markets crisis.

As argued in the next chapter, such uprisings did not yet reflect – or even stimulate – the existence of more visionary, creative and empowering urban social movements. But they are indicative of the enormous contradictions in the application of neoliberalism to fragile

Third World cities. And while resistance to the consequences of neoliberal urban restructuring may have been more intense, Bank rural experts also came under fire for market-centred land reform recommendations (later adopted) made from 1991 to 1993 to the ANC's main rural policy-maker, Derek Hanekom (described by critics as neocolonial smallholder strategies identical to those that failed in Kenya and Zimbabwe) (Box 5.3),[21] and from 1995 to 1998 to the then Water Minister Kader Asmal around the pricing of rural water.

The latter issue is quite illustrative of how far the Bank won the hearts and minds of even the more left-leaning South African politicians (Asmal). Consider the boast by John Roome – a key water sector bureaucrat and task manager of the Lesotho Highlands Water Project – that his 'power-point presentation to Department of Water Affairs' in October 1995 was 'instrumental in facilitating a radical revision in South Africa's approach to bulk water management'. The presentation included advice that

- Asmal must ensure both urban and rural municipalities establish a 'credible threat of cutting service';
- he should drop proposals for a lifeline tariff and rising block tariffs, because municipal privatisation 'will be much harder to establish' (since private firms would not want to supply to consumers if an opportunity for making profit was not available);
- he should be 'very careful about irrigation for "previously disadvantaged"' South Africans; and instead
- the 'key lies in voluntary solutions – trading water rights', assuming that emergent black farmers could compete financially with the larger (and historically subsidised) white commercial enterprises.[22]

Box 5.3: The Bank in the countryside

Why was so little accomplished in the area of land reform? Oxford rural sociologist Gavin Williams examined the role of the World Bank in ANC rural policy-making from 1992 to 1994, and in an article tellingly entitled 'Setting the Agenda' described how the Bank won the hearts and minds of land experts, paying for dozens of reports by an NGO think-tank, the Land and Agricultural Policy Centre (LAPC).

> Over a hundred social scientists and lawyers were involved in producing them. A few declined to participate. Historians, who have done so much to reshape our understanding of social relations and processes of change in the South African countryside, were notably absent from those asked to contribute; the focus was firmly on planning the future.

That planning, Williams showed in convincing detail, was built upon 'misleading intellectual foundations', including distortion of the supposed success of the Kenyan land reform precedent (in which plenty of programme beneficiaries defaulted on loans, other aspects of 'betterment' led to the Mau Mau rebellion, while the most successful small Kenyan farmers were not the preferred 'yeoman' class but instead an expanding 'middle peasantry').

In the meantime, an upsurge in rural protest and policy advocacy by radical social movements required Bank technocrats to disguise their intentions.[23] The Bank's rural mission leader Robert Christiansen and LAPC director David Cooper co-authored a secretive paper in early 1994 for consumption primarily by other Bank staff, conceding 'a suspicion on the part of many South Africans that the focus of the Bank's program in any country was the need to lend and to dictate policy as a precondition to that lending'. Thus 'the typical product blend of Bank-managed sector work followed by lending was not an approach that was viable'.[24]

The mask slipped in October 1993, when the South African Agricultural Union gleefully announced it had won repugnant commitments by the Bank that 'no land should be expropriated or nationalised with a view to establishing small-farmer projects' and 'only land falling within the homelands or within the jurisdiction of tribal authorities, or excess government land, should be used for setting up preliminary pilot projects'.[25] As a result, Christiansen came under fire from environmentalists and progressive peasant advocates.

In Zimbabwe, Christiansen had inherited a floundering rural programme and faced small farmer default rates of 80 per cent (pre-drought, 1988–89) on the Bank's agricultural loan scheme. Yet the Bank continued to endorse the hated 1980 Lancaster House compromise provisions which thwarted land reform.[26]

As happened in Zimbabwe, incoming South African minister Hanekom adopted a 'willing-seller, willing-buyer' policy (with great *chutzpah*, claiming loudly that South Africa would never replicate Mugabe's 1997–98 land appropriation dramas, apparently not drawing any of the logical lessons from the Bank's Zimbabwe disaster). The *RDP* aspiration that 30 per cent of decent agricultural land would be redistributed within five years was reduced to an internal 6 per cent target by 1996; even this was impossible using neoliberal methods, with less than 1 per cent a more accurate reflection of delivery during the ANC's first term, given Hanekom's insistence on maintaining the failed World Bank strategy.

As National Land Committee leader Abie Ditlhake concluded in a 1998 article, the failed market-driven policy was established

> in the context of external influences, in particular the intervention that the World Bank made during the policy-making process. Alternative views and aspirations were not fully integrated into the policy, notwithstanding the perceived consultative process the Department of Land Affairs undertook. Concerns raised [about the land policy] by rural communities in 1994 were outweighed by global imperatives represented by the World Bank and other international interests, and the emerging national petit-bourgeoisie ...
>
> The 'free and open market' has proved its inability to play a meaningful and objective role in the distribution of land as expected by the policy-makers. The market-based approach is not appropriate for South Africa because of huge historical imbalances due to land dispossession and the consequent inequalities in incomes ... A crisis of delivery has resulted, creating frustration and despair amongst the masses of rural people who expected effective delivery of land and consequent improvement in the quality of their lives.[27]

OPPOSITION TO LOANS AND MACROECONOMIC ADVICE

There were enough lapses and criticisms during the early 1990s that progressive South Africans could easily distance themselves from the

Washington financiers. Although some in Cosatu tried to make a distinction between (good cop) World Bank and (bad cop) IMF advice, Rev. Frank Chikane – in 1992 still with the Council of Churches (and later Thabo Mbeki's leading adviser) – warned of the 'universal outcry and misery' in Third World countries following from both institutions: 'We cannot believe that the salvation of our country lies in an uncritical and undemocratic subjection of our country to IMF and World Bank policies.'[28] It was sometimes pointed out that the ANC did not struggle for 72 years to replace the white *baas* in Pretoria with the white financial bureaucrat in Washington, DC.

Most importantly, in early 1994 the ANC endorsed the *RDP*, whose guiding principles appeared to stymie the World Bank's ambitious loan-selling operation in the infrastructure, health, education and industrial sectors:

[Southern African countries] were pressured into implementing [IMF and World Bank] programmes with adverse effects on employment and standards of living ... The *RDP* must use foreign debt financing only for those elements of the programme that can potentially increase our capacity for earning foreign exchange. Relationships with international financial institutions such as the World Bank and International Monetary Fund must be conducted in such a way as to protect the integrity of domestic policy formulation and promote the interests of the South African population and the economy. Above all, we must pursue policies that enhance national self-sufficiency and enable us to reduce dependence on international financial institutions.[29]

This innovative tenet led influential conservative commentator R.W. Johnson to natter (in the London *Times*) that IMF economists believe the ANC is 'living in fairyland' for attempting to finance the *RDP* from domestic resources. Johnson attributed substantial blame for the 'no foreign loans' clause to 'the strength of the SA Communist Party within the ANC and the tendency of many in the ANC to see the Bank and IMF as part of a global capitalist conspiracy'.

Nevertheless, the *RDP* financing principle won praise in surprising quarters. *Business Day* labelled it 'wise', and *Finance Week* asked: 'Well now, is the view that IMF (and other) foreign borrowing should essentially only be used where it helps to create self-financing export-based, or genuinely internationally competitive import replacement capacity in any way "fairyland"? Absolutely not. The complete reverse in fact.' *Finance Week* quoted Nedbank economist Edward Osborn: 'What has to be eschewed is borrowing abroad for borrowing's sake, especially with a likely continuing decline in the value of the rand.'

This was all somewhat counter-intuitive (aside from the remark by Osborn, a noted Keynesian dissident from orthodoxy). In earlier periods, bourgeois sentiment was very pro-Bank and IMF, and the cliché that South Africa was 'underborrowed in international terms' popped up continually. As *Sunday Times* editorialist Ken Owen had argued in 1992, 'There is, according to siren voices in both business and diplomatic communities, one escape from this dilemma: IMF financing, foreign loans and aid payments, and perhaps even foreign private investment.' And in 1993 *Business Day*'s Jim Jones had contended that 'implementing the recommendations of [IMF] professionals who know the conditions capital seeks can only help the cause', as the IMF was persuading the ANC that 'unchecked social spending' was just not on. The early 1994 reversal probably reflected a more immediate panic by bourgeois interests that the ANC would indeed become excessively populist once in power, and receive Bank financial support to do so. (This, after all, was the general sentiment of Zimbabwe's capitalist class, and outright opposition to Bank personnel from the bourgeois press was not unusual by the time the *Economic Structural Adjustment Programme* failed in the early 1990s.)[30]

Indeed, in what seemed to be precisely this spirit – and no doubt sensing that a losing battle for ANC hearts and minds in the wake of Preston's comments about 'communists' (apparently meaning Manuel) to the 1992 annual meetings, and a July 1993 quote by Manuel that 'We will certainly need foreign aid, but not from the IMF or the World Bank'[31] – Bank staff economists published a short booklet entitled *Paths to Economic Growth* in November 1993.[32] The document included a scenario for economic growth of 5 per cent a year based on a *rise* in the budget deficit to more than 10 per cent of GDP from 1995 to 1997 (peaking at 12 per cent), thanks to 'the common assumption about kick-starting the economy with public investment programmes' (and thanks also to a projected rise in foreign debt, no doubt envisaged to come partly from the Bank). Comparing this with the Bank's participation in the June 1996 *Growth, Employment and Redistribution* policy document, which firmly condemned rising deficits as growth-killing, it was clear that Bank models served merely as capricious, erratic tools of political expediency.

But while the Bank told the ANC's left flank what it thought it wanted to hear,[33] the IMF was back to bad cop. Power relations were unveiled when the very first act of South Africa's interim multi-party government – the December 1993–April 1994 Transitional Executive Council – was an application for an $850 million IMF loan purportedly for drought relief but in reality aimed at servicing part of the apartheid foreign debt which had been renegotiated on surprisingly onerous terms a couple of months before (Box 5.4).

Box 5.4: Aggravating the debt burden

Should the $20 billion-plus apartheid foreign debt (and the $50 billion domestic debt) be repaid? It was a question that kept coming up, first in a 1991 ANC handbook on banking: 'Morally, it could be argued that this debt, used to bolster apartheid, should be used to assist economic reconstruction in South Africa.' The handbook called for foreign debt to be repaid not to the commercial banks, but to a reconstruction fund.

The inherited apartheid foreign debt remained an especially important consideration at the back of elite minds, because of the ANC's insistence upon maintaining financial sanctions until the bitter end of apartheid. (Mbeki was an exception, for he consistently and unsuccessfully argued for early normalisation of financial relations, and was joined by enthusiastic if misguided bureaucrats in the Australian and Canadian governments.) Hence when he was ANC general-secretary, Cyril Ramaphosa was particularly tough when warning foreign bankers not to finance Pretoria, on pain of post-apartheid default on such loans.

Nevertheless, several times during the early 1990s, three state agencies attempted – with mixed success – to gain access to new foreign credit (via issuing bonds), claiming they were by then bona fide institutions of the New South Africa. The ANC's Bonn office countered, 'We appeal to the future investors not to co-operate or to participate in a one-sided restructuring of our economy by the apartheid regime ... The bonds are designed to leave costly and heavy burdens of international debts on the future democratic government and people in SA.'[34]

True, but what *would* happen to the existing debt as the elite transition neared fruition? It all became clear in October 1993, when inept Reserve Bank negotiators joined with an ANC foreign debt review team to reschedule $5 billion in foreign debt that had been caught in the September 1985 'standstill'. The deal required downpayment of $500 million in 1994 and a very disadvantageous interest rate (a full percentage point above the standard London inter-bank rate). In short, added to other agreements, South Africa had committed itself to repaying virtually its entire current hard currency indebtedness within the next eight years, with servicing costs averaging some $2 billion per annum.

Commented financial consultant Charles Millward, 'My London contacts think the big European banks just walked all over the Reserve Bank rescheduling team.' When European bankers arrived in Johannesburg in November 1993, the ANC and Reserve Bank reportedly realised their lapse, and begged, unsuccessfully, to renegotiate the $500 million bullet payment. It was a victory for the forces of 'sound' international relations, but nevertheless a defeat for the ANC's econocrats, for as a young democracy in search of macroeconomic growth and stability, South Africa would face hard currency outflows and balance of payments constraints.[35] In turn, such pressures virtually assured that real interest rates would be maintained at extremely high levels notwithstanding the fragility of the recovery.

Later, during the 1994 election, an inconsequential leftist group – the Workers' List Party – posed the question of apartheid debt as a campaign issue, and the November 1994 Conference on Left Unity resolved to fight for repudiation. Two years later the broad-based NGO Coalition also criticised apartheid debt repayment; the Congress of South African Trade Unions and SA Communist Party joined in; and by 1998 a formidable church–labour–NGO–social movement coalition – Jubilee 2000 South Africa – had made progress in embarrassing the Department of Finance on its prioritisation of creditor interests over ANC constituents. In 1999, the issue of apartheid era Swiss and German bank loans was on the agenda, as Jubilee 2000 demanded that instead of waiting an embarrassing half-century to reimburse victims – as Swiss banks did to Jews whose wealth they had exploited in Nazi times – there should be much faster reparations for black South Africa.

But in an extraordinary afront to international solidarity, Finance Minister Manuel implicitly adopted the position, by refusing to question foreign bankers' pre-1994 South African involvement, that the ANC financial sanctions campaign was a paper tiger. This was not only a clear prioritisation of apartheid property rights over keeping ANC constituents alive (as health and welfare cuts literally killed people), it was also a sabotage of any future financial sanctions campaign. Imagine an Aung San Suu Kyi approaching Citibank or Union Bank of Switzerland, begging them to refuse loans to the Slorc junta, and perhaps threatening that when democracy comes to Burma those loans would be looked upon with disfavour – and imagine a three-piece-suited banker smiling back, 'Yeah, we heard that one before ... from Nelson Mandela's ANC. Ha, ha.'

Was there an alternative to the bum deal that emerged from the October 1993 renegotiation? Hard to say, since the ANC had long before dispensed with its international anti-apartheid supporters, and with them the chance of putting popular pressure on London and New York banks for a fair shake. As a result, development would be hindered for years to come by the legacy of odious debt whose repayment in any just world a real national liberation movement would scoff at.

The terms of the IMF loan, which were kept secret until leaked to the press in March 1994, included the rapid scrapping of import surcharges (potentially catastrophic for many local industries), a drop in the government deficit/GDP ratio from around 7 to 6 per cent, and demands not only for a drop in public sector real wages (by roughly 6 per cent), but a decrease in wages across the board. In addition, Camdessus was reliably understood to have put intense pressure on the ANC (in a personal meeting with leaders several months before the election) to reappoint Finance Minister Derek Keys and Reserve Bank governor Chris Stals.

Reactions varied. On the fringe, Robert van Tonder – the cantankerous, racist Boerestaat Party boss – likened the rejoicing over South Africa's renewed access to IMF loans to 'looking forward to your own death'. In a most undignified development, former Cosatu general-secretary Jay Naidoo welcomed the IMF loan – surely a first for a southern hemisphere unionist (not counting Zambia's Frederick Chiluba) – though he did express reservations about a recommendation for South Africa which declared 'real wage growth must be contained' (see Box 5.5). Denying what was universally obvious, SA's ambassador to the US, Harry Schwarz, remained insistent that the

ANC take foreign loans. Schwarz intoned, 'I disagree that, by taking IMF and World Bank facilities, African countries have lost their sovereignty ... Until now, certainly in respect of the $850 million loan from the IMF, it cannot be said that there has been any endeavour to encroach upon sovereignty.'[36]

A more realistic hint of the turmoil ahead could be found in a commentary by *Business Day*'s Greta Steyn:

> The ANC wants to create an almost utopian society, described in the RDP. But it has to build that society while keeping its promises to the IMF and its own commitment to 'macroeconomic balance'. The *RDP* and the TEC statement of policies to the IMF are arguably the two most important clues on future economic policy ... The IMF has subsequently argued a drop in real wages will go some way towards solving SA's unemployment problem. This view is absent from the *RDP*, which 'makes a decisive break with the exploitative cheap labour policies of apartheid'.[37]

Box 5.5: Black workers overpaid, IMF and Bank agree

A few words should be said about the thesis that thanks to unions, the high wages of unskilled and semi-skilled workers were responsible for unemployment – in a country still suffering one of the largest artificial wage gaps between skilled and unskilled labour in the world. Bank economist Peter Fallon and a Bank consultant, Nobel Prize laureate Robert Lucas,[38] used a narrow econometric model in their controversial 1997 draft discussion paper (unchanged on final release in March 1998) to argue that over time, 'a 10 per cent increase in the real product wage would eventually lead to a 7.1 per cent decrease in Black employment' and that 'employment is reduced through union wage-raising effects by about 6.3 per cent'.

The number crunching was dubious, not just because as in all such exercises, vital political-economic context (such as the 1990s tendency of white businesses to substitute capital for labour, no matter the wage levels) was absent, but also in view of the model's supply-side orientation and lack of attention to demand-induced growth resulting from higher wages. (The demand-side effects would be especially important were assumptions to be relaxed about the leakage of spending on imported goods that could be made locally, in the event of a strengthening of political will.) One key Fallon/Lucas recommendation was, hence, to 'avoid excessive wage increases ... The [Employment Conditions] Commission should try to ensure that wage increases do not increase unemployment, which, under present circumstances of very high unemployment, would suggest that *real wages be allowed to fall*' (emphasis added, partly to show that old-fashioned distinctions between the IMF and World Bank on this issue, made repeatedly by labour movement reformists like Jayendra Naidoo during the 1990s, were flawed). Fallon and Lucas also endorsed the big-business demand for dual wage rates ('lower wages for young people and for all workers in areas of unusually high unemployment'). In contrast, for upper-echelon government bureaucrats, they generously argued, 'it is important that government pay to skilled employees does not fall far behind that of competing sectors'.

As the Bank's Pretoria staff realised the politically incorrect implications of this blunt analysis, they backed off a bit, with resident representative Judith Edstrom telling *Business Day*[39] that the study was not an attempt to 'provide ammunition for any particular side'. But the Pandora's box was again open, and in subsequent debate, then Cosatu leader Sam Shilowa rejected the 'so-called gospel of the World Bank that workers should not demand wage increases' and implied that Fallon and Lucas were part of a 'lunatic fringe outside SA [claiming] that one of the economy's main problems was alleged inflexibility of the labour market'. Shilowa argued that 'Labour market flexibility had become discredited among workers who saw it as a euphemism for very few or no regulations at all so employers could hire and fire, pay whatever wages and ensure no worker protection.'[40]

LENDING DROUGHT

As the months passed, try as it did, the World Bank's lending arm (the 'International Bank for Reconstruction and Development') simply could not sell a loan. An October 1995 *Business Day* report had the Bank preparing '$850m in loans to support the RDP in the sectors of education, agriculture, urban renewal and small business development. The World Bank's budget plans were drawn up after SA and the Bank had signed a memorandum of understanding last March which provided for the studies to be undertaken on a number of projects.'[41]

Yet it was only, finally, in May 1997 that an initial face-saving Bank loan – worth a meagre $46 million – was accepted in order to finance the Department of Trade and Industry's 'Industrial Competitiveness and Job Creation' project.[42] These were two areas where South Africa was notoriously weak, as judged both by World Economic Forum rankings consistently in the bottom tenth of all major countries, as well as massive job haemorrhaging. The tiny Bank loan made no noticeable difference.

There were three basic reasons why Bank opponents – in government, Parliament as well as in society as a whole – successfully argued against a financing relationship for so long:

- *The high cost of Bank money.* All foreign loans have this problem, given that the rand tends to decline in value against currencies in which loans are denominated. London School of Economics researchers issued a 1993 study showing that when Eskom borrowed abroad, the country's single largest foreign debtor ran up twice the interest bill of a local capital market loan. Yet the Eskom loans were to fund rand- (not dollar-)denominated expenses – and foreign costed inputs, such as new turbines, could easily have been financed through much cheaper import-export banks.[43] The cost of foreign loans became especially prohibitive in 1996 and again in 1998 when the rand crashed by roughly 30 per cent against the dollar.
- *The existing surplus of money within South Africa.* The financial markets remained ridiculously liquid. Given that pension payments and insurance premiums providing the handful of institutional investors some R60 billion a year in income during the mid-1990s, there was no reason not to divert some of these funds into real economic activity, from their otherwise self-destructive course into overvalued stock market shares, office buildings and shopping malls.
- *The strings attached to foreign loans, which quickly become the hangman's rope.* This was sufficiently well documented, thanks to the tragic lessons of other African countries suffering Bank 'conditionality'.[44]

Notwithstanding these obvious, sensible reasons, poor local leadership was a common explanation for the Bank's failure to lend. It must have been particularly irritating to the Bank head office, for at least $10 million was spent in 1990s policy advisory investments by the 'Knowledge Bank' – as the Pretoria office began to unselfconsciously call itself (even before the Bank's 1998 publication of the *World Development Report: Knowledge and Development*) – at a time Washington desperately sought an African 'success story' for *borrowing* (not just rhetorical parroting). Presiding over the South Africa operations of the Bank in the initial stages was Isaac Sam, a US citizen originally from Ghana. In early 1995, Sam was charged with the rape of an office cleaning worker (which, to the Bank's dismay, was reported on the front page of the *Sunday Times*) although police reportedly 'lost' the critical evidence so the case was dropped. But sufficient public relations damage was done that Sam was replaced in October 1995. At that stage, Wolfensohn appeared on South African television to confirm his willingness to lend.

Nevertheless, notwithstanding Sam's replacement by a much more suave resident representative (with a social democratic sales-pitch) – Judith Edstrom – and renewed promises of a forthcoming $750 million infrastructure loan, there was sufficient resistance to the Bank in pockets of the state and civil society that another year passed before the arduous task of putting the first credit together really got underway. Other explanations for the long delay in lending include the lack of existing constraints to foreign borrowing – the ANC government periodically issued securities to raise hard currency when required – and satisfaction on the part of international financiers with ANC economic bureaucrats, particularly their mimicking of neoliberal policy.

The Bank's own spin control on the period of lending drought was as follows:

At the outset, the Bank had a strongly negative image, particularly among ANC cadres who viewed the Bank through the lens of their experience in other African countries undergoing structural adjustment. The Bank responded by adapting its focus (concentrating on Economic and Sector Work shaped by South African priorities, without being driven by lending expectations) and pursuing an inclusive dialogue with all segments of society, inside and outside the government. Establishment of a more productive relationship with government and other groups has improved the perception of the Bank in South Africa, although distrust and ambivalence about the Bank's motives and agenda persist with certain groups.[45]

In reality, the hostile environment meant that the Bank's own recollection of 'lessons learned' (as articulated in its confidential 1999 *Country Assistance Strategy*) included the 'tradeoff between achieving impact and obtaining acknowledgment: several successful initiatives had no formal outputs or public recognition of our role'. For example, Bank staff quietly sat on a welfare commission which advised cutting the child maintenance grant by 40 per cent (which, thanks to an upsurge of social protest from churches and NGOs, was partially rescinded). A Bank consultant to the Department of Public Works considered the wages paid community-based public works staff (sometimes as little as R8 per day, especially for women workers) *too high*, and instead recommended 'food for work' schemes. Bank staff's pernicious roles in housing, infrastructure, water and land reform policy have been described above. In the field of healthcare, the Bank promoted – through policy and International Finance Corporation investments – 'managed healthcare' (a super-commodification process that sets insurance companies atop a vertically integrated system whose main purpose is to cut costs by closing health facilities and limiting patient access and quality).

And while Edstrom occasionally put a brave public face on the Bank's disastrous macroeconomic advice before leaving her Pretoria job in 1998, by the time of the 1999 *Country Assistance Strategy*, there was, tellingly, no explicit mention in Bank propaganda of its generous contribution – two staffpeople (Luiz Pereira da Silva and Richard Ketley) and an (admittedly erratic) econometric model – to the Department of Finance's *Growth, Employment and Redistribution* strategy and predictions (e.g. 620,000 new formal sector jobs from 1996 to 1998 when in fact at least 400,000 were lost) that had gone so impressively awry.

Indeed, in virtually every chosen area of social policy intervention (education was the sole area in which Bank advice was rebutted, the *Country Assistance Strategy* concedes, but not for lack of offering), Bank staff worked behind closed doors and, 'in several successful initiatives [with] no formal outputs or public recognition', advocated policies which indisputably entrenched status quo wealth and power relations.

Aside perhaps from boisterous, often shrill Democratic Party politicians, there were probably no more effective advocates for the interests of rich white South Africans in post-apartheid South Africa than the quiet, smooth bureaucrats of the World Bank.

But even the Bank's preferred (and apparently triumphant) approach – quietly drawing local bureaucrats more closely into Washington-think ('hundreds' of South Africans were trained by the Bank's Economic Development Institute, according to the *Country Assistance Strategy*) – finally met loud public resistance when Finance Minister Trevor Manuel tried to set up private meetings between the IMF's Camdessus and Democratic Movement leaders in October 1996.

Manuel had just chaired a plenary session at the Bank-IMF annual meeting and was widely celebrated in the international establishment for his success in introducing *Gear*. A few days later, he invited Camdessus to South Africa 'to meet the critics' (specifically, trade unionists, civic associations and students in closed-door sessions facilitated by Manuel). A 'Campaign Against Neoliberalism in South Africa' (Cansa) formed spontaneously, receiving the endorsements of 60 key activists from social movements within two days. Camdessus was greeted by televised protests upon his arrival in Johannesburg and prior to his Cape Town parliamentary session, sharp hostility from several ANC MPs, cancellation of the scheduled meetings by activists scornful of Camdessus, and harsh press statements by the Progressive Primary Health Care Network, South African Students Congress and the SACP. Amidst a surge of anti-IMF publicity, the trip was a disaster. Cansa demanded a publicly televised debate with Camdessus, but in spite of the cancelled meetings, Manuel's aides begged off claiming there was no time on Camdessus's busy schedule (Box 5.6).

It was up to the former workerist – and still SACP member – Alec Erwin, in his role as Minister of Trade and Industry, immediately to defend his government's honour (in a *Mail and Guardian* interview headlined 'Erwin slams loan critics'):

Our policies are consciously designed to prevent the possible pitfalls of a World Bank loan and the effects they've sometimes had on other economies ... [World Bank] influence is negligible; second, we've put in place policies designed to prevent the detrimental effects that some of their projects might actually have ... We often use World Bank expertise and feel sufficiently experienced not to be threatened.[46]

Soon after, apparently smarting from the attacks, Bank resident representative Edstrom wrote to the *Mail and Guardian* to applaud Erwin for drawing his 'own conclusions as to the course South Africa should take' (though without confessing her institution's 'negligible' influence):

> I am baffled by the sentiments of some groups that contact with the Bank constitutes contamination and should therefore be curtailed. The Bank has learnt a lot from groups with differing views. Exchanges with NGOs and civil society groups have had a direct and positive impact on its understanding of and sensitivity to social and environmental aspects of development programmes. We seek more dialogue, not less.[47]

But tellingly, Edstrom refused to rebut or even acknowledge four specific Cansa charges from the previous week's newspaper:

- Two Bank economists and the Bank economic model were utilised in the June 1996 macroeconomic strategy – which aside from its pro-corporate bias has already, after just four months, bombed with respect to 1996 predictions for job creation, interest rates and the strength of the rand (three of the strategy's most crucial targets).
- In 1994–95, the Bank's deputy resident representative led an infrastructure planning team whose proposals will – unless policy is changed dramatically – soon reduce the lot of the urban poor and low-paid workers to pit latrines, water taps within 200 metres and no electricity, instead of the decent sanitation and household water and electricity 'lifeline' supply promised in the *RDP*.
- The Bank-designed land redistribution programme, dating to 1992–93 and endorsed by government in 1994, is yet to get off the ground largely because it relies nearly entirely on market forces.
- And forceful Bank advice from 1991 to 1994 to limit state housing subsidies and to trust commercial banks to make township home loans – instead of the state and community

agencies advocated in the *RDP* – helps explain the present housing delivery fiasco.[48]

Cansa also pointed out in the journal *debate* that it was ironic Erwin was borrowing the $46 million to enhance 'export competitiveness', given the Bank's 'intrinsic tendency to generate overoptimistic market studies in order to promote exports at all costs'. Cansa cited the words of Carlos Lopez, a leading United Nations Development Programme official: 'The World Bank figures are always exaggerated to give a rosy picture of whatever it is they are involved in.'[49]

How competitive was the Bank itself, after all? Cansa noted that 51 per cent of its African projects were considered failures according to the Bank's own internal evaluations. More than $20 billion in approved Bank loans to Africa were still not disbursed in late 1996 because of the damage that the Bank and IMF did to state administrative capacity (as Jaycox had publicly acknowledged in 1993). Indeed, said Cansa, 'Only the largesse of Northern taxpayers, whose leaders regularly recapitalise the Bank, and the foolishness of Third World borrowers, keep the game in play.'

Cansa's closing appeals during the debate with Erwin are instructive:

We hope the IMF will cease sending its managing director here on fruitless missions to sell neoliberal muti to critics. Broader boycotts, tougher demonstrations, even more hostile parliamentarians and louder demands for transparent public debates – such a request was rejected by both Michel Camdessus and the Finance Ministry last week – will result.

The World Bank should close its Johannesburg office and release its economists – with their R700,000 per annum packages – to compete for jobs in the private sector.

Government should remember its election mandate and open the *RDP* document to page 146: 'Above all, we must pursue policies that enhance national self-sufficiency and enable us to reduce dependence on international financial institutions.'

And ordinary citizens and organisations of civil society interested in challenging the drift away from the *RDP* and social justice towards neoliberalism should join the campaign.

Box 5.6: Cansa 'On the IMF Managing Director's visit'[50]

As members of popular organisations and activists of the Democratic Movement, we have come together to launch a 'Campaign Against Neoliberalism in South Africa' ... we must make the following points about the Camdessus visit.

The Finance Ministry's attempt to establish 'good relations' with the IMF follows its promotion of a macroeconomic strategy in June 1996 which bears an uncanny similarity to the IMF's 11 new 'principles for economic success,' also termed the '11 Commandments'. The *Growth, Employment and Redistribution* strategy – emphasising cuts in government expenditure (particularly 'consumption' expenditure which will threaten social services), continuing high real interest rates, export-led growth and trade liberalisation, privatisation and permission for increased capital flight from South Africa – mimics the free market, monetarist policies that across the world favour the interests of powerful conglomerates and banks at the expense of workers, the poor, women, youth and other marginalised social forces. The warm reception received by the South Africa delegation to the IMF/World Bank Annual Meeting in Washington earlier this month follows months of close collaboration in designing South African economic and development policy, marking a fundamental departure from policies outlined in the *RDP* ...

The IMF and World Bank have the ability to psychologically influence prospective foreign investors, in a context in which foreign investment is incorrectly seen by a small group of government policy-makers and advisers as the overarching factor for economic growth. Since the 1980s, South Africa has succeeded in attracting merely large amounts of 'hot money' foreign investment into speculative stock and bond markets (leading to subsequent bouts of currency volatility), with virtually none of the direct foreign investment that might challenge existing monopolistic conditions, transfer technology, or create jobs and products for consumption in the local market. We believe, therefore, that the move towards close relations with the IMF, premised upon attracting what the minister of water affairs correctly termed the 'mythical foreign investor', should be viewed with alarm by all those in South Africa committed to sustainable, people-centred development ...

Across the Third World, Structural Adjustment Programmes imposed by the IMF and World Bank to obtain the repayment of foreign debt have led to famine, environmental destruction, and the dismantling of health, education, infrastructural and social welfare programmes. These programmes nearly always include the same set of measures: currency devaluation, decontrol of exchange rates, higher interest rates, financial deregulation, trade liberalisation, privatisation, wage cuts, reduction in the public service through budget cuts and massive retrenchments, labour market deregulation, and the like. The social costs – typically including large increases in the prices of basic goods and food, intensified poverty, deterioration of public services, and rising unemployment – are nearly always borne by those people, especially women and children, who never received any benefits from the borrowings. Structural Adjustment Programmes have also made small economies vulnerable to transnational corporations that exploit cheap labour (often imprisoned in union-free export processing zones devoid of health and safety regulations with wages that sink to $1 per day) and that dump toxic wastes and poisons produced in the rich industrialised countries.

Debt repayment has become an important mechanism for transferring wealth from the people of the South to financiers of the North. According to the United Nations, developing countries paid $1.662 trillion in debt servicing between 1980 and 1992. This amount is three times the original amount owed in 1980. Yet in spite of the above transfers the total Third World debt still stands at over $2 trillion. It is not commonly known that the Third World has repaid almost a trillion dollars of principle over and above $771 billion in interest.

In Sub-Saharan Africa the ratios of foreign debt to Gross National Product rose from 51 per cent in 1982 to 100 per cent in 1992, and of foreign debt to total exports from 192 per cent in 1982 to 290 per cent in 1992, a period during which the Third World debt crisis was allegedly resolved. The external debt of the Third World has become an eternal debt and stands as the largest immediate obstacle to growth and sustainable development. It is therefore crucial that progressive forces in South Africa add their voice to the calls made internationally to cancel Third World debt as the first step towards building equitable and just relationships between and within different parts of the world.

The meagre gold sales belatedly proposed by Camdessus to help finance extremely limited debt relief – and only for those countries which religiously adopt the IMF's 11 Commandments – are far too little, far too late, and it is a reflection of the exploitative character of Northern political leadership of the IMF that even these gold sales were not approved at the last meetings.

In the light of the near-universal failure of IMF and the World Bank policies in the developing world, we wish to urge extreme caution upon finance minister Manuel. Rather than naively providing Camdessus legitimacy to sell IMF policies to critics in trade unions and social movements, minister Manuel should take up the mantle of leadership by using IMF and World Bank platforms to call for the cancellation of Third World debt, including the inherited apartheid foreign debt ...

Campaign Against Neoliberalism in South Africa
16 October 1996

CONCLUSION: THE BANK'S DIFFUSION OF 'KNOWLEDGE'

It was, as always, difficult to separate structural from struggle factors preventing full capitulation to not just the IMF/World Bank policy framework (which was quite advanced) but to a lending relationship that spelled certain disaster. Although defeats were suffered by the policy advocates of mass-based constituencies, the period since 1990 nevertheless demonstrated that when mobilised, South Africa's progressive forces could at least *partially* hold the world's most powerful institutions at financial arm's length.

In rebuttal, it could be said, the IMF and Bank were not important determinants of South African macroeconomic policy, given the homegrown character of structural adjustment. To take the argument a step further, as did more sophisticated defenders of neoliberalism in the ANC, were it not for *Gear* and fiscal discipline, South Africa would *really* run into economic difficulties, and be forced to take Bank/IMF medicine from a position of weakness. This is how the strategy was deciphered by Frank Chikane, by then Mbeki's main administrator (yet still a weekly preacher to a low-income Soweto congregation):

If you went overboard and pushed lots of resources into social expenditures to uplift the lives of people, you just widen the debt, and the debt servicing becomes higher, and you go tumbling down on your own. And then five years, ten years down the line, the World Bank and IMF will be here, you know, and come and tell you how you can cause more pain to the victims in order to correct the economy.[51]

This reasonable sounding discourse was developed by Manuel and Jay Naidoo in 1994 and became a kind of mantra when replying to Left critics. But the rebuttal begged four questions:

- First, weren't the government's lead promoters of *Gear* – Mbeki, Manuel, Erwin and their staffs – committed to the strategy not as a holding action against future IMF/Bank pressure, but *because they believed in neoliberalism* (or at best that they believed 'There Is No Alternative')?
- Second, wasn't *Gear* failing in reality (as Left critics predicted), thus leading to *increased* vulnerability to international financial flows and hence a *greater* likelihood of an emergency bailout request in future?
- Third, couldn't, in contrast, the act of (intelligently) spending 'lots of resources on social expenditures' *itself* serve as a key component of an alternative economic strategy (alongside an intelligent investment programme aimed at basic-needs infra-structure, as economists Ben Fine and Zav Rustomjee recommended)?[52]
- Finally, weren't the Bank and IMF *already* regularly celebrating *Gear*'s success in translating trade and financial liberalisation plus fiscal discipline into 'more pain to the victims in order to correct the economy' (hence, what indeed was the difference, except that victims were told their suffering was 'non-negotiable' ANC policy, rather than a form of – perhaps more dignified – suffering at the hands of Washington technocrats)?

In short, when Bank economist Manuel Hinds offered his 1990 injunction to macroeconomic policy-makers – that 'they should maintain the real wage low, so that excess profits accrue to capital' – there was no good reason to think that a post-apartheid South African government would wholeheartedly join, rather than buck, the system.

The Knowledge Bank strengthened the neoliberal cause within the ANC, yet at the same time, this chapter has shown, the contradictions were formidable, leading to creative protest which in turn presages the final chapter's survey of the profound weaknesses associated with late twentieth-century capitalist globalisation.

It has been useful, in this chapter's glimpse of the pre-crisis global pressure, to highlight the aggressive stance of the World Bank towards transitional South Africa. Notwithstanding extremely slick marketing, staff from the Bank's Washington and Pretoria offices served controversial – instrumental by some accounts, negligible by others – but demonstrably mediocre roles as policy advisers. But popular forces were not fooled.

And it could have been worse, had the Bank established the sort of lending relationship it desired and that many local neoliberals advocated vigorously. What prevented a tighter hold on South Africa was, simply, the capacity of progressive social forces to think globally and act locally. Ironically, the ANC had shown the way to locating the vulnerabilities of the international system and developing political strategies accordingly during the successful 1980s anti-apartheid sanctions campaign. That capacity did not die. Deepening the resistance to neoliberal globalisation at a time the world economy degenerates into both destructive bouts of volatility and new, dangerous forms of geopolitical arrangement, is the subject of the final chapter.

6

Beyond Neoliberalism?
South Africa and Global
Economic Crisis

The argument: A sea-change in elite strategy and public consciousness quite suddenly became possible as the turn of the century neared, spurred by the East Asian economic meltdown, the unravelling of the 'Washington Consensus' and its potential replacement with a more inter-ventionist set of 'Post-Washington Consensus' reforms; thus finally, the pernicious phrase 'international experience shows' could be used on behalf of social progress, not against it – nevertheless, the translation of increasingly self-confident critique into a shift in the political balance of forces, remained in question throughout the ANC's first term and into its second, and re-emphasised the importance of international solidarity.

TALKING LEFT, ACTING RIGHT

There are many reasons why, in the wake of the 1999 election, South Africa was ripe for dramatic turns of phrase, if not policy, on the political and economic fronts. With respect to its political traditions, the African National Congress locates itself within a community of Third World nationalist governments that resolutely guard their pride of independence. Global processes that once appeared full of promise for post-apartheid South Africa did not deliver the goods. Many observers asked, has globalisation gone too far? If, as even the International Monetary Fund reported in the closing days of 1998,

Malaysia's reaction to financial collapse – the imposition of strong capital controls – did no apparent harm to its immediate economic prospects, might the South African ruling party also be tempted to take a more aggressive stand against imperialism?

After all, on the economic front, there were strong rationales for a change of heart: unemployment worsened (the ANC's first-term total job loss was more than half a million); a serious year-end 1998 downturn in Gross Domestic Product was initially identified in official statistics as a formal recession; several huge corporations – including Anglo American Corporation, Old Mutual, Liberty Life and South African Breweries – voted with their feet by moving large chunks of capital and stock market listings to London; memories remained of the June–July 1998 imbroglio, including Chris Stals's futile expenditure of R33 billion over a single weekend and, when that did not work, his fanatical escalation of the interest rate by 7 per cent to slow the rand's 30 per cent crash; the black elite (far too highly leveraged based on share value) relived the nightmare of the 40 per cent April–September 1998 stock market collapse as more black economic empowerment groups went to the mat.

Looking at the three-year period 1996–98, virtually all *Gear*'s targets were missed. Annual GDP growth fell from 3.2 to 1.7 to 0.1 per cent in 1996, 1997 and 1998, instead of the strategy's projection of 3.5, 2.9 and 3.8 per cent growth. (In view of steady population growth, the per capita wealth of South Africa actually fell by 2.5 per cent.) Formal sector (non-agricultural) job *losses* were 71,000, 126,000 and 186,000, instead of *Gear*'s anticipated employment gains of 126,000, 252,000 and 246,000. The rate of increase in private sector investment fell from 6.1 to 3.1 to a negative 0.7 per cent in 1996, 1997 and 1998 (instead of rising 9.3, 9.1 and 9.3 per cent, respectively). Of private investment, virtually all foreign direct investment was related to the purchase of existing assets through privatisation and merger/acquisition deals (particularly the 30 per cent sale of Telkom) as opposed to new plant and equipment, and South African outflows of foreign direct investment ($2.3 billion in 1997) were far higher than what came in ($1.7 billion that year). Savings also fell (notwithstanding the rise in the real interest rate from 1996 to 1998) from 18 per cent of GDP in 1996 to 15 per cent in 1997 and 14 per cent in 1998; private savings fell from 20 per cent in 1996 to 17 per cent in 1998 (instead of rising to 21 per cent, as *Gear* forecast). The current account deficit worsened from –1.3 per cent in 1996 to

−2.1 per cent in 1998 (instead of remaining stable, as *Gear* predicted). Exports of South African products (other than gold) rose slowly in 1997–98 (5.3 and 2.1 per cent, respectively), confounding *Gear* projections (of 8 and 7 per cent, although 1996 export growth was better than predicted). The real interest rate remained in double digits from 1996 to 1998 (instead of falling from 7 to 5 to 4 per cent, as *Gear* hoped), and the value of the rand collapsed from 3.5 to the dollar in mid-1996 to 6 (at one point, 6.7) in 1998, confounding projections that it would stay relatively stable.[1]

While some alleged South African economic 'fundamentals' appeared strong – low inflation, a declining government budget deficit/GDP ratio – and while the currency and JSE recovered a little in late 1998 and early 1999, and interest rates even fell back to pre-crisis levels by the time of the 2 June 1999 election, very few neoliberals could seriously defend the ANC's first-term economic record. The Democratic Party made a dubious argument that *Gear* was an excellent strategy: the problem was that *it was not being implemented* due to pressure from the ANC Left (big business still hankered for yet more privatisation, more currency liberalisation and more 'flexible' labour markets). Neoliberals were, therefore, on the defensive, for even setting aside the massive job destruction and terribly weak delivery of basic services (housing, land reform, sustainable water projects, decent education, etc.), on its own terms the government's promotion of savings, investments and exports left a great deal to be desired.

So although *Gear* was vociferously defended by Thabo Mbeki at the July 1998 SA Communist Party congress, it fell into such obvious disrepute in ANC circles by October that year that a 'post-*Gear*' era was openly spoken of, in the same tones that the World Bank chief economist declared in early 1998 that it was now high time for a 'Post-Washington Consensus' in economic policy. Most importantly, the 1999 election season provided renewed tapdancing around the political ideology associated with economic policy and development strategy. Mere populist campaigning, or was a more durable shift underway?

Mbeki's erratic, if always eloquent, collection of speeches and articles, published in late 1998 (with the sponsorship of Billiton's Brian Gilbertson), offered hints of this African intellectual's extraordinary range of vision and his poetic capacities, but nothing terribly firm from which to predict second-term ANC political directions.[2] Nor would we gain much from reviewing the slew of advisory reports on the new leader's desk: a technicist (and widely ignored) 1998 Presidential Review Commission study of potential institutional restructuring, a 1998 *Poverty and Inequality Report* greatly influenced by the World Bank and modernisation theory, and the Department of Public Services and Administration 1997 review of provincial shortcomings. (None of these reports – nor, for that matter, opposition platforms unveiled during the 1999 election campaign – questioned government policy, merely implementation tactics.)

Instead, a better perspective is needed on the gap between political discourse and reality – hence between the high road that left-leaning ANC intellectuals (like Mbeki, on some rare days) know they should be taking, in contrast to the swampy, neoliberal climes in which they are actually mired. We can perhaps gain new insights, in this final chapter, from a close reading of a 1998 ANC/SACP/Cosatu ('Alliance') briefing document on the world economy, considered in conjunction with a review of under-reported but strongly held critiques of ANC ministers from former civil society allies. This exercise reveals a classic South African liberation movement tendency to 'talk left, act right,' as scornful parlance within the ANC tradition sometimes has it. The outcome is 'populist', yes, but undergirded by a careful attention to not rock any economic or even development policy boats.

Yet if this tendency is the overarching theme of South Africa's elite transition, and if it fools some of the people all of the time (and here I mainly mean other elite commentators who continue to complain that their interests have not been sufficiently served by the ANC), it bears mention that as the end of the century neared, political fluidity spread dramatically. Here we need to consider regional, continental and international evidence, for most other once-proud nationalist movements to South Africa's north (and west and east) had by the 1990s morphed into venal neoliberal mode. However, this did not represent an immutable end-of-development history, for at least in Zimbabwe, popular backlashes matured from IMF rioting to a new Workers' Party (the Movement for Democratic Change), with 'anybody's guess' as to how political trends associated with neoliberal failure and progressive resistance might unfold in the coming decade. In short, to give context to our concluding assessment of South Africa's position in the world economy after the first five years of democracy requires us to consider first the character and then the fast-changing discourses associated with a world economy in crisis.

GLOBALISATION AS FINANCE-DRIVEN IMPERIALISM

Globalisation – or what many of us used to call imperialism or neo-colonialism – became the watchword of the 1990s. Well before the late 1990s world economic crisis, this clearly was not a healthy development, for even the mere usage of the term seemed to relegate opponents to the meagre role of a local cog in an unchangeable global system. Invoking the name 'globalisation' made it impossible to regulate or transform national and local economies, argued its proponents. Globalisation disempowered anyone advocating anything remotely progressive in terms of social policy, workers' rights, ecological safeguards, people-centred development, gender equality and self-reliant economics. Perhaps influenced by the then director of the World Trade Organisation, Renato Ruggiero – who in 1997 insisted that 'anyone who believes that globalisation can be stopped has to tell us how he would envisage stopping economic and technological progress; this is tantamount to trying to stop the rotation of the earth'[3] – Nelson Mandela himself conceded, at the July 1998 Mercosur meetings of South American nations, that 'Globalisation is a phenomenon that we cannot deny. All we can do is accept it.'[4]

And yet there was nothing all that new and improved about globalisation, compared to other historical appearances of capitalism. Here, for example, is one description of globalisation from another era:

All old established national industries have been destroyed or are daily being destroyed. They are dislodged by new industries, whose introduction becomes a life and death question for all civilised nations, by industries that no longer work up indigenous raw material, but raw material drawn from the remotest zones; industries whose products are consumed, not only at home, but in every quarter of the globe. In place of the old wants, satisfied by the production of the country, we find new wants, requiring for their satisfaction the products of distant lands and climes. In place of the local and national seclusion and self-sufficiency, we have intercourse in every direction, universal interdependence of nations. And as in material, so also in intellectual production. The intellectual creations of individual nations become common property. National one-sidedness and narrow-mindedness become more and more impossible, and from the numerous national and local literatures, there arises a world literature.[5]

This was the analysis of Karl Marx and Friedrich Engels a century and a half ago, in *The Communist Manifesto*. My interpretation is that for Marx and Engels, the benefits of globalisation – intellectual production, culture, arts, music, literature, human engagements, political solidarity and new (appropriate) technologies representing the advancement (not destruction) of the forces and relations of production – had the *potential* to outweigh the costs of disrupting older, less efficient ways of producing and consuming. But that would entail a globalisation of *people*, not of – and by and for – *capital*.

Just as importantly, the quotation hints at the ebb and flow of international economic processes. For if the world witnessed an unprecedented mid-nineteenth-century form of economic globalisation, subsequent (economic crisis-racked) decades saw many of its 'progressive' components warped into features such as the 'Scramble for Africa' (the 1885 Berlin Conference when European powers divided the continent into colonies and territories of imperial influence), the rise of what Hilferding and Lenin termed 'finance capital', and then the geopolitical turmoil of the First World War.

With the Great Depression and then war from 1929 to 1945, globalisation faded (and many semi-peripheral countries, like South Africa, took the opportunity to grow in a much more balanced and simultaneously vigorous manner). But international economic activity returned after the Second World War via the US-controlled Bretton Woods Agreement and associated forms of economic and military hegemony. Even the Cold War allowed Western economic interests increased stability and management of global economic processes, it is now well recognised. The key monetary feature of the Bretton Woods Agreement – the US obligation to pay 1 oz of its hoarded gold for $35 – broke down in the early 1970s because the US simply defaulted. This was followed by currency disorder (until global interest rates were raised in 1979), by intensified Northern-based multinational corporate expansion, and by the rise of speculative financial flows – first in the form of unprecedented lending, then real estate and stock market gambling, and then emerging market investments.

But as in previous cycles, the unsustainability of the current exercise – particularly because of resurgent capitalist crisis tendencies ('over-accumulation' again), rapidly increasing social inequality and the inadequacy of global proto-state regulation in the face of periodic financial meltdown threats – raises the spectre that the finance-driven 'globalisation' is not, after all, omnipotent or irreversible. In reality, its internal contradictions, by the late 1990s, again generated scope and hope for restoring the capacities of nation-states and, indeed, perhaps for even smaller units of social and economic sovereignty.

But how to make the case *not* just to 'accept it', if, for example, one had the ear of a Mandela or other leaders with left-leaning or even humanist tendencies? (for they do exist in the ANC Alliance, as shown below). One might dwell upon the awesome devastation to people (particularly workers, peasants, women, children, the elderly, indigenous groups and disabled people) and environments to make this case. Sufficient spoor from the trail of 1980s–1990s bankers' destruction can seen in the fallout from the Third World debt crisis (1980s), energy finance shocks (mid-1980s), crashes of international stock (1987) and property (1991–93) markets, witnessed in the collapse of several decades' worth of ordinary people's living standards in so many developing countries since the late 1970s, in Eastern Europe since the late 1980s, and in emerging markets since the mid-1990s.

To go further – in effect, to counteract arguments that the dramatic rise in global inequality these past two decades is simply an unfortunate side-effect of the broader prosperity and inevitability associated with globalisation – we would then have to point out the profound contradictions *within* the internal logic of the world economy. That would not be difficult, turning to the sphere of high finance, to the massive over-indebtedness of Northern consumers (especially in the United States), to the enormous disequilibria and volatility in trade and financial ratios (especially for the US), and to the extent to which stock market 'price–earnings ratios' (the main way to judge overvaluation) hit highs in the late 1990s never previously witnessed in history. (Free market guru Milton Friedman commented in mid-1998 – well before Wall Street reached the 11,000 mark – 'If anything, I suspect there is more of a bubble in today's [stock] market than there was in 1929.') In this irrational context, late 1990s examples of gambles turned sour in derivatives speculation, exotic stock market positions, currency trading and bad bets on commodity futures and interest rate futures include Long-Term Capital Management ($3.5 billion) (1998), Sumitomo/London Metal Exchange (£1.6 billion) (1996), I.G.Metallgessellschaft ($2.2 billion) (1994), Kashima Oil ($1.57 billion) (1994), Orange County, California ($1.5 billion) (1994), Barings Bank (£900 million) (1995), the Belgian government ($1 billion) (1997) and Union Bank of

Switzerland ($690 million) (1998). In sum, we have no shortage of symptoms of the underlying crisis of capitalism to point to.

Nor is it hard to make a self-interested case against the finance-driven globalisation of capital, to any patriotic group of national policy-makers. For what of South Africa's insertion into the world economy during the late 1990s? The question was posed in Chapter 1, as a way of explaining the ongoing economic crisis in South Africa, and will appear repeatedly in this chapter.

But what is obvious may not be sufficiently convincing to change course, for in many cases – as discussed in more detail below – there remain rather less patriotic, developmental bureaucrats, politicians and financiers driving policy-making in South Africa. Sadly, we have seen abundant evidence thus far how, as a function of the character of the elite transition, the country's economic and political rulers moved quickly during the 1990s to hoard for themselves the bulk of globalisation's benefits, in the forms of lower tariffs on imported luxury goods and labour-saving machinery; of spoils associated with deregulation, liberalisation, outsourcing and privatisation; of rentier profits associated with South Africa's unprecedented high interest rates and share market appreciation; of the inexplicable permission granted by the ANC to move ill-begotten apartheid era savings to offshore banks; and of an extraordinarily anti-redistributive state capacity – via the destruction of the progressive *RDP* and the imposition of World Bank-friendly social policies – to pass the costs of old and new forms of underdevelopment to the traditional victims.

Although resistance was often impressive, the 'previously-disad-vantaged' (that coy term signifying oppressed South Africans) paid the price in three main struggles over international economic relations:

- *International trade.* South Africa signed the General Agreement on Tariffs and Trade (GATT) in December 1993 following secretive negotiations mainly involving apartheid bureaucrats, big business representatives and labour's team of post-Fordists. Anti-apartheid trade sanctions were finally lifted. And after the 1994 election, trade and industry ministers Manuel and Erwin removed tariffs even faster than GATT required in key areas. But this led to rapid firm closures in key sectors, hundreds of thousands of job losses and a consistently miserable ranking in

World Economic Forum 'Global Competitiveness Reports' with no prospect for improvement at the turn of the century.

- *Foreign investment.* The ANC's energetic campaign for new foreign investments never paid off. In any case, the merits of inviting the likes of American purveyors of cosmetics and sweetened water (Pepsi) to set up shop locally were questionable. Foreign direct investment traditionally intensified the South African economy's apartheid era bias towards both export of raw materials and local production of luxury goods that were affordable only to a small, mainly pale section of the population. Production by state-of-the-art foreign investors was also more highly mechanised, generating fewer jobs and a greater outflow of profits from South Africa.
- *Global finance.* Moral surrender was the only way to describe the ANC's decisions to repay in full apartheid's $20 billion-plus foreign commercial bank debt and to phase out exchange controls in the name of attracting new foreign finance. Debt rescheduling negotiations were carried out by incompetent Reserve Bank bureaucrats and naive ANC economists in 1993, who according to informed financial sources were taken for a ride. Moreover, the destructiveness of foreign speculators demanding convertible currencies should have been obvious in the wake of the 1995 Mexican financial collapse; it took the 1996 crash of the rand for this realisation to hit home in South Africa, yet still financial liberalisation continued.

Indeed, the words of South African-born Kerr Nielson – subsequently associated with Soros Fund Management in Australia – in early 1995 poignantly illustrated how speculators viewed emerging markets like South Africa:

What is being made clear by the Mexican problem is that in traded securities, you are going to have to be very careful about where these flows are going and where the herd is. When everyone is wild to get into a place, it is often better to just stay away ... What a lot of people have missed are the implications of the global flow of equity funds – and the new alignment, where the maniacs, like ourselves, are driving the flow of funds around the world.[6]

The ANC leadership's key problem was in continuing to identify maniacs as friends. It was not because 'the markets' stopped sending clear signals about their trust of the ANC and South African democracy more generally, as this newspaper report three days after the 1999 election (before the final vote tally was released) demonstrates:

> Foreign investors were becoming increasingly anxious yesterday at the prospects of the ANC winning a two-thirds majority in Wednesday's general election, with a major investment fund warning this may have a devastating effect on local financial markets. Mark Mobius, the president of the $40 billion Templeton Emerging Market Fund, said he would fundamentally alter his investment view of the country if the ANC won 67 per cent of the vote. Mobius, one of the most respected emerging market investors, administers the $40 billion fund, one of the largest investors in South Africa's financial markets. It is heavily weighted towards the country, at 8.5 per cent, or about $3.4 billion. 'If the ANC gains the power to unilaterally amend the Constitution, we will adopt a very conservative and cautious approach to further investment.'[7]

FRIENDS AND ENEMIES

Were there, then, any potential alliances to be made as the global crisis gathered pace at the end of the 1990s? To think this through requires delineating five broad tendencies associated with very different reactions to the crisis which appeared, by 1998 or so, to be firming up. They represented (with tentative labels, from left to right) a) 'New Social Movements'; b) 'Third World Nationalism'; c) the 'Post-Washington Consensus'; d) the 'Washington Consensus'; and e) the 'Old World Order'. South Africa's relations to these can be described in more detail once we map the emerging terrain.

The Washington Consensus

Consider, first, the most powerful, the status quo Washington Consensus, which without shame – even after the serious 1995–99 Mexican, South African, East Asian, Russian and Brazilian crises –

dogmatically continued to promote free trade, financial liberalisation and additional foreign investment incentives, business deregulation, low taxes, fiscal austerity, privatisation, high real interest rates and flexible labour markets.[8] If there were problems outstanding in the world economy, they would always merely be temporary, according to the Consensus, to be overcome by more IMF bail-outs (embarrassingly generous to New York bankers though they were), intensified application of 'sound' macroeconomic policies, augmented by greater transparency, a touch more financial sector supervision and regulation, and less Asian cronyism. (An early 1999 IMF attempt to go a bit further, to establish a Washington Consensus 'lender of last resort' was initially discredited, for it was seen as a naked power play.)

Providing political cover for the status quo at the end of the century were Bill Clinton and Tony Blair; providing operational support were US Treasury Secretary Robert Rubin and his deputy (and 1999 replacement) Lawrence Summers, US Federal Reserve chair Alan Greenspan, and IMF Managing Director Camdessus; and offering periodic intellectual justification were IMF Deputy MD Stanley Fischer and Summers. A variety of bank and corporate-sponsored Washington think-tanks echoed the party line, while outside the Washington Beltway, allies were found in the World Trade Organisation, Bank for International Settlements, OECD and numerous university economic departments. (At its core, the Washington Consensus is undergirded by a 'Wall Street–Treasury Complex', in the words of Columbia University's Jagdish Bhagwati; and indeed as another world-famous conservative economist, Rudiger Dornbusch, conceded in 1998, 'The IMF is a toy of the United States to pursue its economic policy offshore.')[9]

The Old World Order

Second, amongst those scornful of the Consensus were conservatives, largely based in reactionary pockets of the United States. But it was a mistake to discount US politicians like Jesse Helms, Trent Lott, Pat Buchanan and their ilk as mere populist rednecks. Their critique of public bail-outs for New York bankers was backed by think-tanks (like the stalwart conservative Heritage Foundation and the libertarian but surprisingly influential Cato Institute in Washington) and closely paralleled by elite conservative concerns – notably of Henry Kissinger and George Shultz, geopoliticians who lost dear friends like Suharto in the 1997–98 financial turmoil – which together led by 1998 to both a formidable attack on IMF policies as unworkable, and opposition to the US Treasury Department's request for $18 billion in further IMF funding.[10]

There were, at these moments, occasional tactical alliances between Buchanan (and his quite active grassroots lobbyists) and left-populist movements, such as the Ralph Nader networks and Friends of the Earth,[11] notwithstanding the danger that political strategies uniting Right and Left, as shown by inter-war Germany, do most damage to the latter. While the right-wing challenge appeared formidable at times, it was also subject to co-option, as occurred in October 1998, when Clinton bought off Republican opposition by agreeing to make IMF conditionality even more fierce, through shortening credit repayment periods and raising interest rates on future bail-out loans. Moreover, xenophobia and isolationism remained the logical political culture of this current, and economically it wasn't hard to envisage (latter-day Smoot-Hawley-style) protective tariffs kicking off a downward spiral of trade degeneration (reminiscent of the early 1930s), as the Old World Order advocates regularly had their way.

The Post-Washington Consensus

Third, there appeared the important reformist position, often taking one step forward, two back, known as the Post-Washington Consensus in honour of a subtitle of the famous 1998 Helsinki speech given by the World Bank's Joe Stiglitz.[12] Aimed at perfecting the capitalist system's 'imperfect markets', Stiglitz cited organic problems like 'asymmetric' (unbalanced) information in market transactions – especially finance – and anti-competitive firm behaviour as key contributors to the late 1990s instability. Likewise speculator George Soros attributed financial volatility to bankers' herd instincts.[13] However, by merely advocating somewhat more substantive national regulatory interventions (tougher anti-trust measures, and even dual exchange rates to slow capital controls) and more attention to social development, Stiglitz was as reluctant to tamper with underlying capitalist dynamics as Soros, whose call for a global banking insurance fund to protect speculators, to be embedded within the IMF, looked suspiciously self-interested (particularly coming at a time, in August

1998, when he had lost several billion dollars of his Russian investments due to Boris Yeltsin's default on state debt).[14]

Others from a neoliberal economic background who abandoned the Washington Consensus ship as the crisis unfolded included Massachusetts Institute of Technology economist Paul Krugman, who claimed both a temporary fondness for capital controls to halt speculative runs, and responsibility for Mohamad Mahathir's September 1998 restrictions on trading the Malaysian ringgit.[15] Likewise, Jeffrey Sachs, director of the Harvard Institute for International Development, offered critiques of IMF austerity economics so vociferous as to (nearly) disguise his own previous life as 'Dr Shock' Therapy.[16]

Unexpectedly, perhaps, a local South African variant of George Soros was Donald Gordon, the Liberty Life insurance magnate. After losing enormously to speculators running away from his $350 million 'euro-convertible bond' issue (in the process crashing Liberty's share value), Gordon remarked ruefully in 1999, 'In the name of short-term gain for a few, these people have been allowed to undermine most of the emerging markets. In South Africa [foreign traders' speculation on local assets] was the financial equivalent of allowing hostile war boats free rein along our coast. It is a destructive activity that undermines the very core of our sovereignty.' As his interviewer interpreted:

> Gordon reckons it [the eurobond] opened a Pandora's box of arbitrage activity that attacked the very substance of Liberty for four years. It marked the beginning of a period that saw stock lending, asset swaps and derivative trading take off on a grand scale, activities which seemed predicated on the devaluation of liquid blue chip stocks. Four years on and having devoted much energy and four annual reviews to the problem, Gordon remains perplexed by the previous unwillingness of global authorities to rein in the destructive powers of arbitragers.[17]

More durable than the growing chorus of reform-oriented neoliberals (and burned financiers) were institutions which had an actual material stake in promoting human welfare, such as several key UN agencies including the UN Conference on Trade and Development (whether they ever succeeded or not was another matter).[18] More confusing than any of the other reformers was the World Bank itself, whose president, James Wolfensohn, allowed Stiglitz space to attack the IMF but whose own unoriginal contribution to the debate – a January 1999 paper on the Bank's 'new paradigm' reminiscent of dusty modernisation theory – described his institution's function as the opposite side of the same coin of the IMF, one doing macroeconomic 'stabilisation', the other 'development'. As David Moore concludes:

> If James Wolfensohn's memorandum on the Bank's post-millennium project is indicative, it seems that in the wake of failed structural adjustment programmes and a 'second-fiddle' image in the Asian financial crisis, the 'knowledge bank' is attempting to control (or at least coordinate) the whole gamut of international development activities through the construction of a panopticon-like grid of surveillance available to all who have access to the World Wide Web. In the age of diminishing resources for 'social development' this may be the essence of leadership in that realm.[19]

More potentially significant than any of the above were the shifting political sands of social-democratic (and Green or otherwise left-leaning) party politics in Germany, France, Italy and Japan. While the proposed 'Miyazawa Initiative' (named for Japan's Finance Minister) – an 'Asian Monetary Fund' to promote growth not austerity as a response to crisis – was beaten back by Rubin and Summers on three occasions in 1997–99, and while the departure of Oskar Lafontaine in March 1999 represented a profound setback for this current and appeared to realign Germany away from France and towards Britain, nevertheless it wouldn't be easy for Washington to continue having its way in G-8 meetings (where the industrialised world's leading officials regularly gathered).[20] More and more, the presence of Keynesian-oriented officials from Tokyo and Paris would benefit from the mid-1999 realisation that state fiscal stimulation actually produced, finally, some results in Japan. Moreover, given its importance to the South African debate, the Stiglitz 'information-theoretic' approach to economics is worth revisiting again a bit later.

Third World Nationalism

Fourth, the equivalent groupings in a very broadly constituted Third World Nationalist camp could hardly claim to share ideological-economic traditions in any respect. While China and India forthrightly resisted financial liberalisation and Russia formally defaulted in August 1998 (if only temporarily – but in the process avoided seizure of assets by creditors), it was in rather different nationalist regimes in Asia, Africa and Latin America that discourses of opposition to the Washington Consensus emerged most vociferously by the late 1990s. From Malaysia to Zimbabwe to Venezuela, IMF-bashing was back in style by 1999, even if the respective leaders' rhetorical flourishes had different origins: one, Mahathir, Muslim; another, Mugabe, a self-described socialist; the third, Hugo Chavez, simply populist. Yet, self-evidently, the trajectory chosen by all three amounted, at best, to attempts to join the system, to play by its rules and, having discovered that the game was set up unfairly, to adjust these rules somewhat in the Third World's favour.[21]

Not even reflective of the 1970s call for a New International Economic Order, this strain faded badly over the subsequent two decades, as demonstrated by a quick recollection of national leaders from previously disadvantaged Second and Third World societies who, at one point (at least momentarily), carried the aspirations of a mass popular electorate – Aquino (Philippines), Arafat (Palestine), Aristide (Haiti), Bhutto (Pakistan), Chavez (Venezuela), Chiluba (Zambia), Dae Jung (South Korea), Havel (Czech Republic), Mandela (South Africa), Manley (Jamaica), Megawati (Indonesia), Musoveni (Uganda), Mugabe (Zimbabwe), Nujoma (Namibia), Ortega (Nicaragua), Perez (Venezuela), Rawlings (Ghana), Walensa (Poland) and Yeltsin (Russia) – but who then reversed allegiance, imposing ineffectual and extremely unpopular structural adjustment programmes. In the cases of Mahathir, Mugabe and others, 'talking left' also entailed repression of public interest groups and trade unions (and women and gay rights movements), which was less publicised in 1998–99, but just as chilling to democratic processes as the arrests of a high-ranking Malaysian politician (of the Washington Consensus ideological ilk) and of several Zimbabwean journalists.

Not just a problem of Third World nationalism, selling out the poor and working classes on behalf of international finance was also the general fate of so many labour and social democratic parties in Western Europe, Canada and Australia. Even where once-revolutionary parties remained in control of the nation-state – China, Vietnam, Angola, and Mozambique, for instance – ideologies wandered over to hard, raw capitalism. It is striking that the two leaders with the most impressive working-class organisations active in their ascendance, certainly since the mid-1970s, namely Kim Dae Jung in South Korea and Nelson Mandela, rolled over and played dead most convincingly before financial speculators and their local allies during attacks on national currencies. And yet, too, the very universality of financial crisis would necessarily allow counter-hegemonic voices to emerge.

Thus there was still talk within the ANC of potential interlocking interests of major Southern Hemisphere nations, which would potentially reflect renewed muscle in the Non-Aligned Movement, Group of 77 and various other fora of revived nationalisms. Indeed, whether the ANC might fit itself comfortably within a nationalist critique of global capitalism was an open question, and is revisited below.

New Social Movements

Which brings us, fifth, to the New Social Movements, whose goal typically was to promote *the globalisation of people and halt or at minimum radically modify the globalisation of capital*, and which spanned Old Left forces (many labour movements, and some ex-Stalinist Communist Parties like those of the Philippines, South Africa, parts of Eastern Europe and Cuba), other newer political parties (from the Brazilian Workers Party, Sandinistas and their São Paolo Forum allies in Latin America, to the emergent new workers' party – the Movement for Democratic Change – in Zimbabwe), progressive churches, human rights and disarmament movements, democracy activists, urban/rural community and indigenous peoples movements, organisations of women, youth and the elderly, HIV and health activists, disability rights lobbyists, consumer advocates and environmentalists who work from the local to the global scales (Greenpeace and Friends of the Earth in the latter group, along with international environmental justice networks).

Virtually all countries provided evidence, by the turn of the century, of coalitions and networks of anti-globalisation activists, many of which were fairly well grounded in mass democratic organisations that acted locally, but thought globally: for example (here we cite only a few simply to give a flavour of this current), Mexico's Zapatistas, Brazil's Movement of the Landless, India's National Alliance of

People's Movements, Thailand's Forum of the Poor, the Korean Confederation of Trade Unions, Burkina Faso's National Federation of Peasant Organisations, the Canadian Halifax Initiative, the US '50 Years is Enough' campaign against the Bretton Woods institutions, and so on.

Some localised efforts were already having inspiring results, such as anti-dam struggles in parts of South Asia and the unveiling of Chile's repressive legacy as part of an international campaign to bring General Pinochet to justice. But it was always vital to question whether these sorts of organisation could forge links, so as not only to think globally and act locally, but also act globally? Local struggles to make housing and food social entitlements – expanding the sphere of human rights discourse beyond 'first-generation' liberal political rights into more radical socio-economic spheres – were aggregated into the Habitat International Coalition and FoodFirst International Action Network. The Zapatista 'Intercontinental Encounters for Humanity, Against Neoliberalism' planted seeds, as did growing anarchist-inspired networking and activism (like People's Global Action) in London, Davos and other sites of Northern power. The most successful of these groups during the late 1990s tackled three global issues: landmines (nearly victorious were it not for the United States), the Multilateral Agreement on Investment (where several stunning stalemates were won mainly in European settings) and the Third World debt.

Indeed, it was possible to locate within the 'Jubilee 2000' debt cancellation movement (particularly its Asian, African and Latin American components) an extremely effective campaigning spirit that not only attracted the likes of celebrities Muhammad Ali and U2 singer Bono, but also drew tens of thousands of activists to protest at G-8 meetings in Birmingham in 1998 and Cologne in 1999. (Admittedly, classic South versus North sentiments arose not only in Jubilee 2000 critiques of the Washington Consensus and the highly conditional debt relief schemes on offer from Washington, but also in Jubilee 2000 *South* critiques of their northern advocacy counterparts, who often appeared extremely pliant to Northern politicians' gambits.)

Not only did social movements show that in some settings they could move from marginal sideline protest to shake ruling-class confidence in major neoliberal initiatives (the North American Free Trade Agreement and US support for the General Agreement on Tariffs and Trade were threatened as much by radical US farmer and labour activists, as by the Republican right-populists). They also claimed quite substantial resources for future struggles, including effective advocacy networks (again a handful of examples will suffice, e.g. the Third World Network based in Penang and Accra, the Third World Forum in Senegal, the International Rivers Network in Berkeley), and a few progressive nerve-centres in sites of power, particularly Washington DC (the Nader organisations, Alliance for Global Justice and Center for International Environmental Law, for instance). There were, in addition, several radical economic think-tanks associated with the social movements (e.g. Focus on the Global South in Bangkok, the Preamble Center and Institute for Policy Studies in Washington, Amsterdam's Transnational Institute and International Institute for Research and Education), a few university allies (with critical masses of political economists at London's School of Oriental and African Studies, the University of Massachusetts/Amherst, and American University in Washington), and a handful of accessible international activist-oriented periodicals (in English, including *Third World Resurgence*, *Monthly Review*, *Z*, *International Viewpoint*, *Multinational Monitor*, *The Ecologist*, *International Socialism*, *Red Pepper* and *Left Business Observer*) and publishing houses (Pluto Press, Zed Press, Monthly Review, Verso, amongst just the English-language presses).[22]

In the same illustrative spirit, some of the leading anti-neoliberal spokespeople, activist leaders and leftist luminaries of the late 1990s deserve mention: Subcommandante Marcos of the Zapatistas, Lula (Luis Ignacio da Silva) of the Brazilian Workers Party, Cuban premier Fidel Castro, Guatamalan Nobel laureate Rigoberto Menchu, Alejandro Bendana of Nicaragua, Samir Amin of the World Forum for Alternatives in Dakar, the poet Dennis Brutus of the debt cancellation movement, the Indian anti-dams and social movement campaigner Medha Patkar, Martin Khor of Third World Network, Indian writer Arundhati Roy, feminist-scientist-environmentalist Vandana Shiva, Walden Bello of Focus on the Global South, former Tanzanian President Julius Nyerere, the Australian journalist John Pilger, the Russian intellectual Boris Kagarlitsky, Susan George of the Transnational Institute, the French intellectual Pierre Bourdieu, the US consumer activist Ralph Nader, the *Monthly Review* co-editor Ellen Meiksins Wood, the Irish journalist Alexander Cockburn, the Palestinian literary critic Edward Said and the US intellectual Noam Chomsky.

The global balance of forces, to be sure, was very clearly weighted against Third World Nationalists and New Social Movements as the millennium dawned, and there appeared little real basis for any forms of alliance between the two given the former's penchant for authoritarianism and patriarchy. There were also a variety of other important, organised social forces which didn't fit neatly into any camp (such as Muslim fundamentalists, Andean left-wing guerrillas, Chinese 'communists' or still stodgy US trade unionists) but which had the potential to influence local or regional matters. In addition, the global crisis resurrected platforms for well-meaning economist-technocrats: for instance James Tobin, author of the international 0.05 per cent cross-border financial transaction tax proposal which bears his name; John Eatwell and Lance Taylor, who argued for a World Financial Authority; futurist Hazel Henderson, who suggests means to prevent currency 'bear raids' by focusing on electronic funds transfers (and a transparent transaction reporting system); or post-Keynesian Paul Davidson, who wanted an international clearing union providing for capital controls.[23]

Moreover, amongst the New Social Movements there were two fault-lines. One was a dangerous tendency amongst the more conservative Washington NGOs and environmental groups – some even derisively called Co-opted NGOs, or CoNGOs – to cut pragmatic, yet ultimately absurd, untenable deals with the establishment (the 1999 US–Africa free trade deal – the Clinton–Leach 'Africa Growth and Opportunity Act' – provided an example, as did numerous negotiations over the environment). Jubilee 2000 nearly fractured around strategy in 1999 because of this fault-line. Not only did major environmental organisations often cross the line into co-option, so too others in the field of development advocacy – such as Oxfam's Washington office, the Center for Concern and the Structural Adjustment Participatory Review Initiative (a project driven by the Development Group for Alternative Policies) – seem naively to believe their work with Bank and IMF leaders on 'reform' would benefit society more than the delighted Bretton Woods institutions.[24]

And indeed the other ongoing debate concerned whether energy should be invested in aggregating post-Washington Consensus reforms into a global state regulatory capacity – expanding upon embryos like the IMF and Bank, WTO, United Nations and Bank for International Settlements – or whether in contrast the immediate task should be defunding and denuding of legitimacy the various sites of potential international regulation, so as to reconstitute a progressive politics at the national scale. This latter problem we must return to, for it raises important issues around 'the politics of scale', but to do so requires considering further economic rhetoric – and harsh reality in the fields of domestic socio-economic policy – emanating from South and Southern Africa (and South Korea).

RHETORICS OF CRISIS

Back in Johannesburg, the October 1998 Alliance statement on the world economy provided a very different interpretation of contemporary political economy than was normally available in the South African media, and it is worth briefly dwelling on this and a parallel mid-1998 ANC discussion document entitled 'The State, Property Relations and Social Transformation'. Key Alliance intellectuals and representatives – government communications chief Joel Netshitenzhe, lead SACP officials Blade Nzimande and Jeremy Cronin, and then Cosatu leader Mbhazima Shilowa – regularly set out the main lines of argument about the course of the 'National Democratic Revolution'. True to ANC traditions, such papers were enthusiastically photocopied and circulated to a hungry young intellectual strata of the liberation movement (and often published in the *African Communist*, amongst other Alliance publications), but aside from attracting predictably dusty liberal critiques (by, especially, Howard Barrell in the *Mail and Guardian*) they generally had no bearing on actual government policy or practice.

Nevertheless, evolving rhetorics are themselves important markers of material processes. In 'The State, Property Relations and Social Transformation', a document released prior to the October 1998 Alliance Summit (and attributed to Netshitenzhe), a revival of Marxian phraseology was evident:

If in the past the bourgeois state blatantly represented the interests of private capital, today its enslavement is even the more pronounced, with its policies and actions beholden to the whims of owners of stupendously large amounts of capital which is in constant flight across stocks, currencies and state boundaries. More often than not, governments even in the most advance countries assert their role in the economy merely by 'sending signals to the markets,' which they can only second-guess. If in the past, the Bretton Woods institutions (the IMF and World Bank) and the

World Trade Organisation pursued the same interests as these powerful corporations and governments, today their prescriptions are turned on their heads as 'the animal spirits' sway moods in a set of motions that have no apparent rhythm or logic.

Yet there is rhythm and logic. It is the logic of unbridled pursuit of profit which has little direct bearing to production.[25]

Were these the meanderings of Netshitenzhe, as merely a lone ANC intellectual (albeit an exceptionally important strategist and Mbeki loyalist who was widely understood to be a future deputy President or Finance Minister)? Clearly not, for soon afterwards, the 'Global Economic Crisis' – a formal Alliance position paper – provided a flavour of how extraordinarily far *official* thinking shifted in a few months following the mid-1998 run on the rand and Mbeki's caustic attack on the SACP for its disloyalty to *Gear*:

The current instability and volatility in the global economy over the last year is seriously affecting the economies of both developed and developing countries ... The present crisis is, in fact, a global capitalist crisis, rooted in a classical crisis of overaccumulation and declining profitability. Declining profitability has been a general feature of the most developed economies over the last 25 years. It is precisely declining profitability in the most advanced economies that has spurred the last quarter of a century of intensified global-isation. These trends have resulted in the greatly increased dominance (and exponential growth in the sheer quantity) of speculative finance capital, ranging uncontrolled over the globe in pursuit of higher returns ...

As the depth and relative durability of the crisis have become apparent, the dominant economic paradigm (the neoliberal 'Washington Consensus') has fallen into increasing disrepute ...

The dominant assumption in the 1990s has been that alignment with globalisation would guarantee economies more or less unin-terrupted growth. The paradigm of an endlessly expanding global freeway, in which, to benefit, individual (and particularly developing) economies simply had to take the standard macro-economic on-ramp (liberalisation, privatisation, deregulation, flexibility and a 3 per cent budget deficit) is now in crisis.[26]

The document's authors, drawing for inspiration upon Robert Brenner's seminal (if controversial) May–June 1998 *New Left Review* article (later a major book, *Turbulence in the World Economy*), were absolutely correct. Since the 1970s, the crisis had indeed evolved from overproductive 'real' sectors of the world economy into speculative financial markets (stocks, debt instruments, real estate, and the like). That this was not an accident was illustrated by the cyclical pattern associated, historically, with this process (at least one third of all nation-states fell into effective default during the 1820s, 1870s, 1930s and 1980s–1990s, following an unsustainable upswing of borrowing; likewise corporations and consumers went to the mat).

The radical tone of 'Global Economic Crisis' was unprecedented in recent years and amazingly condoned by Mbeki and Manuel, for citing overaccumulation as the underlying problem (for now this meant that it was *capitalism*, not just finance-driven imperialism, that was under intellectual attack).[27] But the language belied the managerial, decidedly non-transformative character of the strategic vision laid out next, which called for action on several fronts:

- The struggle to introduce a much more effective international regulatory system for speculative financial flows ...
- Joint action with other developing economies, which may provide more immediate results. In particular we need to engage with some of the more significant economies of the South (eg. Brazil, India, China, etc.). Can we forge a Brasilia–Pretoria–Delhi–Beijing Consensus in the absence of any Washington Consensus?
- Continuously enhancing a southern African and African perspective.[28]

Excellent intentions these, but a sense of how to build relationships with counter-hegemonic geopolitical forces – in South Africa, Africa and across the South – was yet to be articulated. (After all, what 'consensus' could possibly emerge from the key countries' then ruling parties: Brazil's crisis-ridden liberal-corporate regime, the ANC's neoliberal proto-Africanism, Hindu nationalism in India, and a conservative bureaucratic-Communism-cum-rampant-capitalism in China?) Indeed, South Africa's official 'Southern African and African perspectives' left a great deal to be desired, in reality, as shown below.

Thus in the 'talk left, act right' tradition, the 'Global Economic Crisis' document was better understood as a (very fortuitous) opportunity to displace massive contradictions that existed within the Alliance – as witnessed by Mbeki's pro-*Gear* harangues to the SACP and Cosatu in mid-1998 – to the global sphere. ('Thank goodness for the global economic mess', I was told by one ANC insider just prior to the document's release.) Yet in international economic relations, the ANC government would continue its record of foreign policy confusion. To borrow from the five-part typology offered above, ANC leaders deplored the protectionism and often naked imperialism of the Old World Order; followed loyally the dictates of the Washington Consensus; made occasional noises about joining the Post-Washington Consensus (through the Socialist International, for example);[29] shied away from amplifying – or even effectively utilising – Third World nationalist platforms (when heading, for example, the Non-Aligned Movement, or holding a World Bank/IMF director's seat);[30] and *eschewed entirely the New Social Movements from which the ANC, as a liberation movement, had emanated and for so long sought and found nurture.*

Likewise on the domestic front, talking left, acting right would continue. In its details, the 'Global Economic Crisis' offered much more – reading further into the document – to bring the Alliance partners into the Finance Ministry's export-led, budget-cutting *Gear* philosophy than the other way around.[31] Thus while the penultimate paragraph began, 'At the ANC's NEC of last weekend, the notion of an Alliance "post-*Gear*" consensus was mentioned in passing', the document quickly denied the merits of 'engag[ing] polemically with each other along these lines' – and so in the process vanquished the earlier radical critique.

At a point when a global rethink about development policy was underway, and a shift from *laissez-faire* to more interventionist approaches widely anticipated, the ANC's left flank expected more. By way of contrast, not only did the Korean Confederation of Trade Unions adopt the analytical orientation of the ANC–Alliance Left, they also took the logical political conclusion and in 1998 broke off corporatist ties with their business and state elite compatriots (see Box 6.1). But in South Africa, the disappointments did not end there. Not only at the macroeconomic scale but throughout contestations of social policy, virtually all ANC ministers encountered friction with their civil society constituencies, as a brief review demonstrates.

Box 6.1: Korean workers echo Alliance versus global capitalism

Entirely independently, the dynamic young general-secretary of the Korean Confederation of Trade Unions, Koh Young-joo analysed global capitalism in ways reminiscent of the South African ANC Alliance, in this extract from a March 1999 paper:

> The intensification of the fantastic and imperialistic neoliberal offensive and the economic crisis is the dual expression of one entity: the overaccumulation (overproduction) of capital since the 1970s. The global economy is characterised by overproduction and a decline in the rate of profit. Efforts of capital are concentrated on increasing the rate of profit, leading to greater monopolisation. And the global monopolies and their metropoles are intent on driving out state intervention in the process of reproduction. This is what is undertaken under the name of 'deregulation'.
>
> Furthermore, the decline in the rate of profit due to overproduction has meant that capital can no longer find sufficiently profitable areas for investment in production or distribution. This has forced capital to turn to speculation. The birth of mammoth speculative capital, fostered by the changes in global financial practices, has transformed the system into a 'casino capitalism'.
>
> Monopoly capital, while calling for the exclusion of the state from the process of reproduction, is however intent on mobilising the power of the state to extract greater pain and sacrifice of workers and people, and to exercise and step up the states' imperialist influence on their behalf in international interactions.
>
> We cannot, at the same time, overlook the influence of the science and technology revolution. It is, on the one hand, a consequence of the deepening of overproduction and the intensification of competition, and on the other hand, a cause for their greater acceleration in the science and technology revolution.
>
> The result is the deepening of the neoliberal offensive and the worsening of the crisis. And workers are forced into greater unemployment, deepening poverty, and oppression and repression.[32]

ACTING RIGHT, ATTRACTING LEFT CRITIQUE

An argument made throughout this book is that South Africa's immediate post-apartheid domestic policy was excessively influenced by conventional neoliberal wisdom, in many cases imported through 'international experience' (a pseudonym for advice by the World Bank and its allies). As confirmed by Netshitenzhe in 'The State, Property Relations and Social Transformation', speaking more broadly about the era of neoliberalism,

> What this in fact means is that, in terms of the broad array of economic and social policy, information and even political integrity, the state has lost much of its national sovereignty. This applies more so to developing countries. While on the one hand they are called upon to starve and prettify themselves to compete on the 'catwalk' of attracting limited amounts of foreign direct investment, they are on the other hand reduced to bulimia by the vagaries of an extremely impetuous and whimsical market suitor![33]

The worsening bulimia was not widely understood in South Africa, for typical media reports during the ANC's first term religiously avoided interrogations of what forces truly influenced state 'economic and social policy, information and even political integrity'. Instead, especially as the ANC's first term of office drew to a close and some kind of assessment might have been expected, the media offered only a steady fare of junk food news, highlighting personality squabbles within the Alliance and nearly all of the opposition parties (and futile competition within the latter over just a third of the electorate), musical chair movements of often irrelevant politicians, and – in the major daily papers – a drumbeat of criticism of the ANC, mainly over crime and declining standards, from centre-right and right-wing political parties and vocal white citizens, perhaps very occasionally augmented by often-caricatured perspectives of trade unionist or Africanist dissent. There was virtually nothing on offer to question why much of South Africa's national sovereignty continued to be offered up on a plate to impetuous and whimsical local and international financial markets.

All the more reason, in contrast, to revisit briefly the continued radical instincts of a few high-quality unions, community-based organisations, women's and youth groups, NGOs, think-tanks, networks of CBOs and NGOs, progressive churches, political groups and independent leftists. Their 1994–96 surge of shopfloor, student and community wildcat protests had subsided, true, yet IMF riots continued to break out in dozens of impoverished black townships subject to high increases in service charges and power/water cut-offs. Yet while virtually invisible to the chattering classes, this mode of South African politics was just as – perhaps far more – likely to inform ANC Alliance rhetoric in coming years as was the banal defensiveness about the first democratic government's failure to fully appease the privileged.

What, then, did radical civil society think about post-apartheid policy? Those most often in the firing line were the ANC economic team. Manuel and his bureaucrats were condemned by left critics not only for sticking so firmly to *Gear* when all targets (except inflation) were missed, but also for sometimes draconian fiscal conservatism; for leaving VAT intact on basic goods, and amplifying (especially in 1999) his predecessors' tax cuts favouring big firms and rich people; for real (after-inflation) cuts in social spending at the same time the Finance Ministry demonstrated a fanatic willingness to repay apartheid era debt; for restructuring the state pension funds to benefit old guard civil servants; for letting Anglo American, Old Mutual, and South African Breweries (three of the country's largest corporates) shift headquarters to London; for liberalising foreign exchange and turning a blind eye to capital flight (in particular allowing Standard Bank to give £50 million to its London subsidiary to cover bad Russian loans); for granting permission to demutualise the two big insurance companies; for failing to regulate more aggressively financial institutions (especially in terms of racial and gender bias); for not putting discernible pressure on Chris Stals to bring down interest rates; for initially proposing legislation that would have transferred massive pension fund surpluses (subsequent to the stock market bubble) from joint-worker/employer control straight to employers (though Cosatu prevented this); and for publicly endorsing controversial figures like Camdessus and Harvard Business School's Michael Porter, whose deregulatory, export-oriented advice generated none of the promised benefits.

Likewise, the Minister of Trade and Industry, Alec Erwin, was attacked for the deep post-1994 cuts in protective tariffs leading to massive job loss (including a 1999 European Free Trade deal which would deindustrialise South Africa even further, and endorsing a controversial US version of the same strategy); for his weakness, as president of the UN Conference on Trade and Development, in allowing the neoliberal agenda to prevail on issues such as the Multilateral Agreement on Investment and continuing structural adjustment philosophy; for giving out billions of rands in 'supply-side' subsidies (redirected *RDP* funds) for Spatial Development Initiatives, considered 'corporate welfare'; for cutting decentralisation grants which led to the devastation of ex-bantustan production sites; for inserting huge loopholes in what was once a tough liquor policy; for a dreadful record of small business promotion; for lifting the Usury Act exemption (i.e. deregulating the 32 per cent interest rate ceiling on loans) at a time when even Manuel was decrying moneylenders' extortionate interest rates; and for failing to impose a meaningful anti-monopoly and corporate regulatory regime.

Land Affairs and Agriculture minister Derek Hanekom was jeered by emergent farmers associations and rural social movements for failing to redirect agricultural subsidies; for allowing privatisation of marketing boards; for redistributing a tiny amount of land (in part because he adopted a World Bank-designed policy); for failing to give sufficient back-up support to large communal farming projects and for not fighting Constitutional property rights with more gusto.

Housing Minister Sankie Mthembi-Mahanyele (and her former Director-General Billy Cobbett and indeed Joe Slovo before his 1995 death) came under fire from the civic movement for lack of consultation, insufficient housing subsidies; for 'toilets in the veld' developments far from urban opportunities; for a near-complete lack of rural housing; for gender design insensitivity; for violating numerous detailed *RDP* housing provisions; and for relying upon bank-driven processes – via behind-closed-door agreements that the banks immediately violated with impunity – which were extremely hostile to community organisations.

Welfare Minister Geraldine Fraser-Moleketi was bitterly criticised by a church, NGO and welfare advocacy movement for attempting to cut the child maintenance grant by 40 per cent; and for failing to empower local community organisations and social workers.

Education Minister Sibusiso Bengu was censured by teachers' unions, the student movement and movement education experts for often incompetent – and typically not sufficiently far-reaching – restructuring policies; for failure to redistribute resources fairly; and for a narrow, instrumentalist approach to higher education.

Minister of Constitutional Development Valli Moosa was condemned by municipal workers and communities unhappy with the frightening local government fiscal squeeze; for intensifying municipal water cut-offs; for the privatisation of local services (on behalf of which he tried to divide-and-conquer workers and community activists); for low infrastructure standards (such as mass pit latrines in urban areas); and for preparations underway to effectively end – by siting at vast distances – local democracy for millions of South Africans (by closing half the country's 843 local municipalities through amalgamation).

Aside from his role in certifying arms sales to regimes like Algeria (which he defended for having had recent 'elections', no matter that the government refused to recognise their results), Water Minister Kader Asmal earned the wrath not only of unions for his privatised rural water programme, but also of beneficiary communities for whom the majority of the new taps quickly broke (the vast majority of waterless South Africans remained without water, notwithstanding Asmal's *RDP* commitment to supply all with at least emergency supplies); and he was condemned by environmentalists and Gauteng community activists for stubbornly championing the unneeded Lesotho Highlands Water Project expansion.

Defence Minister Joe Modise and Deputy Minister Ronnie Kasrils were denounced for their R30 billion 'toys-for-boys' approach to rearmament (with obfuscating 'spin-offs' justification); as well as for arms sales to repressive regimes in and beyond Africa. Likewise, intelligence head Joe Nhlanhla was criticised for not shaking up the National Intelligence Agency, which cannibalised itself in spy-versus-spy dramas.

Safety and Security Minister Sydney Mufamadi was considered weak for not transforming policing services more thoroughly (thus generating active protest from the Popcru union); for allocating far more resources to fighting crime in white neighbourhoods and downtown areas than in townships; for allowing a top-down managerial approach to overwhelm potential community-based policing; and for failing to sustain his battle with George Fivas.

Foreign Minister Alfred Nzo was ridiculed by Democratic Movement solidarity organisations for chaotic and generally conservative foreign policy, including flip-flops on both Nigeria generals (first hostile then friendly) and Laurent Kabila's Democratic Republic of the Congo (once friendly then hostile); for cosying up to Indonesian dictator Suharto

(Cape of Good Hope medalist a few months before popular revulsion sent him packing); for the Lesotho invasion fiasco; for often playing a role as US lackey; for prioritising arms sales over human rights; and for the failure of South African leadership to put forward or sustain progressive positions in the Non-Aligned Movement, the Southern African Development Community, Organisation of African Unity, the Commonwealth, and other venues.

Environment Minister Pallo Jordan was seen to be exceedingly lazy in enforcing environmental regulations, particularly when it came to mining houses; as well as for failing to generate innovative community-based tourism opportunities to attract the ANC's international supporters. His department, while paying lip-service to 'consultations' with environmentalists, was considered an inactive, untransformed bureaucracy, which failed to conduct rudimentary monitoring and inspection and instead passed the buck to ill-equipped provinces.

Labour Minister Tito Mboweni was, while in cabinet (before taking up a position as governor-designate of the Reserve Bank in June 1998), attacked by trade union experts for a Labour Relations Act that disempowered unions by overemphasising what were seen as co-optive workplace forums. His successor, Membathisi Mdladlana, was understood to have won the job because, as the *Mail and Guardian* put it, 'he was so vocally contemptuous of trade unions in the ANC caucus that Mbeki decided he was the man to sort out the workers'.

Notwithstanding periodic denials, Posts and Telecommunications Minister Jay Naidoo was regularly criticised not only for condoning the Americanisation of broadcasting (under an excessively heavy hand of the state), but for his partial sale – and hence rapid commercialisation – of Telkom, which entailed dramatic increases in local phone tariffs and price-cuts for international calls.

Health Minister Nkosazana Dlamini-Zuma was attacked by progressive health workers not only for lethargy on HIV/AIDS (such as the refusal to provide cheap anti-virals to pregnant women, and for deep pedagogical confusion as evidenced by her sponsorship of the blame-the-victim in the Sarafina 2 drama, an educational play mired in financial corruption and mismanagement) but also for cutting too deeply into hospital budgets before promised clinics materialised; for de-emphasising community health workers and more innovative primary healthcare strategies, and for failing to mobilise allies in civil society before going into sometimes suicidal (though salutary) battle against tobacco companies, international pharmaceutical corporations (and with them Al Gore and the US government), urban doctors, medical aids firms and insurance companies.

Transport Minister Mac Maharaj became notorious for ignoring his *RDP* mandate to promote public transport ('It is a living document', he would quip); for deregulating many areas of formerly regulated transport; for failing to curb violence convincingly and bring order to the murderous taxi industry; for allowing the train system to decay; for privatising and outsourcing large sections of his department (and pushing the commercialisation ideology on municipalities); and for allowing subsidies to impoverished commuters to stagnate (and indeed suffer phase-out) without sufficient changes in apartheid era socio-economic and geographical relations (yet Maharaj described himself, as late as 1998, as a 'Marxist').

No one understood Public Works Minister Jeff Radebe's dramatic reduction in national staff capacity (retrenching most of his civil servants and subcontracting many functions); his department's tendency to favour old-guard consulting firms and leave communities out of local 'community-based' projects (which in any case received a surprisingly low priority); the high level of provincial public works incompetence and corruption; the lack of progress on establishing an indigenous construction industry (notwithstanding tendering oppor-tunities); and extremely low pay for contract workers on rural public works projects.

Energy Minister Penuell Maduna's critics included many concerned about the corrupt nexus he nurtured involving local and Liberian con artists; his baseless, unsuccessful attack on the auditor-general's *bona fides* (which, he later conceded in court, he 'couldn't be bothered' to remedy publicly once proved wrong); the liberalisation of nuclear energy (and, via a state bureaucrat, the scandalous deal that exempted mining houses from radiation regulation); his failure to transform power relations in the mining and energy industries; and his lack of attention to the needs of small-scale miners and to most new electricity consumers whose tariffs were five to ten times as much as those paid, per kilowatt hour, by Alusaf, Billiton and other favourites of Eskom.

Public Services Minister Zola Skweyiya was criticised for not moving quickly enough in slimming down apartheid era bureaucratic activity in the state and establishing new, more appropriate, developmental job opportunities for the unemployed and unskilled.

Public Enterprises Minister Stella Sigcau was criticised for a completely shallow, foreign-influenced approach to privatising parastatals (but applauded for being extremely inefficient in winning support and carrying privatisation through).

Justice Minister Dullah Omar was considered weak for leaving enormous residual power in old guard judicial and prosecutorial hands; for allowing enormous problems in the criminal justice system to develop; for his uncreative approach to formalising community-based justice institutions; for failing to reform court procedures in cases of sexual offences against women; and for not transforming the legal aid system, hence effectively ignoring constitutional guarantees of access to courts which for most South Africans are denied due to lack of affordability.

Sports Minister Steve Tshwete was considered excessively lenient in allowing sports bodies to retain existing race, gender and class privileges; and especially for failing to establish viable recreational opportunities for the mass of low-income South Africans.

To be sure, there were occasions when at least one minister, Dlamini-Zuma, revelled in (and was praised by civil society activists for) taking on extremely powerful corporations and vested interests. Yet as noted, these fights also showed a penchant for going it virtually alone, bringing on board none of Dlamini-Zuma's likely civil society allies. In that context, her public image as a heat-seeking missile was never effectively countered, even though it would not have hard to have positioned herself as intermediary between protesting grassroots social movements and corporate titans. And this indeed sums up the broader character of 'talk left, act right' politics; for even the exception proves the rule.

The contrast with what *could* have been done, were ANC ministers in true alliance with the grassroots social-change movements, was hinted at in 'The State, Property Relations and Social Transformation', where Netshitenzhe insisted that, in view of 'counter-action by those opposed to change',

> Mass involvement is therefore both a spear of rapid advance and a shield against resistance. Such involvement should be planned to serve the strategic purpose, proceeding from the premise that revolutionaries deployed in various areas of activity at least try to pull in the same direction. When 'pressure from below' is exerted, it

should aim at complementing the work of those who are exerting 'pressure' against the old order 'from above'.[34]

This honourable strategy – essentially, encouraging ruling politicians to build (and offer public respect to) a 'left flank' in civil society as a buffer against the old guard – was, frankly, *void* in reality. Virtually all first-term ministers' gaping digression from Netshitenzhe's approach cannot be explained simply by the perceived need for emergency social stabilisation measures – such as calling out the army to quell mid-1994 wildcat strikes by transport workers – or Mandela's often stern, consensual-patriarchal approach to governance. Lumping mass action protests together with the shooting of policy, Mandela warned at the opening of parliament in 1995,

> Let it be clear to all that the battle against the forces of anarchy and chaos has been joined ... Some have misread freedom to mean license, popular participation to mean the ability to impose chaos ... Let me make abundantly clear that the small minority in our midst which wears the mask of anarchy will meet its match in the government we lead ... The government literally does not have the money to meet the demands that are being advanced ... We must rid ourselves of the culture of entitlement which leads to the expectation that the government must promptly deliver whatever it is that we demand.[35]

The conflict-ridden gap between ANC rulers and subjects stems, more, from the conflict between neoliberal social policies adopted by the government in the mid-1990s, and the policies that people actually required to have a chance to change their lives. The result was a need to *demobilise* the left-flank movements, or when not demobilising them (for instance, in giving the SA National Civic Organisation more than a million rand during the mid-1990s so as to keep it alive), *controlling* them.

But given South Africa's traditions of militant civil society self-organisation and autonomy, controlling or even channelling the 'pressure from below' was not always easy. One of the most confident (and, pre-1994, left-leaning) of ministers, Derek Hanekom, exemplified relations between neoliberal politicians and radical civil society in early 1996, when – in the context of Constitution-writing and a march to Pretoria against the property rights clause – Hanekom disdainfully remarked of the National Land Committee advocacy group, 'They don't understand.' Not: 'The Old Order must now realise that any defence of land based on property rights will come under attack not just from government but from social movements.' Or: 'The tempestuous history of rural struggle in South Africa is a warning to us all that it would be suicidal to not deliver the goods.' Or even: 'The National Land Committee is a serious network of the major social movements and we must listen carefully to their grievances.' Instead, on a national public radio broadcast: 'They don't understand.' Later, Hanekom would publicly accuse rural critics of being 'frivolous' and 'ultra-left' when they raised complaints about the shockingly slow pace of land reform and his thoroughly deregulatory orientation when it came to state support for black farmers.

The second-term ANC ministers, announced in mid-June 1999, were not anticipated to do any better (Box 6.2). Changes in Mbeki's 'new' cabinet – he was, after all, considered to be a key architect of the first – were widely considered as arbitrary and capricious as the earlier (March 1996) cabinet reshuffle. The deployment of Maduna to Justice, of Tshwete to Sports, of Sigcau to Public Works, of Kasrils to Water, of Mufamadi to Provincial and Local Government, of Patrick Lekota to Defence and of Phumzile Mlambo-Ngcuka to Minerals and Energy appeared to have no logic. Perhaps this reflected the last-minute refusal of Inkatha boss Gatsha Buthelezi to move from the Home Affairs Ministry to the deputy presidency, on condition (he confirmed to the media) that the KwaZulu-Natal premiership be taken away from the obstinate Inkatha stalwart Lionel Mtshali and given to the ANC (Mbeki had overestimated Buthelezi's ego, and moreover to everyone's surprise, sufficient pressure existed in Inkatha for Buthelezi to retain the provincial power-base rather than – as it appeared – take a job that by implication would have led to Inkatha's slow liquidation). That meant that instead of the anticipated promotion of ANC Deputy President Jacob Zuma to the Defence Ministry, Zuma was made National Deputy President, which in turn threw off other (perhaps more logical) appointments.

Certainly some changes were in order. Three first-term ministers not regarded as strong performers (Modise, Nzo and Bengu) retired for reasons of ill-health or old age. Two others (Maharaj and Naidoo) resigned, by some accounts, because tensions with Mbeki were so severe that there was little hope of reappointment (in both cases, no social support base existed, especially after Naidoo had tastelessly attacked his former comrades in Cosatu for opposing *Gear*, and there were no obvious defenders elsewhere). Another two – Jordan and Hanekom – were simply fired, it appeared, for reasons perhaps related to personality clashes with Mbeki. (Hanekom was terribly bitter; Jordan, having been fired once before as Communications Minister after a clash with Mbeki over whether to broadcast state developmental propaganda, must have known his days were numbered.)

Surprisingly, Peter Mokaba (formerly Deputy Minister of Tourism) was not promoted or even reappointed, notwithstanding his strong role, while serving as ANC Youth League president a few years earlier, in Mbeki's own political recovery (following his downgrading during the early 1990s negotiations process). Nor, surprisingly, was a ministry reserved for Winnie Madikizela-Mandela – widely tipped to be rewarded for her continuing grassroots popularity and tough campaigning in squatter camps and the hotly contested Eastern Cape (as well as for having swallowed her earlier vicious critiques of Mbeki's leadership clique). However, as if to assure continuity in personnel controversies, Mbeki also appointed as Mpumalanga premier Ndaweni Mahlangu, a former bantustan minister who not only rehired three provincial ministers under investigation for corruption, but cheerily endorsed lies allegedly told by one of them regarding an illegal R340 million promissory note secured by world-famous provincial game parks, on grounds that lying 'is accepted and is not unusual anywhere in the world. It wasn't the end of Bill Clinton's life.'[36]

The extended cabinet, to Mbeki's credit, was composed of nearly 40 per cent women (eight ministers and eight deputy ministers, including a pacifist as deputy Defence Minister). But aside from the illogical swaps of portfolios – perhaps a way for Mbeki to elevate his personal authority by loosening relations between ministers and their departments (hence boosting the importance of civil service directors-general, whom Mbeki also then took a much greater role in choosing for the second term) – the most telling indicator of power in Mbeki's cabinet was the much lobbied retention of the two most business-friendly ministers, Manuel and Erwin. 'Market confidence' was restored, and the rand gained value after the reappointments.

Box 6.2: The ANC's second cabinet

Ministers
1. President: Thabo Mbeki
2. Deputy President: Jacob Zuma
3. Agriculture and Land Affairs: Thoko Didiza
4. Arts, Culture, Science and Technology: Ben Ngubane (IFP)
5. Correctional Services: Ben Skosana (IFP)
6. Defence: Patrick Lekota
7. Education: Kader Asmal
8. Environmental Affairs and Tourism: Valli Moosa
9. Finance: Trevor Manuel
10. Foreign Affairs: Nkosazana Dlamini-Zuma
11. Health: Manto Tshabalala-Msimang
12. Home Affairs: Mangosuthu Buthelezi (IFP)
13. Housing: Sankie Mthembi-Mahanyele
14. Justice and Constitutional Development: Penuell Maduna
15. Labour: Shepherd Mdladlana
16. Minerals and Energy Affairs: Phumzile Mlambo-Ngcuka
17. Communications: Ivy Matsepe-Casaburri
18. Provincial and Local Government: Sydney Mufamadi
19. Public Enterprises: Jeff Radebe
20. Public Service and Administration: Geraldine Fraser-Moleketi
21. Public Works: Stella Sigcau
22. Safety and Security: Steve Tshwete
23. Sport and Recreation: Ngconde Balfour
24. Trade and Industry: Alec Erwin
25. Transport: Dullah Omar
26. Water Affairs and Forestry: Ronnie Kasrils
27. Welfare and Population Development: Zola Skweyiya
28. Intelligence: Joe Nhlanhla
29. Presidency: Essop Pahad

Box 6.3 What Mozambique is *owed*

With approximately $5.6 billion in foreign debt by 1998, in the wake of at least $20 billion in apartheid-generated damage (not counting a million lives), Mozambique found itself repaying more than $100 million a year. Although this was a small fraction of what in fact should have been repaid (in a context in which the state budget was virtually entirely funded by foreign aid), it represented a huge drain on resources that should have gone to education, health and basic infrastructure. Mozambique is amongst the most destitute countries in the world, with 70 per cent of the population living below the poverty line.

As a result, when in 1996 the World Bank and IMF responded to demands (largely from progressive church groups) for debt reduction with its 'Highly-Indebted Poor Countries' (HIPC) initiative, Mozambique was a logical place to begin. But notwithstanding a write-down of approximately $1.4 billion in debt owed to the IMF and Bank, the actual repayment relief amounted to only just a bit more than $10 million a year, leaving Mozambique to continue servicing the debt at a level of more than 20 per cent of its foreign exchange earnings.

Thus HIPC allowed merely a write-off of unserviceable debt – which no one ever expects Mozambique to repay – yet virtually no real relief. Worse, in return, there were harsh conditions attached to the debt relief. Only in December 1998 did these begin to emerge as a matter for public debate, at an unprecedented foreign debt conference at the Assembleia da Republica, attended by 500 members of the parliament and civil society leaders. In order to comply with HIPC, parliamentarians learned, they would have to pass legislation effectively quintupling patient fees for public health services over a five-year period. The demand was part of a report accompanying a March 1998 letter by World Bank president Wolfensohn, agreed to by government leaders and major donors, but not previously disclosed to either the parliament or civil society. According to the letter, the terms of HIPC also include the privatisation of municipal water. Already, acknowledged the Bank report, water 'tariffs have been increased sharply in real terms over the past 18 months and are to be increased even further prior to the signing of management contracts'.

Frelimo's parliamentary deputies were angry about their leaders' capitulation to the HIPC deal, and warmly welcomed delegates from trade unions and the Mozambican Debt Group who reinforced the general demand for a total cancellation of the foreign debt. A special parliamentary debt investigation commission was established. The Bank's Maputo representative could only testify, grimly, that Mozambique's $1.4 billion in debt relief was far more than other HIPC countries received, and Mozambique should probably not expect further relief. Ironically, the G-7 countries had the previous month announced a new $90 billion IMF fund to be used for emergency rescues of financiers exposed to large emerging markets considered 'too big to fail' – unlike the world's poorest country, Mozambique, which remained out of sight, out of mind, to international economic managers.

Finally at the end of June 1999, a groundswell of Jubilee 2000 pressure (and bad publicity for the IMF) led to slightly greater concessions. Instead of the average 1995–98 debt repayment of $114 million a year, only $73 million would be squeezed out of Mozambique from 1999 to 2005. Still, even with debt payments dropping from 17 per cent of the state budget in 1999 to 11 per cent in 2001, that year more money would still be spent on Northern creditors than on public health in Mozambique. Moreover, to get the relief, the IMF imposed 71 new conditions on Mozambique, among which were a prohibition on resurrecting the cashew processing industry using traditional industrial policy tools and effectively ending state attempts to provide clean water to the rural poor.

Notwithstanding a national debate about the World Bank's mistaken 1994 decision to force both privatisation and trade liberalisation on the cashew processing industry, which led to the closure of ten major plants and the layoff of 10,000 workers (half of whom were women), the IMF prohibited Mozambique from imposing a 20 per cent export tax on raw nuts which the parliament was on the verge of approving in order to save the processors from subsidised international competition. The IMF also encouraged the parliament to adjust the overall tax structure to make it more regressive (i.e. the rich would pay a decreasing share of their income).

And following in the tradition of South Africa's failed rural water supply projects, the IMF also used new jargon in applying neoliberal conditionality, insisting on the Mozambican government quickly 'transforming the planning and delivery of rural water and sanitation services from a supply-driven model to a sustained demand responsive model, characterised by community management, cost recovery, and the involvement of the private sector'.

The word 'recolonisation' comes to mind. A few days later, at the Durban World Economic Forum Summit, President Joaqim Chissano argued that 'The [debt-reduction] rules should be reviewed.' Even Alec Erwin offered a long-overdue outburst at the same meeting: 'For the G-7 to be cautious on debt is criminal. It's criminal.'[37]

Box 6.4 Zimbabwe's zig-zags

An even more criminal case of neoliberalism gone awry was the mismanagement of Zimbabwe's economy and political system. The problems were often portrayed as derived from the maniacal ravings and corrupt schemes of Mugabe and a few powerful cronies like Defence Minister Moven Mahachi. These were indeed serious impediments to progress, but there remained much more formidable structural barriers to economic revival as the crucial 2000 elections approached.

For two decades, Zimbabwe suffered a strange mix of populist government rhetoric from a nominally 'Marxist-Leninist' ruling party; white corporate domination of the industrial, agricultural, financial and services sectors; and inability to break into global markets. Since independence, Mugabe steadily condoned an ever-greater role for the private sector in Zimbabwe's development, in the process taking on vast quantities of international debt (whose repayment cost 35 per cent of export earnings by 1987), culminating in the 1990 adoption of a structural adjustment programme that parroted the Washington Consensus.

The programme failed decisively, and not simply because of two bad droughts in 1992 and 1995. The overall structure of Zimbabwe's economy and society left it ill-suited for rapid liberalisation, extremely high real interest rates, a dramatic upsurge in inflation and devastating cuts in social welfare spending. For even while Mugabe often confused matters – with rhetoric hostile to the Washington Consensus – three extremely conservative Finance Ministers (Bernard Chidzero, Ariston Chambati and Herbert Murerwa) and Reserve Bank governors (Kenneth Moyanda and Leonard Tsumba) loyally followed a fiscally-conservative, deregulatory agenda.

As a direct result of funding cuts and cost-recovery policies, exacerbated by the AIDS pandemic, Zimbabwe's brief 1980s rise in literacy and health indicators was dramatically reversed. In contrast, the stock market reached extraordinary peaks in mid-1991 and mid-1997, but these were followed by crashes of more than 50 per cent within a few months, along with massive hikes in interest rates. More steadily, manufacturing sector output shrunk by 40 per cent from peak 1991 levels through 1995, and the standard of living of the average Zimbabwean worker fell even further.

Although growth was finally recorded in 1996–97, it quickly expired when international financial markets and local investors battered Zimbabwe's currency beginning in November 1997, ultimately shrinking the value of a Z$ from US$0.09 to $0.025 over the course of a year. As a result, unprecedented inflation was imported, leading in January and October 1998 to urban riots over maize and fuel price hikes, respectively.

Mugabe's reactions included a claim in November 1998 – widely disparaged – that he would return to socialist policies. Yet there were some small hints of reasserted Zimbabwean sovereignty in the face of financial meltdown, such as a mid-1998 price freeze on staple goods, a late 1998 tariff imposed on luxury imports, and several minor technical interventions to raise revenues, slow capital flight and deter share speculation.

For example, the 1990s liberalisation of a once-rigid exchange control system had created such enormous abuse that new regulations on currency sales had to be imposed. Yet two days after a 5 per cent capital gains tax was introduced on the stock market, a broker boycott forced a retraction. Indeed, the government was not, apparently, powerful enough to reimpose full (Malaysian-style) exchange controls – which had been widely expected in the event an IMF loan fell through, given the perilous state of hard currency reserves.

As economic grievances and more evidence of political unaccountability mounted, trade union leaders Morgan Tsvangirai and Gibson Sibanda called several successful national stayaways beginning in December 1997. Mugabe's increases in general sales and pension taxes to fund a large pension pay-out for liberation war veterans were vociferously resisted, and government backed down slightly.

Simultaneously, an October 1997 threat to redistribute 1,400 large commercial farms (mainly owned by whites) scared agricultural markets, allowed Mugabe extensive populist opportunities to critique worried foreign donors (especially the British), while giving land-starved peasants only passing hope – unrealistic, considering Mugabe's past practice of rewarding farms to political elites. Peasant land invasions of several large farms were quickly repelled by the authorities.

In another unpopular move, Mugabe also sent several thousand troops to defend the besieged Laurent Kabila in the Democratic Republic of Congo in mid-1998, according to rumour in order to protect the investments of politically well-connected Zimbabwean firms (dozens of body bags soon returned). The homophobic leader also had to contend with the conviction of his former political ally Canaan Banana – Zimbabwe's first (then ceremonial) president – on charges of raping at least two male staff members, and claims that Mugabe had turned a blind eye to the abuse.

By early 1999, government coffers were nearly dry. The IMF sent a high-level team to negotiate the disbursement of a $53 million loan (which in turn would release another $800 million from other lenders). The conditions attached were reported to include a prohibition on acquiring commercial farms unless payment was in full – not just for buildings and infrastructure, as Mugabe had desired – and was made ahead of time. Once satisfied that Mugabe had surrendered on the land issue, the IMF then insisted on the lifting of price controls and the luxury import tariffs – the only two really redistributive measures Mugabe had taken in recent years. (In 1999, studies were released documenting the fact that Zimbabwe had become Africa's most unequal country.)

In opposition to Mugabe, not only did workers mobilise more actively within a new 'Movement for Democratic Change' (MDC, known popularly as the 'workers' party' when launched in July 1999). A popular front grouping (the National Constitutional Assembly) emerged parallel – under Tsvangirai's leadership, with church, human rights and some liberal business support – devoting itself to rewriting the Zimbabwe Lancaster House constitution. If somewhat akin to Zambia's early days Movement for Multiparty Democracy, the Frankenstein metamorphosis of Frederick Chiluba from trade union democrat to neoliberal authoritarian was obviously a model Tsvangirai and Sibanda would try to avoid.[38]

REGIONAL REACTION

Would anything shake the ANC from its status quo orientation? At least in neighbouring Mozambique (Box 6.3) and Zimbabwe (Box 6.4), the perils of orthodox economics, financial globalisation and debt were gradually affecting political discourses. Post-apartheid South Africa was not much help, in part because it imposed upon the region a neoliberalism born of its own free trade philosophy and the ambitions of its largest extractive (mining and agricultural), firms, merchants and banks. Other Southern African countries' political-economic interrelationships were beset with confusion, on the one hand because of South Africa's – especially Erwin's – continuing neoliberal obstinance. But on the other hand, notwithstanding the homogenising aspects of structural adjustment programmes adopted across the region during the 1990s, the attention of national elites was often largely focused on each country's domestic concerns and insecurities: democratic transitions in South Africa, Namibia and Malawi; ongoing war in Angola; the slowing of Botswana's diamond boom; enormous pain associated with adjustment in Zimbabwe, Zambia, Tanzania and Mozambique; political instability in Lesotho; and civil society attempts to get reform to spark in feudal Swaziland. The Democratic Republic of the Congo's initial liberation from Mobutuism was followed, tragically, by regional factionalism (with a showdown between Central and Southern African countries who lined up on different sides in the 1998–99 war). South Africa's own hypocrisy in denying support to Zimbabwe, Angola and Namibia so as to prop up Kabila – by mid-1998 under siege – was exemplified by its own invasion of Lesotho shortly afterwards (mid-September) so as to prop up a government.

These elemental questions of state legitimacy had answers that were often either inward-gazing or too influenced by bilateral relations with traditional international partners. The Southern African Development Community (SADC) – the countries noted above, plus prosperous Mauritius (but minus the island nation of Madagascar) – remained feeble as an institution. Rarely did regional integration arise as a priority and rarely were regional geopolitical issues addressed seriously. And, until a free trade deal between South Africa and the European Union was cut in 1999, followed by a World Economic Forum session in Durban featuring obnoxious hectoring by the US Undersecretary of Commerce, only rarely was the looming intensification of international economic relations perceived in a realistic manner. The underlying problem remained partly intellectual in nature: regional bureaucrats tended to place enormous faith in the merits of global markets.

And yet it was common cause that if Southern Africa's major states did not take advantage of regional economies of scale and if production and consumption linkages were not explored and re-established on a less uneven footing, then the whole would not only be far less than the sum of the individual parts, it would be a shaky basis for conducting any political and economic activity. As development economist Fantu Cheru of the American University commented in 1993, 'With the end of the cold war, the old military blocs are being replaced by trading blocs, signalling the emergence of a "global apartheid" system, separating North and South.'[39] Against three huge trading zones – encompassing the US-led Western Hemisphere, the Far East and Europe plus the former Eastern bloc – 'Africa will find itself becoming ever more vulnerable and isolated if it chooses, or is obliged, to remain a collection of 50, small, competing exporters.' The same was true for Southern Africa.

Objective conditions remained dire in SADC countries: war, flimsy infrastructure, high debt burdens and weak management capacity were only the most glaring barriers to growth. The limits to regional integration opportunities were not only a function of apartheid desta-bilisation, for as Cheru argued, 'After years of structural adjustment efforts in Africa, progress with trade liberalisation has been slow and accompanied by serious reversals. In fact, trade liberalisation vis-à-vis the outside world, initiated by adjustment programmes, has definitely contributed to the stagnation of intra-regional trade, opening up the SADC market to cheap supplies from outside the region.'

SADC's failed efforts to reduce intra-regional tariffs exemplified the problems. According to Cheru:

> Most governments are likely to exhibit excessive preoccupation with politics over economics, as ruling alliances try to deflect the pain that accompanies fundamental economic restructuring. Reform in the areas of pricing, exchange rate, privatisation, liberalisation of trade, public sector reform and the like will be slow. This is especially true in the face of dwindling external assistance, the uncertain commodity environment and shifting global trading patterns.

The only potential bright spot, by all accounts, would be a far more regionally conscious post-apartheid Pretoria. But a variety of factors converged against this happening during South Africa's own transition. One of the most important was South African businesses' failure to conceive of the region as a potential industrialising market, as opposed merely to a hinterland from which to draw raw materials and migrant labour.

Emerging from a waning home market – one still more than three times as large as that of the combined SADC countries – South African firms initially appeared most hungry to capture mining and construction work in Angola and Zambia. Mozambique was nearly sewn up between the South African-based tourist trade and several major multinational agribusinesses and mining operations in the hinterland.

Fears of domination by the South African octopus were real during the early 1990s, as Johannesburg's mining-based conglomerates began what some referred to as a 'recolonisation' of the region. De Beers sought diamonds in Angola and Zimbabwe. Genmin was after Mozambican coal, with oil in Angola and the mineral wealth of Zambia also likely prospects. Zambian Consolidated Copper Mines – owned by Anglo American prior to the 1970 nationalisation – was put up for privatisation, even though it was responsible for 90 per cent of Zambia's forex earnings. In construction, Murray & Roberts signed deals with Angolan officials to construct prefabricated schools, hospitals, houses, roads and harbours, and even mining and agricultural ventures. In Zambia, roads, housing and building materials were also seen as good prospects.

Notwithstanding selected business opportunities, though, most of South Africa's elites still preferred to ignore the region. This was foolish, not only because Africa bought a fifth of South African exported goods, but because wars, coups and urban riots in the Frontline States had increased in tempo over the previous decade, leading an estimated 2–3 million illegal immigrants to find refuge and economic opportunities in South Africa.

Thus after a period of regional optimism by a few Johannesburg firms, a harsher reality emerged. Zambia's major privatisations were continually held up, Angola's recovery was derailed, and other South African inroads – several banks' move into Zimbabwe, for instance – occurred more through buying existing assets (cheapened through rapidly devalued currencies) than through the anticipated wave of new direct investments. Trade issues remained paramount, particularly the re-emergence of intra-regional tariffs, mainly following pressures from domestic firms in Zimbabwe and Zambia which faced extinction from South Africa exports. As a result, by 1994 when the ANC finalised the *RDP*, most policy-makers in the region were desperate for any potentially coherent initiatives from a democratic South Africa.

Mandela himself expressed ANC regional policy in gracious terms: 'We want to state quite categorically that the integration of the South African economy into the regional economy should scrupulously avoid the domination by the South African economy of the regional economy.' A number of recommendations surfaced in ANC discussions, including infant industry protection, creation of a regional Development Bank, stronger industrial location policies and strategic industry protection. And as a result of persuasive inputs by the University of the Western Cape's Centre for Southern African Studies (particularly Rob Davies, subsequently a leading progressive ANC MP), the *RDP* was extremely eloquent on regional policy (Box 6.5).

The Centre for Southern African Studies researchers had spent the early 1990s carefully considering three main competing approaches, terming them 'cooperative regionalism', 'hegemonic bilateralism' or 'neomercantilism'. Advocates of cooperative regionalism intended to undo apartheid era damage and explore Southern African economies of scale in manufacturing and minerals beneficiation. As the 1990s began, South African exports to Africa represented only around 2 per cent of the total import bill of 39 major African countries. During the transition period, vast increases in exports of plastic, rubber, steel, food, chemicals, motor vehicles, machinery and appliances gave succour to South African conglomerates (albeit with little gains for small businesses). In addition, there were potential benefits to South Africa through access to Southern Africa's infrastructure and resources (such as an electricity grid extending to the Congo River and water from Lesotho and in future Swaziland), construction and engineering contracting, minerals extraction, technical and managerial cooperation and food security.

But attempts by Pretoria to circumvent cooperation and instead establish dominance in one or another aspect of regional relations – hegemonic bilateralism – were more likely. After all, negotiators from across the region had other priorities of their own: preferential access to the South African market; higher earnings from resources such as hydropower and water; guarantees that migrant labourers wouldn't be repatriated; financial and technical contributions by South Africa to regional programmes; more equitable arrangements in existing relations with neighbouring countries; and more balance in Southern African transport infrastructure, capital investments, and location of industry. Likewise, there were firm powerful opponents of regional cooperation in Pretoria. Chris Stals once worried about the 'huge burden' the region presented South Africa, and the SA Chamber of Business more explicitly argued that 'closer [i.e. cooperative] economic ties with African countries would merely worsen the Republic's own problems'. According to this line of argument, Pretoria should remain lukewarm towards integration, though some concessions would have to be made to bilateral partners within the framework of South African hegemony.[40]

And indeed by late 1998, Erwin was reduced to self-consciously pursuing the bilateral hegemonic approach, in view of widely acknowledged strife within the SADC and the many difficulties associated with cutting a European Union free trade deal that would allow for regional economic integrity.

An even worse outcome, however, would be neomercantilism, with South Africa taking advantage of globalisation solely to promote its short-term partisan interests. It was, the Centre for Southern African Studies researchers argued, a 'default option that could, unintentionally, materialise from a passive approach to regional issues, from a sense that the region is a mere side show to the main business of becoming more involved in global markets'. There were important developments which pointed pessimistically to such an outcome. In particular, the two-year appointment of Manuel as Minister of Trade and Industry was disastrous from the region's standpoint, as South African trade surpluses mushroomed and Manuel showed no inclination to even sweet-talk his neighbouring colleagues. After a strong start – forging a 1996 SADC protocol to establish a free trade area – Zimbabwe-born Erwin failed to establish confidence. Trade surpluses continued to rise, fostering regional anger at Pretoria's perceived protectionism (refusing to renew a 1964–92 South Africa–Zimbabwe preferential trade deal, for instance).

Moreover, few observers understood the rapid spread of informal relations between South Africa and its neighbours, even though these had the potential to intensify polarisation and damage the integrity and culture of business of all parties and sour both bilateral and multilateral relations. Such relations included the black professional brain drain from Africa to South Africa; tensions emerging from hybrids of unknown African traditions and the modern township economy; and illicit traffic in people, AK-47s, drugs and currency, to name a few. Most ominously, the ANC's failure to transform the operating policies and international philosophies of the Department of Foreign Affairs and the SANDF during the ministerial careers of Nzo and Modise, respectively, contributed to the rejection, not fulfilment of *RDP* regional promises. And although an initial agreement gave citizenship to long-time SADC residents living in South Africa, the fate of millions of other shorter-term continental African residents – a small fraction of whom were engaged in legal mine labour – represented a test of New South African–Southern African relations which Pretoria (especially Home Affairs Minister Buthelezi) and many xenophobic South Africans failed profoundly.

But so too most other visions of indigenous regional development faltered. The great danger was that neoliberalism would impose its own mode of integration on the region, at the same time many of its components entailed disintegration. For left to the market and to the inherited bureaucracy in Pretoria, South Africa's contribution to regional economic development had more continuities with the apartheid era than not.

This in turn was partly a function of the role of neoliberalism in breaking down states and reconfiguring trade, financial and investment flows. On the one hand, this integrated Southern Africa by virtue of the relatively homogeneous, 'harmonious' economic approach – shrinkage of states, lowering of taxes, dropping of border barriers to capital (if not labour), convergence of currency and financial decontrol, and universal welcome to foreign investors – adopted during the 1980s and 1990s. But on the other hand, there was danger of tremendous disintegration, as the ill-effects of open trade, investment and financial policies accumulated. This was obvious in the region as a whole, but also increasingly within South Africa.

Box 6.5: Regional rumours, dreams and promises

The *RDP* promised a new spirit of teamwork, harking back to the Lagos Plan of Action and the Abuja Declaration:

> If South Africa attempts to dominate its neighbours it will restrict their growth, reducing their potential as markets, worsening

their unemployment and will lead to increased migration into South Africa. If we seek mutual cooperation, we can develop a large stable market offering stable employment and common labour standards in all areas.[41]

The *RDP* aimed to 'break down apartheid and colonial geography, and open up new economic potential in the areas of production and tourism'.[42] Such cooperation would entail a regional bloc or other measures to 'combine to develop effective strategies for all Southern African countries', and hence 'to strengthen the Southern African region in its relations with emerging global trading blocs'.

There were several concrete suggestions along these lines. 'Harmonisation of infrastructure, legal and operational aspects of regional Southern African transport must be considered a priority.' Telecommunications, energy, water resources, food and health care were considered high-priority items for regional cooperation. In addition, the *RDP*'s mining section insisted that the first democratic government 'extend across our borders by using our considerable expertise in mineral exploration and exploitation to rehabilitate and develop the mineral potential of our neighbours. In this regard a special facility should be created to promote investment in the subcontinent.'

As for trade, the *RDP* noted the severe imbalances and called for 'policies in consultation with our neighbours to ensure more balanced trade'. Moreover, South Africa's (relatively highly paid) manufacturing workers who were worried that when regional trade barriers fell, their products would be uncompetitive, could at least take heart from another provision: 'minimum standards with regard to rights of workers to organise should be established across the region as a whole so that a process of greater integration becomes one of levelling up rights and conditions of workers rather than of levelling them down to the lowest prevailing standard'.

But soon after the April 1994 election, it became clear that trade, labour and foreign policies were not being made with *RDP* promises in mind.

BEYOND THE (POST-)WASHINGTON CONSENSUS

It was, by the time of South Africa's second democratic election, no longer controversial to point out that *Gear*'s predictions for GDP

growth, interest rates, employment, fixed investment, the value of
the currency and practically every other indicator except inflation
and the budget deficit were in shambles. But more than just failed
targets was at stake; it was crucial to get to the very bottom of the
free-market philosophy to challenge the underlying dynamic of the
theory that inspired *Gear*.

Some of the South African Left's confidence to challenge orthodoxy
had come from the January 1998 speech in Helsinki, by Joseph Stiglitz
(previously Bill Clinton's chief economic adviser). Defending *Gear* at
an ANC leadership meeting in October, Manuel was reported to have
cautioned his colleagues – especially left-leaning Max Sisulu – against
validating a 'new high priest of economics'. And yet many on the
South African Left initially looked to Stiglitz the way they viewed John
Maynard Keynes in the 1930s: as ushering in a revolution in
economic thinking at a time the 'dismal science' was disgraced.

(To illustrate the discipline's demise at a peak moment of Stiglitz's
own rise in September 1998, a $3.5 billion hedge fund – Connecticut-
based Long-Term Capital Management – came spectacularly undone.
LTCM had used a financial model devised by two 1997 Nobel Prize
laureates in economics, was backed by more than $100 billion in
investments, and established a portfolio of more than $1.5 trillion in
gambles on obscure financial instruments. But instead of hedging
against risk, the model amplified market volatility, requiring a
massive, 'crony-capitalist' – to cite Stiglitz – bail-out coordinated by
the New York Federal Reserve. In a desperate bid to restore lost
credibility, the Nobel economics committee, which so regularly
honoured vicious neoliberal 'rational-expectationists' and financial
market modellers, hurriedly redirected the 1998 prize to a poverty
economist, Amartya Sen.)

Did Stiglitz deserve this status? The subtitle of his Helsinki speech
– 'Moving Toward a Post-Washington Consensus' – suggested a
fundamental sea-change in thinking. Stiglitz's most important
professional critic, Professor Ben Fine of the University of London
School of Oriental and African Studies, summarised:

Essentially, the capitalist economy is seen [by Stiglitz] as a construct
of imperfectly informed individuals, imperfectly coordinated through
the market place ... Indeed, it is simply a matter of identifying in
practice the wide variety of informational imperfections and how

they are handled in particular contexts. Policy is concerned with handling them better than leaving them to the pure market.

If, for Stiglitz, contemporary financial crises were the function largely of market information 'asymmetries', the policy implication was to avoid the pre-Keynesian 'Treasury view' (the phraseology that Keynes used to deride his predecessors for very similar hard-line monetarist perspectives that at the end of the century prevailed at the IMF and US Treasury Department). In fact, Stiglitz remarked to me, had Fischer – one of his students many years previously – provided the Treasury view answer (austerity policies) to a hypothetical East Asia crisis question – *which the IMF did answer in reality in 1997–99* – in a Stiglitz economics exam, 'he would have received a D or F'.[43]

At first blush there was merit to transcending the Washington Consensus on these grounds. The effect of the Helsinki paper was striking, leaving many of the NGOs that dabbled in international economics convinced a new ally had emerged from within the belly of Washington. As the *Mail and Guardian* reported after a high-profile January 1999 trip to South Africa, 'Reflecting the changing face of the World Bank, Joseph Stiglitz is a hero in some left-wing circles ... His intention is noble: to free the poor from the powerlessness that is such a feature of poverty.'[44] Development journalist Joe Hanlon interpreted for NGO readers,

The World Bank's new chief economist and senior vice president has challenged virtually the entire package of conditions that the Bank and the International Monetary Fund have been imposing on developing counties for more than a decade ... Stiglitz attacks virtually every sacred cow ... And writing like one of the Bank's critics, he attacks economists who 'fly into a country, look at and attempt to verify the data, and make macroeconomic recommendations for policy reforms all in the space of a couple of weeks' ... Stiglitz calls for 'a greater degree of humility, the frank acknowledgement that we do not have all the answers'. And he says that any post-Washington Consensus 'cannot be based on Washington'.

This leads to the bizarre position that the IMF and some of Stiglitz' own staff are making debt relief conditional on policies Stiglitz says are not conducive for long term growth. Stiglitz may say 'we do not have all the answers,' but his own staff disagree. The IMF's 'power flows from the institutions carefully constructed image of infallibility. To disagree publicly with the IMF is widely viewed as a rejection of financial rectitude,' comments Jeffrey Sachs, director of the Harvard Institute for International Development. But if top IMF and World Bank officials do not agree on any of the policies being imposed on Asia and on poor countries of the south, perhaps it is time to take a closer look at the emperor's wardrobe.[45]

Following Stiglitz and Soros, it was particularly easy, in the wake of macroeconomic crises in countries (like South Africa), all ostensibly following 'sound' policies, to turn populist wrath against the fickle financiers who irrationally flooded 'hot money' in and out of stock, bond and currency markets based on bad information: for example, a rumour that Mandela was ill (February 1996), or on the skin colour or former socialist inclinations of a new Finance Minister (March 1996) and Reserve Bank governor-designate (July 1998). As Stiglitz had pointed out,

Making markets work requires more than just low inflation, it requires sound financial regulation, competition policy, and policies to facilitate the transfer of technology, and transparency, to name some fundamental issues neglected by the Washington Consensus. At the same time that we have improved our understanding of the instruments to promote well-functioning markets, we have broadened the objectives of development to include other goals like sustainable development, egalitarian development, and democratic development.

Stiglitz explicitly pointed out the limits to orthodox development strategy, such as the key pillar of privatisation:

Even when privatisation increases productive efficiency, there may be problems in ensuring that broader public objectives, not well reflected in market prices, are attained, and regulation may be an imperfect substitute. Should prisons, social services, or the making of atomic bombs (or the central ingredient of atomic bombs, highly enriched uranium) be privatised, as some in the United States have advocated?[46]

In short, Stiglitz, if not the Bank's Pretoria staff (as shown in Chapter 5), recognised the need to consider a variety of goods not as privatisable commodities, but as 'public goods', with positive 'externalities' – such as preventing the spread of disease – that require consumption of municipal services like water and electricity beyond what individual affordability might dictate. But would the post-Washington Consensus be sufficient? Indeed, was Stiglitz himself – and his allegedly path-breaking theory – a reliable international ally?

Soon enough, the integrity of the Post-Washington Consensus was thrown into question, in the same way that the 'post-*Gear*' reforms alluded to above proved, under a microscope, to melt into the status quo. According to Fine, Stiglitz's Post-Washington Consensus shared some of the same fundamental flaws as the Washington Consensus. 'It can deal with the regulation of the financial system, for example, its efficiency, and the protection of shareholders, without once mentioning the economic and political power structures embodied in a financial system.'

Moreover, even if Stiglitz could claim in late 1998 that 75–80 per cent of his senior Bank colleagues agreed with him, the 'information-theoretic' analytical innovations could not be seen in an institutional vacuum. Brown University political economist Robert Wade attributed the Bank's new open-mindedness to an acknowledgement of internal intellectual sclerosis, Japan's increasing donor role (and its own self-interest in expansionary not contractionary policies for countries in which its firms invested), and self-reflective case study, including the counter-intuitive East Asian miracle.[47] Hence the freedom that Bank president Wolfensohn gave his chief economist to critique the neighbours at the IMF should also have been read as an institutional survival mechanism, even when Stiglitz regularly got under the skin of his former student Stanley Fischer (the South Africa-raised deputy managing director of the IMF), and his Bank predecessor Lawrence Summers (deputy US Treasury Secretary).

But the disjuncture between the status quo-oriented Clinton–Rubin–Camdessus–Greenspan–Fischer–Summers bloc and reformers centred on Stiglitz boiled down, ultimately, to an elite fight between hostile brothers. As Fine concluded, 'The social content of [Stiglitz's] theory – based on the methodological individualism of neoclassical economics – seems incapable of explaining the presence of social structures and institutions, let alone classes and the state, whose existence is glaringly obvious.'

And precisely the institutional role Stiglitz had to continue playing – defending a key Washington Consensus institution, the World Bank

– led soon enough to his South African delegitimisation. In January 1999, his colleagues set up a formal conference to debate a forthcoming Bank *World Development Report* on poverty, co-sponsored with Anglican Archbishop Njungonkulo Ndungane, the premier spokesperson for South Africa's dispossessed. As Fatima Meer later remarked in the *Sunday Times*:

> The workshop did not, however, discuss the elimination of poverty. Most of the time was spent defining poverty and on methods of measuring it. Neither did the workshop 'consult' civil society: it had flown in its own experts and a body of academics mainly from Europe and the US to propound on these issues. The Bank had, in effect, set the limits of the debate and decision-making and protected the discussion from deviating into a critique of its policies of the global economic system.[48]

A few days later, in a meeting with 50 members of the SA NGO Coalition (Sangoco), and alongside an entourage of local Bank staff, Stiglitz went on to reverse tack on the larger economic issues (including his consent to allowing inflation rates to rise to 40 per cent – he reduced the figure to 8), once some embarrassing questions about 'moral hazard' were put to him. As recounted by Sangoco vice president Mercia Andrews and Campaign Against Neoliberalism in South Africa coordinator George Dor:

> We asked him for his views on the contradiction between his speech in Helsinki and the World Bank contribution to the *Gear* strategy. He told us he didn't know much about South Africa ... We put it to him that perhaps the Bank should take action against its staff members on the *Gear* team who got the employment predictions so horribly wrong by suggesting that *Gear* would generate hundreds of thousands of jobs each year when, in reality, hundreds of thousands are being lost. Everything in his tortuous reply suggested that he was not particularly concerned whether Bank staff members produce work of poor quality and that staff members can get away with shoddy work that has a profound impact on people's chances of finding employment ...
>
> Our engagement with him highlights a significant retreat from his Helsinki position. There are a number of possible reasons. His Helsinki speech may have been a deliberate strategy to create the

impression of change. He may have been reigned in by the World Bank after Helsinki. Perhaps he felt restrained in Johannesburg by the need to talk the language of his entourage. He portrays the confidence that he has the ear of the institution but insider talk suggests that he is a maverick who is not to be taken too seriously. Whatever the reason for his retreat, his hero's halo has now vanished.[49]

CONCLUSIONS: WAYS FORWARD

'In general', pondered Kim Moody (a leading US labour movement intellectual-activist), 'the Left in the twentieth century has tended to blame the failure of the potential of basic social and economic struggle to produce socialist consciousness or organisation on either the economic-political dichotomy, leadership betrayals, or the "incorrectness" of one or another party's positions or type of organisation.'[50] The Left critique of South Africa's elite transition falls into several of these categories, and uncomfortably so.

For this was an unsatisfying outcome – not just because crying 'sell-out' is disturbingly shallow and dangerously personalistic – but because ANC leaders could still self-righteously insist that the balance of forces at the end of the century provided insufficient room for manoeuvre. It was also unsatisfying when, implicitly, the South African 'alternative' was represented by, at best, progressive (though ideologically extremely diverse) organisations in 'civil society' which had not yet regained anything like the confidence and militancy of the late anti-apartheid era, and whose portentous but still marginal fragments of political resistance included:

- an on-again, off-again contestation of macroeconomic policy and economic processes (Chapter 1);
- ambivalence about fora – like Nedlac – and processes characterised by 'stakeholder'-based scenario-planning-style compromises that were debilitating for analysis and politics alike (Chapter 2);
- a somewhat radical (but fragmented and politically impotent?) residual programme of 'policy,' namely, the *RDP* of the Left (not Right or Centre), but without ministers who would take forward their 1994 mandate (Chapter 3);

- uneven, sometimes violent, and largely ineffectual responses to the massive contradictions thrown up by urban (and to some extent rural) housing/infrastructure neoliberalism (Chapter 4);
- a healthy dislike of the World Bank (Chapter 5); and
- as this chapter has highlighted, growing – but still unseasoned – prospects of internationalist networking and multifaceted solidarity in a global context of neoliberal crisis.

Realistically, could more be expected? To come straight to a point regularly speculated upon by commentators, there was always the possibility that the SACP – the only party on the South African Left with more than a few hundred cadres[51] – would break free from the Alliance early in the twenty-first century. As an institution, argued leftists hoping for an Alliance split, the SACP would soon realise that there was no future in maintaining a political-operational responsibility that appeared, so depressingly often (dating to the 1930s), mainly to entail mediating (or at best spin-doctoring) the rightward drift of its Alliance partner the ANC. Doubters insisted that this would require a fundamental break by (or more likely, against) some quite conservative leaders whose ministerial (including at provincial level) or even parliamentary seats/salaries/power had grown comfortable. ANC loyalists in the SACP would continue to insist upon the existence of space to change the movement, by referring, for example, not only to the 'rhetoric of crisis' discussed above, but to positionality: the late 1990s lineup of Alliance executives – ANC, SACP and Cosatu general-secretaries and deputies Motlanthe and Mthintso, Nzimande and Cronin, Shilowa and Vavi – who were also SACP politburo members. Still, under the leadership of Blade Nzimande, there was the potential for more honesty and organic-intellectual socialism than in living memory, and a young Left SACP grouping had as much of a role as ever following a difficult 1997–98 (featuring not only Mbeki's attack but internal pressure from conservatives).

The 'talk left, act right' problem looked set to continue, no matter the outcome of future SACP internal power struggles. As explained by ex-activist Firoz Cachalia (by then a leading ANC politician in Johannesburg) to a *Business Day* readership just prior to the 1999 election:

Fiscal and monetary constraint and liberalised trade and capital movements ... which aim at the structural repositioning of SA's economy in response to globalisation, whatever their long-term benefits, have severe short-term costs for constituencies of votes who are among the current supports of the governing party. The ANC has, however, indicated that it will persist on its chosen path ... Contrary to the conventional wisdom that the alliance between the governing party and trade unions limits economic growth, there is considerable evidence that such relationships make growth possible through wage restraint.[52]

Echoing Cachalia just after the election, Saki Macozoma, chief executive of Transnet, remarked that 'Mbeki's term will be an opportunity to revisit legislation of the past, like making labour regulations more business-friendly'. Within weeks, Transnet announced the forthcoming retrenchment of 27,000 workers as a prelude to privatisation. 'The ANC are not fools', observed Gordon Smith, economist with Deutsche Morgan Grenfell Bank. 'They know where the balance of economic power lies.'[53] Reflecting on that power, Mbeki expressed ANC economic assumptions in the wake of the 1999 victory: 'In the last budget in March, we ... further reduced the budget deficit and corporate taxes, because we need to create the best possible conditions for people to invest in the economy.'[54]

There was always the hope that, *perhaps*, Cosatu would move leftwards again. Without a leader (Shilowa – under Mbeki the premier of Gauteng Province) seen as inordinately close to the Mbeki kitchen-cabinet during the mid-1990s, could the heady post-election days of national stay-aways over the Labour Relations Act (1994), privatisation (1995) and the Constitution (1996) be recreated? It was not inconceivable, for as Moody noted, a major trend in international social-movement trade unionism beginning in the mid-1990s was

the growing separation or independence of the unions from political parties they had been dominated by (usually Communist or nationalist) or dependent upon (social democratic) but whose leaders and professional politicians had moved closer to the neoliberal, pro-market policies of the parties of capital. While the unions might continue to support the parties of the left electorally, they would now shape their own political agenda. This was partly the case for many unions in Canada, and even more so for those in Europe formerly associated with Communist Parties, as in France,

Spain and Italy, and for labour federations across Asia, Latin America, and Africa.[55]

After all, under generally less propitious conditions than South Africa, Moody observed, a series of political mass strikes by national workers' movements had shaken Nigeria, Indonesia, Paraguay and Taiwan in 1994; Bolivia, Canada and France in 1995; Argentina, Brazil, Canada, Greece, Italy, South Korea, Spain and Venezuela in 1996; Belgium, Colombia, Ecuador, Haiti and South Korea in 1997; and then with the 1998–99 crisis, many other important sites of East Asian, East European, African and Latin American proletarian suffering due to neoliberal economic disaster.

Rising militancy as the long economic downturn proceeded was logical enough. As global uneven development heightened during the 1980s–1990s, the displacement (or what we termed in Chapter 1, 'stalling/shifting') of the overaccumulation crisis – particularly footloose financial capital – into new areas of the world, or into new (and increasingly unbearable) kinds of class/labour/gender/ethnic relations in the advanced industrial countries, became more frenetic. Observers became increasingly aware of the symptoms: rising inequality, widespread child labour, booming sweatshops, declining social wages, unemployment-enhanced xenophobia and nationalist resurgences, super-exploitation of women, massive ecological destruction, and the like. But it was not just 'space' – and relatively weaker conditions of eco-social solidarity in favoured transnational corporate investment zones – that served capital's need to move the crisis around. The use of time as a means of displacing overaccumulation was also critical to late twentieth-century capitalist crisis management: not just more rapid transport and communications, and 'speed-up' on the production line in the context of flexibilised labour markets, but also rising indebtedness so that today's consumption (personal, corporate and sometimes government) could be paid back with income *later* (debt/GDP ratios hit unprecedented and untenable levels by the 1990s).

This meant that even if the South African Left desired, ultimately, a 'globalisation of people, not of capital', global capital flows would have to be more explicitly confronted, and with more and more sophisticated kinds of solidarity. Thanks to the internet, e-mails and faxing, the movements' attacks upon neoliberal global economic managers were becoming incredibly surgical, exemplified by the 1997–99 obstruction of the Multilateral Agreement on Investment (that 'multi-national corporate bill of rights', as it was known). But at the turn of the century, the political basis for new international networking was still uncertain. Peter Waterman's typology of six kinds of solidarity – Identity, Substitution, Complementarity, Reciprocity, Affinity and Restitution – helped contextualise the uncertain ways forward. As Waterman explains, 'Each of these has its own part of the meaning of international solidarity; each is only part of the meaning, and by itself can only be a limited and impoverished understanding of such':

- Identity is expressed by the slogan 'Workers of the World Unite!', implying one long-term general interest;
- Substitution is exemplified by development cooperation, or 'standing in' for the poor, exploited and powerless;
- Complementarity is the solidarity of 'differential contribution' to a common interest or aim (which could be between workers, or North–South);
- Reciprocity is the exchange of similar quantities or qualities over time;
- Affinity suggests personal identity/friendship between, say, eco-feminists, socialists (of a particular hue), or even stamp-collectors;
- Restitution is recognition and compensation for past wrongs.[56]

South and Southern Africa would probably play quite an important role in defining which kinds of solidarity would emerge and synthesise amongst the world's political-economic, cultural, single-issue and political movements of the early twenty-first century. If so, the influence of 'CoNGOs' in promoting international reformism as the goal of international solidarity would logically wane, and the search for radical local, regional and conceptual 'alternatives' – a matter taken up again below – would intensify.

CoNGO declarations of victory notwithstanding, with respect to conceptual and intellectual trends, the possibility of uniting with Post-Washington Consensus reformers was as bleak and fruitless as the prospect of mass-popular alliances with Mahathir, Mugabe and other rabid nationalists. By 1998, Stiglitz was being consistently challenged from the Left through, for example, a formidable set of seminar papers given at the London School of Oriental and African Studies, which documented the merely ameliorative effects that Post-Washington

Consensus reforms (greater transparency, more active competition policy, enhanced regulation, less focus on inflation, etc.) would have on a world economy drifting dangerously towards depression and financial chaos. A new intellectual project – perhaps a '*post*-Post-Washington Consensus' (e.g. from meetings of church/NGO/social movements in Lusaka and Nairobi in 1999, an 'Africa Consensus') – with respect to development, economics, ecology and global-local processes was sorely needed, and began emerging from diverse quarters.

With respect to resistance strategies, the need to reduce the stranglehold that international financiers maintained on national leaders was considered an extremely high priority on the South African Left, and was systematically addressed initially by Cansa and then through the global Jubilee 2000 debt cancellation initiative. The South African J2000, chaired by Molefe Tsele of the SA Council of Churches and supported by the Alternative Information and Development Centre in Cape Town and Johannesburg, with patrons including Ndungane, Meer and Brutus, had phenomenal success in 1998–99, publicising not only the $20 billion-plus apartheid era foreign debt, but expanding the country's regional consciousness with respect to the $50 billion 'apartheid-caused debt' and destabilisation costs faced by the rest of Southern Africa, forcing Manuel's bureaucrats onto the defensive about debt repayment while social programmes were cut to the bone. In addition, along with left-leaning chapters in Nicaragua, Argentina and Philippines, the Southern African J2000 helped intensify pressure on G-7 leaders in mid-1999, at a time when cutting a highly conditioned debt relief deal appeared seductive to northern J2000 leaders and CoNGOs.

As an important aside, the representativeness and accountability of progressive internationalists – especially as reflected in petit-bourgeois, self-appointed (and generally male) NGO spokespeople – would also have to be thrown into question. As Sonia Alvarez remarked, 'Though civil society is certainly crucial to the democratisation of dominant national and international publics, it must remain a central "target" of the democratising efforts of feminists and other progressive activists worldwide.'[57]

Indeed, continually humanising the Left movements would not be easy under the circumstances. Drawing upon women's movement experiences, Leila Rupp sent out a challenge that applies to progressives active in challenging capitalist political-economy as much as feminists challenging capitalist patriarchy:

> If nationalism and internationalism do not have to act as polar opposites; if we can conceptualise feminisms broadly enough to encompass a vast array of local variations displaying multiple identities; if we work to dismantle the barriers to participation in national and international women's movements; if we build on the basic common denominators of women's relationship to production and reproduction, however multifaceted in practice; then we can envisage truly global feminisms that can, in truth, change the world.[58]

Finally, as noted above, within the domestic sphere – but certainly hampering prospects for South African version of radical internationalism – political dynamics remained very uneven. One day not far off, South Africa might repeat a process unfolding in, for example, Zimbabwe at the turn of the century (Box 6.4). There, a nationalist government with enormous social prestige began a project of redistribution after Independence (in 1980), but quite quickly fell under World Bank sectoral advice (by 1982 or so) and IMF macroeconomic policy influence (1984). The marginal social progress attained after independence was soon reversed. Organised labour, NGOs, human rights groups, social movements, environmentalists and other progressive forces began making links between their woes and government policy. Rising levels of state corruption and official interference in NGOs together made opposition to the ruling party less lucrative and indeed more dangerous than anyone had ever expected. Yet after a time, the contradictions had presented themselves in such stark terms that a new movement emerged in 1998 based not on opportunistic, petit-bourgeois, personality politics (although that was always a problem), but on a chance to contest the 2000 parliamentary election (and 2002 presidential contest) with enormous popular support – and potentially a post-nationalist *and* post-neoliberal programme.

Matters won't, probably, degenerate so far in South Africa given the far higher levels of democratisation and the strength of organisations of working-class and poor people. Still, enormous energies will be required to pull together the intellectual, strategic, tactical and political threads into an oppositional discourse and practice that doesn't stop at the Post-Washington Consensus, but moves towards more genuine transformative possibilities than have been on offer from Washington elites, half-hearted reformers who aim to restore credibility to global economic rules, and their conservative allies in Pretoria.

But for progressive South Africans and their international allies, the most immediate political conclusion should be just as obvious, paralleling the argument by world systems theorists Giovanni Arrighi, Terence Hopkins and Immanuel Wallerstein in their 1989 book *Anti-Systemic Movements*, that the most serious challenge to the capitalist mode of production (which, after all, lies behind the vast bulk of problems described throughout *Elite Transition*), occurs when 'popular movements join forces across borders (and continents) to have their respective state officials abrogate those relations of the interstate system through which the pressure is conveyed'.[59]

And as civil society pressure increasingly compels politicians and bureaucrats to question the inter-state relations which convey neoliberal pressure, then what? From Samir Amin, the most important of Africa's radical economists, variations have emerged on the theme of regional 'delinking'.[60] As unrealistic as this appears at first blush (recall this chapter's long list of populists-turned-neoliberals), the recent, present and forthcoming conditions of global economic crisis appear to both demand and supply the material grounds for a profound change in power relations. The ideological hegemony and financial stranglehold that neoliberalism and its sponsors have enjoyed are discredited and could fast disappear. Out of nowhere (East Asia!), after all, suddenly appeared system-threatening contradictions. And out of radical social and labour movements come, increasingly, demands that can only be met through greater national sovereignty and regional political-economic coherence. The global scale may one day appear as a likely site of struggle (for example, through the United Nations system which at least conceptually could be democratised, unlike the Bretton Woods Institutions). But realistic 'alternatives' are probably going to have to be fought for and won at national and regional scales.

This means that to 'de-globalise' – as Southern Africanist Dot Keet terms it – is also to regionalise, drawing on the best traditions of alternative development (and in some cases, alternatives *to* development), and to make alliances with those in the North seeking 'innovative alternatives to over-producing/consuming capitalism'.[61]

And yet, such alternatives themselves need to be contextualised in power relations that are still to be fought for, Canadian labour radical Sam Gindin reminds us:

> The real issue of 'alternatives' isn't about alternative policies or about alternative governments, but about an alternative *politics*. Neither well-meaning policies nor sympathetic governments can fundamentally alter our lives unless they are part of a fundamental challenge to capital. That is, making alternatives possible requires a movement that is changing political culture (the assumptions we bring to how society should work), bringing more people into every-day struggles (collective engagement in shaping our lives), and deepening the understanding and organisational skills of activists along with their commitment to radical change (developing socialists).[62]

In a previous epoch – one recent enough in the collective memory and still bursting with the pride of authentic struggle – not more than a few thousand South African radical civil society activists took up a task of similar world-scale implications. In part, the struggle was to open up space for a *developmental* liberation (even if that space was quickly closed, and unnecessarily so, we have argued). A core component of the strategy was severing international elite relations with (and support for) apartheid, as Arrighi et al. propose for the anti-neoliberal struggle.

As impossible as the activists' anti-apartheid mission appeared during the darkest days, *they won!* Given the rapid shifts in power and the crisis of elite interests now being played out across the world, the multifaceted campaigns against Washington – and against those in southern capitals who serve as its parrots – still rank amongst the very highest priorities of South African progressives and their allies. 'From apartheid to neoliberalism in South Africa' is not simply a wrong turn due to elite pacting, therefore, but is also a signpost along an admittedly arduous road of social struggle, leading our comrades from one century to the next.[63]

Notes and References

FOR FURTHER READING

This book is part of a diverse tradition of left analysis from a synthetic anti-apartheid, anti-capitalist standpoint, and hence some of its gaps are due to very strong treatment of many related issues found elsewhere. To cite books published merely over the past decade that I have found invaluable, one of the best background studies, by Robert Fine and Dennis Davies, *Beyond Apartheid* (London: Pluto Press, 1991) contemplates the problems and possibilities faced by nationalist and communist forces during the 1950s and early 1960s. The failure of the ANC (and SA Communist Party) to set the stage for transformation during the subsequent long (1963–90) exile drought is treated by Dale McKinley (*The ANC and the Liberation Struggle*, London: Pluto Press, 1997).

As for subsequent internal political developments, political interventions across the progressive spectrum are worth consideration: by Neville Alexander, one of the most accomplished South African left intellectuals (amongst his collections of essays, see *Some are More Equal than Others*, Cape Town: Buchu, 1993); by John Saul, the model scholar-activist of the international solidarity movement (*Recolonization and Resistance in Southern Africa*, Trenton: Africa World Press, 1993); and by the premier Trotskyist critic Alex Callinicos (*South Africa between Apartheid and Capitalism*, London: Bookmarks, 1992). Each addresses the first stage of ANC capitulation to elite pacting temptations. Sadly, rebuttals and interventions on such matters from formidable ANC and Communist Party intellectuals Pallo Jordan, Joel Netshitenzhe, Blade Nzimande, Jeremy Cronin, Langa Zita and Rob Davies, amongst others, are not yet available in book form, although the *African Communist*, *Links* and ANC publications often carry their work. For earlier works from the ANC perspective, however, see Govan Mbeki's *The Struggle for Liberation in South Africa* (Cape Town: David Philip, 1992) and Ronnie Kasrils's biography *'Armed and Dangerous': My Undercover Struggle Against*

Apartheid (Oxford: Heinemann, 1993). Books that presaged the contemporary debates include edited collections produced by Vincent Maphai (*South Africa: The Challenge of Change*, Harare: SAPES Books, 1994) and Gordon Naidoo (*Reform & Revolution: South Africa in the Nineties*, Dakar, Codesria and Johannesburg: Skotaville, 1991).

The parallel turmoil within the National Party and Afrikaans society as a whole has again been treated brilliantly by Dan O'Meara (*Forty Lost Years*, London: James Currey, 1996), in a book that also rigorously tackles the main theoretical debates about the character of the state, capital and society. For a general work that provides an overview of the mid-1990s political transition there is hardly as good a study as that by Martin Murray (*Revolution Deferred*, London: Verso, 1994; see also his *Myth and Memory in the New South Africa*, London: Verso, 1999). A book on African politics which treats South Africa with great insight is Mahmood Mamdani's *Citizen and Subject: Contemporary Africa and the Legacy of Late Colonialism* (Princeton: Princeton University Press, 1996). An important statement about the early years of ANC rule that I consider a general empirical (and to some extent analytical) prerequisite for much of the argument presented here – and whose author is the most eloquent of South African left journalists – is Hein Marais's *South Africa: Limits to Change* (London: Zed Press, and Cape Town: University of Cape Town, 1998). (The other two essential journalists of the SA Left are *Natal Mercury* columnist and sociologist Ashwin Desai – see his audacious *South Africa: Still Revolting*, Durban: Natal Newspapers, 1999 – and *Business Report* labour correspondent Terry Bell.) At the human scale, the book *Fault Lines: Journeys into the New South Africa* by David Goodman (Berkeley: University of California Press, 1999) offers a superb, compatible complement to structural accounts of 'liberation'.

Moving to more obscure academic terrain, one current model for radical South African social-historical analysis – a nuanced biography of sharecropper Kas Maine – is Charles van Onselen's monumental *The Seed is Mine* (London: James Currey, and Cape Town: David Philip, 1997). The strongest economics text is certainly Ben Fine and Zav Rustomjee's *The Political Economy of South Africa* (London, Hirst and Johannesburg: Wits University Press, 1996). And I could add any number of specialist works on sectors of the economy, gender politics, history, the legacy of apartheid, new social problems, crime and security, race and ethnicity, trade unions, urban movements, the gay/lesbian scene, the youth, churches, culture, and the like.

It must said, however, that such important recent books have been relatively unstimulating and uncontroversial, if we are to judge by their quiet reaction in political and intellectual circuits – with the exception, perhaps, of McKinley's attack on the exiled ANC (as well as various debates about, for instance, the historical character of Zulu nationalism) – because they have by and large gone unread, unreviewed and undebated, at least in South Africa itself. Does this reflect the quality of those contributions mentioned above? Or instead, is it a sign of the times, namely the terribly weak intellectual and political conditions that exist for robust radical argumentation – perhaps caused by the sea-change of opinion-makers from an opposition culture infused with curiousity, to smug self-satisfaction?

I think the latter, not simply because a large group of progressive leaders went into the state in 1994 and were hence positioned as the target of critics. In addition, as shown in the journal *debate* (3, 1997: 'Retreat of the Intellectuals'), hundreds if not a few thousand university leftists and shopfloor/grassroots organic intellectuals who during the 1970s–1980s awaited with great anticipation for the latest issues of *Work in Progress, SA Labour Bulletin, South African Review, Review of African Political Economy* and (later) *Transformation* and *Agenda*, had every reason for deep disillusionment, subsequently, about the character of contributions from dozens of erstwhile left commentators, who were by the 1990s far more engaged in consulting gigs and policy drafting than in the production of searching analysis.

Thus whereas social historians would have had, during the 1980s, ongoing and powerful debates with neo-Poulantzians and whereas Saul/Gelb 'racial capitalism' advocates would have bumped into Two-Stage Theory adherents or Permanent Revolutionaries at the campus pub and perhaps even a union hall, the 1990s witnessed only low-key, uninspired attempts to compare notes (for a good example of disappointing 'post-Marxist' caricatures of radical positions, see David Howarth and Aletta Norwal (eds), *South Africa in Transition: New Theoretical Perspectives*, London: Macmillan, 1998). As we shall soon see, the 1987–91 rise and collapse of the seminal (if profoundly flawed) poli-econ perspective, 'Regulation Theory', is indicative of the dog days of South African radical analysis.

All is not lost, for as Chapter 6 hints, there is renewed space for a revival of forthright critique of neo-apartheid, neoliberal *capitalism* as a function, at least in part, of the recent global crisis. It is in this context that I feel my relatively journalistic input, with its dash of idiosyncratic theory, can clarify for international and local readers alike the terrain of debate in a South Africa that will undoubtedly soon retake its place amongst the foremost of global sites of social struggle, perhaps including struggle over intellectual innovation.

INTRODUCTION: DISSECTING SOUTH AFRICA'S TRANSITION

1. Karl Marx, *Capital*, Moscow: International Publishers, 1967 edn, ch. 27, p. 15.
2. For a brief summary, see my 'Uneven Development', in P. O'Hara (ed.), *The Encyclopaedia of Political Economy*, London: Routledge, 1999.

3. Harold Wolpe (ed.), *The Articulations of Modes of Production*, London: Routledge & Kegan Paul, 1980.
4. Neil Smith, *Uneven Development*, second edition, Oxford: Basil Blackwell, 1990, p.156.
5. Alain de Janvry, *The Agrarian Question and Reformism in Latin America*, Baltimore: Johns Hopkins University Press, 1982.
6. Rudolf Hilferding, *Finance Capital*, London: Routledge & Kegan Paul, 1981 edn.
7. This was also the case in neighbouring Zimbabwe; see my *Uneven Zimbabwe: A Study of Finance, Development and Underdevelopment*, Trenton: Africa World Press, 1998.
8. From 1996 to 1998, the SA Human Sciences Research Council funded studies that have been encapsulated in Chapters 4 and 5 below, as did Community Aid Abroad (Australia) and Misereor (Germany) from 1990 to 1994 when I worked at Planact. Prior to that, the US Social Science Research Council made available resources to allow me to come to the region in the first place and conduct doctoral studies. Academic journals which have published some of the argumentation, though in different format and sometimes with co-authors, include *Geoforum, Urban Forum, South African Geographical Journal, International Journal of Health Services, Socialist Studies Bulletin, Journal of World Systems Research* and *Africa Today*. Academic books within which chapters played the same function include *Transformation in South Africa? Policy Debates in the 1990s* (edited by Ernest Maganya and Rachel Houghton, Johannesburg: IFAA, 1997); *Socialist Register, 1996: Are There Alternatives?* (edited by Leo Panitch, London: Merlin Press, 1996); *Debating Development Discourses: Institutional and Popular Perspectives* (edited by David Moore and Gerald Schmitz, London: Macmillan, and New York: St. Martin's Press, 1995); *Money, Power and Space* (edited by Stuart Corbridge, Ron Martin and Nigel Thrift, Oxford: Basil Blackwell, 1994); *The Limits of Capitalist Reform in South Africa* (edited by Andrew Nash, Bellville: University of the Western Cape, 1994); and *The Apartheid City and Beyond: Urbanization and Social Change in South Africa* (edited by David Smith, London: Routledge). Parallel arguments are found in two other books, *Commanding Heights and Community Control: New Economics for a New South Africa* (Johannesburg: Ravan Press, 1991) and *Cities of Gold, Townships of Coal: Essays on South Africa's New Urban Crisis* (Trenton: Africa World Press, 2000). A variety of other periodicals also carried articles written during 1990–98 from which I draw in the pages below. I wrote most often for *African Agenda* and *Africa South* magazines (edited by Gwen Ansell and Tony Hall), and was given regular columns for occasional periods by the Harare *Financial Gazette* (edited by Trevor Ncube), the *Southern African Review of Books* (edited by Rob Turrell) and

Reconstruct/Work in Progress (edited by Devan Pillay). I also wrote about South Africa for *African Communist* (Johannesburg), *Against the Current* (Detroit), *BankCheck* (Berkeley), *Business Day* (Johannesburg), *City Press* (Johannesburg), *Cross Sections* (Toronto), *Debate* (Johannesburg), *Development Update* (Johannesburg), *Environmental Justice Networking Forum Newsletter* (Pietermaritzburg), *Finance Week* (Johannesburg), *The Guardian* (New York), *i'Afrika* (Copenhagen), *Indicator SA* (Durban), *Journal of Southern African Studies* (Oxford), *Land and Rural Policy Digest* (Johannesburg), *Left Business Observer* (New York), *Local Government Chronicle* (Johannesburg), *The Mail and Guardian* (Johannesburg), *Multinational Monitor* (Washington DC), *New African* (Durban), *Neue Zuricher Zeitung* (Zurich), *New Ground* (Johannesburg), *New Nation* (Johannesburg), *Red Pepper* (London), *Searchlight South Africa* (London), *South African Labour Bulletin* (Johannesburg), *SouthScan* (London), *Southern Africa Chronicle* (Harare), *Southern Africa Report* (Toronto) and *Sunday Independent Reconstruct* (Johannesburg). All the editors and publishers associated with these periodicals and books are warmly thanked.
9. Cited in Alex Callinicos, *Making History*, Cambridge: Polity Press, 1987, p. vii.

1 NEOLIBERAL ECONOMIC CONSTRAINTS ON LIBERATION

1. Editorial, *Business Day*, 20 January 1990.
2. Ben Fine and Zav Rustomjee, *The Political Economy of South Africa* (London, Hurst and Johannesburg: Wits University Press, 1996), Chapters 4 and 5.
3. Dave Kaplan, 'Machinery and Industry: The Causes and Consequences of Constrained Development of the South African Machine Tool Industry', *Social Dynamics*, 13, 1, 1987.
4. For the argument that the luxury character of import substitution industrialisation generally deformed the strategy, see Fred Nixson, 'Import-Substitution Industrialization', in M. Fransman (ed.), *Industry and Accumulation in Africa*, London: Heinemann, 1982; for a light historical discussion which treats luxury goods overaccumulation during the 1970s as a core process marking the onset of the long economic decline, see my *Commanding Heights and Community Control*, Chapter 2: A Crisis of Overaccumulation.
5. Since 1994 there has been a general sentiment – though hardly well-enough documented to be convincing (given the rapidly rising unemployment rate) – that South Africa is gradually improving on its

appalling inequality, as measured in narrow United Nations Human Development Index reports, although it is conceded that gaps between highest-tier and lowest-tier black households have become as great as the division between whites and blacks (*Mail and Guardian*, 11 September 1998). More realistic is the 1994 UNDP characterisation of white South Africa as having living standards nearly equivalent to Canada, while on average black South Africans enjoy lifestyles equivalent to those of the Congo.

6. Ministry of Reconstruction and Development, *Key Indicators of Poverty in South Africa*, Pretoria, 1995.

7. Full details are provided in my 'A History of Finance and Uneven Geographical Development in South Africa', *South African Geographical Journal*, 80, 1, 1998.

8. William G. Martin, 'From NIC to NUC: South Africa's Semiperipheral Regimes,' in W. Martin (ed.), *Semiperipheral States in the World-Economy*, New York: Greenwood Press, 1990.

9. Jill Nattrass, *The South African Economy*, Cape Town: Oxford University Press, 1981.

10. Nicoli Nattrass, *Profits and Wages*, London: Penguin, 1992, pp. 4, 6.

11. Such arguments are debunked in Charles Meth, 'Productivity and South Africa's Economic Crisis', Unpublished research monograph, University of Natal Department of Economics, 1990.

12. Steven Gelb, 'Making Sense of the Crisis', *Transformation*, 5, 1987, and Steven Gelb (ed.), *South Africa's Economic Crisis*, Cape Town: David Philip, and London: Zed Press, 1991.

13. World Bank, 'South Africa: Post-Apartheid Economic Options', Unpublished paper, Washington DC, 1991.

14. The price rise from $35/oz in 1971 to $250/oz by 1979 to nearly $850/oz in 1981 was itself a consequence of global factors such as intensifying inter-capitalist competition, bottlenecks in trade and currency, and overaccumulation which were all displaced, in part, monetarily – through inflation – during the 1970s. With currencies weak, gold played its traditional role of ultimate store of value. Then in 1980 with global real interest rates at extremely high levels and a myriad of financial assets hence now far more attractive to institutional investors, the gold price crashed back to $400/oz. Gold dropped even further over the subsequent two decades, reaching what is probably an historic low point of under $270/oz in 1998.

15. *South African Reserve Bank Quarterly Bulletin*, various issues.

16. David Harvey, *The Limits to Capital*, Chicago: University of Chicago Press, 1982.

17. Urban Foundation, *Regional Development Reconsidered*, Policies for a New Urban Future Series, 3, Johannesburg, 1990.

18. For evidence of the late 1980s tension in capital's consciousness, see Michael Morris and Vishnu Padayachee, 'State Reform Policy in South Africa', *Transformation*, 7, 1988.

19. John Pickles, 'Industrial Restructuring, Peripheral Industrialization, and Rural Development in South Africa', *Antipode*, 23, 1, 1991.

20. Harry Magdoff and Paul Sweezy, *Stagnation and the Financial Explosion*, New York: Monthly Review Press, 1987; see also my 'The New United States Class Struggle', *Capital and Class*, 40, Spring 1990.

21. See my 'Are Mining Houses Bleeding SA of Profits?', *Financial Gazette*, 17 February, 1994; see also Zav Rustomjee, 'Capital Flight under Apartheid', *Transformation*, 15, 1991.

22. Bob Aldworth, *The Infernal Tower*, Johannesburg: Contra Press, 1996.

23. Blank – a prototype yuppie in his late twenties – defrauded Old Mutual on 48 occasions for at least R2 million. Yet he painted a murky picture in which it appeared that Old Mutual's Harper, Celotti and Schapiro ran an insider trading syndicate. The latter three would identify stocks (including offshore trades), Blank would buy large amounts for the syndicate's private accounts, Old Mutual would buy them back, and the traders would clean up pensioners' monies. Blank contended that his behaviour was not unusual – such scams are commonplace on Diagonal Street. Celotti and Schapiro fled overseas, and in 1992 Blank received an eight-year sentence which, in a controversial 1996 decision, was reduced for good behaviour.

24. In 1993, South Africa's best-known bank entrepreneur, Jan Marais (founder of TrustBank), was fingered by police on possible corruption charges. Marais, a former National Party MP, was a non-executive director in Fundstrust, which was founded a decade before to place funds in the money markets. Then, in 1991, a company substantially owned by Anton Rupert's giant Rembrandt empire attempted to recoup a R45 million placement in Fundstrust that was being mishandled, with the result that Fundstrust was liquidated. At that point it was revealed that key Fundstrust employees were engaged in massive internal fraud, leading co-founder Ansi Kamfer to flee the country. Investigators ultimately made their way to an angry Marais.

25. Lombard (brother of Jan) was found guilty of US$1 billion in foreign exchange fraud while a leading official at the Durban branch of the Reserve Bank.

26. See my article, 'Are Mining Houses Bleeding SA of Profits?'.

27. *Business Day*, 11 September 1992.

28. *Star*, 12 February 1993.

29. *Star*, 30 September 1992.

30. Thompson allegedly misled the London diamond trade about supply conditions. The *Financial Times* said simply: 'His credibility has been

dented', while Johannesburg *Star* finance guru John Spira suggested that De Beers 'might well have damaged its reputation irreparably'. *Sunday Times* writer John Cavill called the subsequent 'dumping' of De Beers' stocks 'traumatic', while *Business Day* editorialists raised a more damaging spectre: 'Investors who had overcome antipathy to SA and had their fingers scorched [on De Beers] are morosely wondering about the way South Africans do business. De Beers' handling of its dividend cut has inadvertently done this country's investment hopes a disservice.' For more, see my 'Politics Subsides, Eskom Slides, Anglo-De Beers Accused of Lies', *Financial Gazette*, 27 August 1992.

31. Jan Lombard, 'Housing Finance and the National Economic Scenario', Address to CSIR Conference: Finance – The Pathway to Housing, Council for Scientific and Industrial Research, Pretoria, 2 June 1988. For more on the rise of finance, see my 'Township Housing and South Africa's Financial Explosion', *Urban Forum*, 1, 2, 1990.

32. Steven Mayo, 'South African Housing Sector Performance in International Perspective', Paper presented to the 21st World Housing Congress, Cape Town, 10–14 May 1993.

33. Reflecting the chaos, *Business Day* editor Jim Jones had rough words for one of ABSA's pillars: 'The name TrustBank has for years been a byword for many of the things which can go wrong with a bank. Control systems were atrocious, and that gave rise to any number of opportunities for fraud or for covering incompetence.' Plenty of TrustBank and other ABSA loans were illustrative of the decay. Tollgate Holdings (R250 million to be written off) and Bester Homes faced bank-initiated liquidation, while Rusfern got a new ABSA-chosen board. Other ABSA credits to FSI/W&A group (R1.3 billion in debt) went badly sour, and ABSA reportedly forced FSI into a bail-out merger. See my 'Tale of Forsaken Financiers', *Financial Gazette*, 4 March 1993.

34. I made this point in an article printed in the *Mail and Guardian* in 1998 ('Time again for the Finrand?', 16 October); but that particular paragraph was censored. The capital flight engendered by the main banks should have been a national scandal, particularly when foreign subsidiaries of Standard made bum loans to Russia and Brazil, but reflecting the hegemony of banking capital, it was rarely remarked on and virtually ignored by regulators.

   To some degree the early 1990s expansion affected Africa. Standard Bank bought Grindlays in Zimbabwe and other affiliates in Zaire, Uganda, Nigeria, Madagascar and Ghana. Nedcor bought part of Merchant Bank of Central Africa.

35. See my 'Is There a Way to Halt Capital Flight?,' *Financial Gazette*, 24 June 1993. Soon afterwards, Gencor bought international minerals/metals subsidiary Billiton from Shell Oil in a suspicious deal

in which Finance Minister Derek Keys gave the company permission to use hard currency; after his quick departure from the 1994 Government of National Unity, Keys won a top Billiton job.

36. See, e.g., *Sunday Business Times*, 6 June 1992; *Star*, 19 April 1993. To make matters worse, the Usury Act (with its 32 per cent interest rate ceiling through most of the 1990s) was liberalised in 1998 to allow lenders of up to R10,000 to charge any interest rate that the market would bear.

37. See Aldworth, *The Infernal Tower*, for details.

38. As an aside, the popular disgust with banks over their undemocratic impulses in mid-1992 was mirrored by a different breed of racist-populists a few months earlier. At a time that banks' agricultural portfolios were slouching under the weight of unrepayable loans to reactionary white farmers, the rural right wing grew angry that financiers contributed heavily to F.W. de Klerk's pro-reform referendum fund in 1992. 'This shocking action by certain financial institutions ought to be stopped immediately,' griped a Transvaal Agricultural Union spokesperson, who called for more contributions to the TAU bail-out fund instead. A Conservative Party official even threatened a boycott against two allegedly 'ANC-linked' banks (Standard Bank and First National), on the grounds they were scaring their employees into voting Yes for reform. The Yes vote won, by 68–32 per cent.

    Historical precedents of such right-populist, anti-banking Afrikaans anger are found in Dan O'Meara, *Volkskapitalism*, Cambridge: Cambridge University Press, 1983; and Tim Keegan, *Rural Transformations in Industrializing South Africa*, Johannesburg: Ravan Press, 1986.

39. The banks never convincingly showed that the shortage – which had peaked in late April at R11 billion and fallen to R6 billion at the time of the rate increase in mid-May – was actually resolved by the 1 per cent increase. Instead, the fact that the liquidity shortage trend was down, and that during the period that the rate was increased by 1 per cent the downward trend actually slowed, leaves room for doubt.

40. Standard and Nedbank publicly debated whether the new products (a 17.5 per cent capped bond) were priced transparently. Nedbank argued that its own capped bond was a better product than Standard's, for the latter's included a monthly fee that brought the effective interest rate up to 18.4 per cent (hence raising issues of accuracy in advertising).

41. *Weekly Mail*, 12 January 1993.

42. Greta Steyn, 'Ultimately, Revival of SA Investment needs an Act of Faith', *Business Day*, 26 November 1992.

43. *Sunday Business Times*, 15 November 1992.

44. Sipho Pityana and Mark Orkin (eds), *Beyond the Factory Floor: A Survey of Cosatu Shop-stewards*, Johannesburg: Ravan Press, 1992.

45. Andrew Levy and Associates, quoted in South African Institute of Race Relations, *Race Relations Survey 1992*, Johannesburg: SA Institute of Race Relations, 1992, p. 366.

46. *Business Day*, 24 August 1992.

47. *Business Day*, 1 September 1992. Safto finally was defunded by trade and industry minister Alec Erwin, and split into several parts. By 1999, the *Financial Mail*'s Adrienne Roberts ('SA's Export Drive is still too Pedestrian', 4 June) lamented the lack of the 'cut-throat, hard-core, well-oiled export machine [South Africa] needs to compete', in part because 'SA exporters, in general, are not well informed'.

48. Nevertheless, throwing caution to the wind, the same economists even called for the 'selective liberalisation' of basic wage goods such as wheat, shoes and garments, a liberalisation 'that goes beyond that of the Bank', a sure route to more retrenchments in sectors that were extremely vulnerable. See Avril Joffe, Dave Kaplan, Raphael Kaplinsky and Dave Lewis, 'Meeting the Global Challenge: A Framework for Industrial Revival in SA', in *South Africa and the World Economy in the 1990s*, David Philip: Cape Town, 1994.

49. *Business Day*, 11 March 1993.

50. Locally, the (non-homeland) clothing sector was decimated by a series of post-Fordist innovations – the output of informal cottage manufacturing, home sewing, residual homeland export-processing industrial suburbs, second-hand imports, etc. – and as a result the sector's output dropped 40 per cent during the 1980s, even before tariff reductions began in earnest. It is worth noting that the World Bank industrial strategy for Zimbabwe also hinged on clothing and textile sales to niche export markets, but there too the industry collapsed (see my *Uneven Zimbabwe*, Chapters 11 and 12).

51. *Sunday Business Times*, 27 September 1992.

52. For Turok, see *Mail and Guardian* articles collected in his *Beyond the Miracle: Development and Economy in South Africa* (Cape Town, Fair Share, 1999, Chapter 7). Mlambo-Ngcuka, later to become Minerals and Energy Minister, was widely cited, including in the smug book by Heribert Adam, Frederick van Zyl Slabbert and Kogila Moodley, *Comrades in Business: Post-Liberation Politics in South Africa*, Cape Town: Tafelberg, 1997, p. 201.

53. *Business Report*, 10 October 1997; Mvundla quoted in *Business Report*, 6 November 1996. Thanks to Omano Egidheji for pointing out these references, in his fine University of Durban-Westville Master's thesis.

54. Sam Nolutshungu, *Changing South Africa*, Cape Town: David Philip, 1982, pp. 206, 207.

55. John Kane-Berman's books include *South Africa's Silent Revolution*, Johannesburg: Institute of Race Relations, 1990 and *Political Violence*

in South Africa, Johannesburg: Institute of Race Relations, 1993. See also my 'Taxis Fail as Black Model', *Financial Gazette*, 23 July 1992, and 'Behind the Jo'burg Taxi Riots: The Spectre of Declining Profits', *Financial Gazette*, 18 February 1993.

It is important to point out that the drivers were not passively oppressed by their owners and the state. Johannesburg driver riots included demands to the Johannesburg Traffic Department such as ending police harassment and excessive ticketing, improving taxi ranks and drop-off points, and providing transport subsidies. By all accounts the drivers put on a massive display of disruptive power, and won immediate release of their jailed colleagues and impounded vehicles, as well as drawing international attention to their plight (and forcing the free-marketeers onto the defensive).

56. Meshack Khosa, 'Capital Accumulation, the Apartheid State and the Rise of the Black Taxi Industry,' DPhil thesis, Oxford University, School of Geography, 1992.

57. By the early 1990s South Africa claimed 200,000 registered small companies and 625,000 informal sector businesses, including many of the most celebrated vehicles of black economic empowerment: services ranging from hairdressers to sangomas to childminders, domestics and musicians; retail distributors (especially street hawkers and *spaza* shops); small-scale financial enterprises; productive and secondary activities (such as dressmaking, cement-block making, and furniture-making); repairs; transport (especially taxis); building construction; accommo- dation; and illicit activities (prostitution, gambling). But poor research and vast hyperbole characterised the informal sector. For example, Sanlam's 1993 *Platform for Investment* study – discussed in the next chapter – claimed that the size of the informal sector rose from 5 per cent of GDP in 1980 to 17 per cent in 1991, and Professor Brian Kantor of the University of Cape Town once estimated that as much as 40 per cent could be added to South Africa's GDP through informal sector activity. The first official estimate (by the Central Statistical Service in 1990) suggested 2.6 million informally employed Africans were responsible for at least 7.3 per cent of GDP. But another estimate of informal sector income in 1993 (by students at the UCT Graduate School of Business) was just R6 billion – i.e. under 2 per cent of GDP.

58. Government's small business agencies – Khula Enterprise Finance for credit guarantees, the Ntsika Enterprise Promotion Agency, and the National Small Business Council – were, respectively, ineffectual (just over 600 loans were guaranteed by Khula in its first 18 months, a pitiable figure showing how little the major banks regarded the scheme), represented in only a few token offices scattered around the country, and corrupt (the Council had to be shut down). A long-awaited state National Empowerment Fund, saving 10 per cent of each privatisation

deal for black shareholders, was meant to be introduced, following the Malaysian bumiputra financing model.

59. Cited in my 'In 1993, Will South Africa Halt the Worst Trends?', *Financial Gazette*, 7 January 1993. Ironic, this quote, in relation to Nyati's own notoriously fabricated c.v.

60. Upon (perhaps temporarily) quitting politics due to his defeat in a major power struggle with Thabo Mbeki in 1995, Ramaphosa – who once in his career had been close to the Trotskyist Marxist Workers Tendency – celebrated his entry into the business world by calling for the liberalisation of exchange controls. The more government followed such neoliberal advice, the more fragile the economy became (with the currency crashing in 1996 and 1998) and the more interest rates needed to be raised in order to keep local money in and attract more foreign hot money to support the balance of payments. The more interest rates went up, the faster that debt-addicted BEE deals, like Ramaphosa's Nail, went down. After being fired, effectively, by his colleagues, Ramaphosa went to head the only organic, bottom-up BEE firm, Molope Bakery (in doing so he violated official King Commission recommendations that the positions of chairman and chief executive be split).

61. Frantz Fanon, *The Wretched of the Earth*, New York: Grove Press, 1968. *Financial Mail*, 4 June 1999. As the *FM* advised its readership, 'Beware of companies fundamentally grounded in financial services, which grow not by creating wealth, necessarily, but by facilitating the trading of assets or the generation of debt. Look for people who want to *make* things.'

    This appeal recalls another Third World (Caribbean) Marxist who critiqued actually existing BEE, Clive Thomas: 'The emerging capitalists in the periphery are, *as a social class*, underdeveloped in comparison to their counterpart in the centre. In spite of the emergence of some "vibrant" business elites and the increasing sophistication of some state classes, I believe that at this stage peripheral capialists are incapable of seeing their class project in terms of the need for historic reforms. To most of these ruling groups, reform is anathema. Also, the capitalist classes in the periphery generally rely on the exploitation of economic rents through strategic control of assets instead of pushing a constant revolution in productive techniques' ('Restructuring of the World Economy and its Implications for the Third World', in A. MacEwan and W.K. Tabb (eds), *Instability and Change in the World Economy*, New York: Monthly Review, 1989, p. 335).

62. Pedro Belli, M. Finger and A. Ballivian, 'South Africa: Review of Trade Policy Issues', Informal Discussion Papers on Aspects of the Economy of South Africa, Paper 4, Southern Africa Department, Washington DC, World Bank, 1993. The unevenness of the tariff system was the critical issue, with South Africa claiming more than 2,800 different types of surcharges; Nepal was next in complexity, with just 87 surcharges.

63. *Star*, 31 July 1992.
64. *Business Day*, 28 October 1993.
65. *Business Day*, 17 December 1993. See also my 'GATT Attack Requires more than a Regional Defence', *Africa South and East*, February 1994; 'GATT will Prove a Rude Shock', *Financial Gazette*, 6 January 1994; and 'Economic Diary', *Southern African Review of Books*, November–December 1993.
66. High profits prevailed in spite of the fact that US multinationals' South African wages were more than a third higher than Latin America, and twice as high as most of Asia. According to the *Sunday Business Times*, the survey provided another 'reason not to be optimistic about major infusions of US investment – at least until SA can demonstrate that it has a healthy and growing market for products made by American affiliates'. Only 10 per cent of US companies' South African output was exported in 1989 (*Sunday Business Times*, 4 April 1993).
67. Frankel Max Pollak Vinderine Inc., Sanlam, Ernst & Young and the Human Sciences Research Council, *Platform for Investment*, Johannesburg, 1992, p. 112.
68. *Business Day*, 25 November 1993, 30 November 1993.
69. See my 'Neoliberalism Comes to South Africa', *Multinational Monitor*, May 1996; Patrick Bond, Yogan Pillay, and David Sanders, 'The State of Neoliberalism in South Africa: Developments in Economic, Social and Health Policy', *International Journal of Health Services*, 27, 1, 1997; my 'Globalization, Pharmaceutical Pricing and South African Health Policy', *International Journal of Health Services*, 29, 3, 1999; and John Judis, 'K Street Gore', *The American Prospect*, 45, July–August 1999.
70. Alec Erwin, 'Building the New South Africa's Economy', *African Communist*, third quarter, 1996.
71. Two reflections of the (still self-described communist) minister's unusual role were first, the extraordinary optimism in the stock market when, in March 1996, rumours abounded that Erwin (not Manuel) would replace Liebenberg at the Finance Ministry; and second, the fact that *Business Day* published Erwin's Gramsci reference with the preface '*As a Marxist ...*' (the *AC* must have received an edited copy from Erwin, as opposed to *Business Day*'s verbatim transcript), which probably had the reassuring effect, for banqueters, of denuding Marxism of any meaning whatsoever.

2 SOCIAL CONTRACT SCENARIOS

1. African National Congress, *The Reconstruction and Development Programme: A Policy Framework*, Johannesburg: Umanyano Publications, 1994.

2. Heribert Adam and Kagila Moodley, *The Negotiated Revolution: Society and Politics in Post-Apartheid SA*, Berkeley: University of California Press and Parklands: Jonathan Ball, 1993.

3. Bob Tucker and Bruce Scott (eds), *South Africa: Prospects for Successful Transition*, Kenwyn: Juta, 1992.

4. Pieter le Roux, *The Mont Fleur Scenarios*, Bellville, University of Western Cape, 1993.

5. Nicoli Nattrass, 'Evaluation of Old Mutual/Nedcor Scenario Planning', *Innes Labour Brief*, 1992.

6. Clem Sunter, *The World and South Africa in the 1990s*, Cape Town: Human & Rousseau Tafelberg, 1987.

7. *Neue Zuricher Zeitung Folio*, April 1994. Ramaphosa and Golding both reverted from active politics to positions in big business in 1996, and by 1998 were each estimated to have accumulated personal wealth in excess of R40 million.

8. Mzwanele Mayekiso (*Township Politics*, New York: Monthly Review Press, 1996, pp. 243–4) assessed the 'underclass' analysis of Scott and his allies, Maude Motanyane, Mamphela Ramphele and Sheila Sisulu, and concluded: 'Nedcor and Old Mutual are, it seems, satisfied with a democratic political system only if it specifically does not lead to political empowerment of the oppressed, redistribution of wealth and restructuring of the economy in the interests of poor and working people – this led their analysts to construct a method for dealing with political demands which treats them as cultural weaknesses.'

9. Frankel Max Pollak Vinderine, Sanlam, Ernst & Young, and Human Sciences Research Council, *Platform for Investment*.

10. Joffe et al., 'Meeting the Global Challenge'.

11. Raphael Kaplinsky, 'Is and What is Post-Fordism', Unpublished paper presented to the Economic Trends Group, 1990; and 'A Policy Agenda for Post-Apartheid South Africa', *Transformation*, 16, 1991.

12. *Business Day*, 28 October 1993.

13. *Sunday Times*, 4 September 1996.

14. Duncan Innes, 'Towards the Year 2000: Megatrends Shaping Industrial Relations', *Innes Labour Brief*, 3, 2, 1991.

15. Samir Amin, 'SA in the Global Economic System', *Work in Progress*, February 1993.

16. Joffe et al., 'Meeting the Global Challenge'.

17. Jeremy Baskin, 'Corporatism: Some Obstacles Facing the SA Labour Movement', Social Contract Series, Research Report 30, Centre for Policy Studies, Johannesburg, April 1993.

18. Consultative Business Movement (1993), *Managing Change: A Guide to the Role of Business in Transition*, Johannesburg, Ravan Press.

19. Professional Economists Panel (1993), 'Growing Together', Johannesburg: Nedcor/Old Mutual.
20. The 'Great Sale' of public housing begun in 1983 received only a 35 per cent take-up a decade later.
21. J. French, 'Hitting Where it Hurts Most: Jamaican Women's Livelihoods in Crisis', in Pam Sparr (ed.), *Mortgaging Women's Lives: Feminist Critiques of Structural Adjustment*, London, Zed Press, 1994; S. Jayaweera, 'Structural Adjustment Policies, Industrial Development and Women in Sri Lanka', in *ibid*.
22. Pierre Wack, 'Scenarios: Shooting the Rapids', *Harvard Business Review*, November–December 1985.
23. Indeed, years after *Prospects* was unveiled, did Nedcor/Old Mutual put its money where its mouth is in order to advance the mythical social compact? No, for although Nedcor's NedEnterprise small business unit was set up as a direct response to *Prospects* (according to the bank), none of the other areas where Old Mutual had overwhelming market power – continuing speculation in the JSE and commercial real estate markets, and repudiation of municipal bonds – showed even a hint of a more enlightened policy. Emblematic was Mutual's 1992 decision to red-line the securities offered by city governments, in the process denying Johannesburg the capital needed to make vital infrastructural investments in Soweto. Moreover, Mutual's forays into residential real estate shied well clear of low-cost housing. The effective termination of the Perm's low-cost housing initiatives in 1994 merely confirmed the overall trend.
24. A slight revival was signalled by three 'labour scenarios' developed by Wits sociologist Karl van Holdt and considered by Cosatu's September Commission in late 1996, and in early 1997 KwaZulu-Natal's Inkatha rulers ran a 'scenario planning' workshop on provincial economic development.
25. Alec Erwin believed differently, arguing, dubiously, that 'In that publication [the Harare conference] you will note that the basic building blocks of the current policy were there, including that of nationalisation' (Erwin, 'Building the New South Africa's Economy', p. 26).
26. Merg's other proposals were nothing out of the ordinary: continuing exchange controls for domestic residents (but not foreign investors); a 2 per cent real interest rate; massive construction of (fairly low-standard) rental housing for the poor; labour market interventions such as human resources investment, a 'conservative and cautious' minimum wage, and the like. Merg argued against 'dismantling the conglomerates'. Skews in industry were targeted and export prospects identified. Merg's proposed reforms of import protection and export support were unremarkable, and generally supported exposure to international

competition. More R&D investment was proposed and financial markets received attention. In addition to Reserve Bank nationalisation, Merg proposed a People's Bank based on the Post Office Savings Bank infrastructure, prescribed assets for insurance companies and pension funds, and capital market controls. Bank relations with industry were criticised as being unimaginative. See MacroEconomic Research Group, *Making Democracy Work*, Bellville: Centre for Development Studies, 1993.

27. Department of Finance, *The Key Issues in the Normative Economic Model*, Pretoria, 1993.
28. *Business Day*, 3 March 1993.
29. Department of Finance, *Growth, Employment and Redistribution: A Macroeconomic Strategy*, Pretoria, 1996.
30. *Mail and Guardian*, 21 June 1996.
31. Dale Mckinley, Vishwas Satgar and Langa Zita, 'Critique of Government's Macroeconomic Strategy: *Gear*', *debate*, 1, 1996.
32. Above quotes cited in my 'Gearing up or down?', *South African Labour Bulletin*, 20, 6, August 1996.

   Mandela was inconsistent on *Gear*, having conceded in his address at Cosatu's 1997 national congress 'the ANC learnt of *Gear* when it was almost complete' (*Business Day*, 17 September 1997), but denying on subsequent occasions that the process was politically impulsive and undemocratic. Wags soon realised that instead of achieving growth, employment and redistribution, *Gear* was, quite objectively, a decline, unemployment and polarisation economics (*Dupe*), and worker songs – 'pansi *Gear*' – took on a humorous tone, to the stern Mandela's enormous irritation.

3 RUMOURS, DREAMS AND PROMISES

1. *Business Day*, 23 November 1993.
2. *Business Day*, 3 May 1994.
3. RDP Council, 'Rebuilding the MDM for a People-Driven *RDP*', *African Communist*, second quarter 1996.
4. Everyone has their own definition of 'people-driven development', and this writer's own background in the civic movement and urban service NGOs leads me to the following characteristics: an emphasis on basic needs as *entitlements*, financed and delivered in a non-commodified form, through a 'strong but slim' state that is capable of capturing and redistributing the social surplus, complemented with additional state-supplied resources for building the organisational capacity of democratic, non-profit, community-controlled institutions. For more, see, e.g., Mayekiso, *Township Politics*, Chapters 13–15; and South African National Civic

Organisation Commission on Development Finance, *Making People-Driven Development Work*, Johannesburg: Sanco, 1994.

5. So initially enthusiastic was Buthelezi, as Home Affairs Minister, that in September 1994 he pronounced that 2 million illegal immigrants were 'undermining the *RDP*'. In fact, had Buthelezi actually read the *RDP*, he would have found ample evidence of regional solidarity, hints at reparations for apartheid's regional destabilisation, and a commitment to far more balanced economic growth and rising wages as solutions to the influx of Southern Africans. (Later, on the advice of Professor Schlemmer and the Human Sciences Research Council, Buthelezi extrapolated some samples and guessed that there were 8 million illegal immigrants.)

Within a week, the National Intelligence Service visited the development NGO Planact, demanding to know the dynamics behind Southern African immigration to inner-city Johannesburg. It was, the agent commented to two staff without a trace of irony, the NIS's (self-appointed) contribution to the *RDP* to find out such things. Unpersuaded by xenophobic attempts to create a new 'Other' (in the NIS's case to justify a R500 million-plus budget), Planact refused to cooperate.

6. *Sunday Times*, 1 May 1994.

7. Cited in my 'The *RDP* of the Left: An Interpretation of the *Reconstruction and Development Programme*', *African Communist*, second quarter 1994.

8. *Ibid*.

9. *Mail and Guardian*, 13 May 1994.

10. Cited in my article, 'The *RDP* of the Left'.

11. Alec Erwin, '*The Reconstruction and Development Programme*: A View from the Tripartite Alliance', *South African Labour Bulletin*, 18, 1, 1994, p. 42.

12. *Work in Progress*, January–February 1994.

13. Without the mechanisms which the *RDP* demands, I argue in Chapter 4, housing would ultimately be bought and sold subject only to financial means, and more privileged class fractions within the townships and rural areas would quickly crowd out the poorer beneficiaries of the subsidies, leading to landlordism and 'downward raiding'. In turn, the insider–outsider dichotomy which grew so rapidly since neoliberal economic policies were adopted during the late 1980s, would be exacerbated. Dexter was correct, but didn't take his argument further than one magazine article.

14. *African Communist*, first quarter 1994.

15. *South African Labour Bulletin*, July–August 1993.

16. But how to carry out *RDP* implementation? Here Sanco took an important, if controversial, initiative: a Commission on Development Finance whose report, *Making People-Driven Development Work*, was

authored by London-based journalist Joe Hanlon. *Business Day* newspaper (13 April 1994) appeared stunned that Sanco's 'unrehabilitated Marxists' could generate 'a great deal of food for thought. It is not a blind attempt to destroy so as to allow the new society to rise from the ashes – as has been the tone of some previous Sanco statements.'

17. Still possibly the finest work in the field is Jim Ferguson's study of the 'depoliticisation' of development in Lesotho via a discourse analysis of a World Bank country report and a dissection of a Canadian CIDA project (*The Anti-Politics Machine*, Cape Town: David Philip, and Cambridge: Cambridge University Press, 1991). Also in the emerging post-structuralist camp are contributions by radicals – see, e.g., Franz Schuurman's edited collection *Beyond the Impasse: New Directions in Development Theory* (London, Zed Press, 1993) – which confirms that no matter how disillusioned with dependency theory and with the ultra-Marxism of the Warren School, the development intelligentsia has not taken the political right-turn characteristic of some strains of postmodernism. Another interesting volume, *Debating Development Discourse* (London: Macmillan, 1995), edited by David Moore and Gerald Schmitz, revitalises historical materialism but also includes Ferguson's discourse-critique of Zambian structural adjustment.

18. *Business Day*, 30 May 1994.

19. This is how it appeared to this author, who was given the responsibility of drafting the *White Paper on Reconstruction and Development* nearly from scratch during a two-week period in August and September. One experience worth recounting was drawing to Naidoo's attention a passage from *Washington Post* journalist Bob Woodward's recent book about the Clinton Administration, *The Agenda* (New York: Simon and Schuster, 1994, p. 84): 'You mean to tell me that my whole programme, and my reelection, hinge on the Federal Reserve and a bunch of fucking bond traders?', asked Bill Clinton (a week before taking office) of his top economic advisers, who nodded their heads affirmatively. 'That's exactly how it feels here', Naidoo grimly responded. Due consultations occurred between two top business intellectuals and Naidoo's team, and 'the markets' replied positively to the signals. (For confirmation, see *Business Day*, 7 September 1994.)

20. The most significant amendment was, following the inclusion of an endorsement of the *RDP* – (section 0.4) 'The original document is considered the basic starting point for the *RDP White Paper*; in the text it is referred to as the *RDP* "Base Document"' – the telling erasure of these subsequent lines: 'The Base Document's statement of existing problems, its commitment to new policy directions, and its many direct programmatic suggestions should still be considered as underlying the

Government National Unity's approach to reconstruction and development.'

21. *Business Day*, 8 September 1994.

22. See my 'Under the Microscope: The ANC in Power', *Southern Africa Report*, March 1995.

23. Ministry of Reconstruction and Development, *White Paper on Reconstruction and Development*, Cape Town, 1994, sections 7.6.6 and 7.6.7.

24. Alistair Sparks, *Tomorrow is Another Country*, New York: Hill and Wang, 1994; for a critique of the whole exercise see my 'Fly-Fishing', *Southern African Review of Books*, May–June 1995.

25. For the strongest treatment of NGOs and their lot, see Marais, *South Africa*, Chapter 7.

26. Indeed, sporadic rent boycotts in the Western Cape, East Rand and other sites pre-date the 1983 launching of the United Democratic Front, and represented informal modes of struggle based on the survival mechanisms implicit in the township moral economy. At root cause, the quality of the services – and of the matchbox houses for which residents paid rent without any secure urban tenure rights – was generally abominable.

27. Traditional complaints about much higher average payments per unit of service than in white areas were based on the fact that whites had long ago paid off capital charges but for blacks these were internalised because services were newer, and that infrastructure provision was far more costly in peripheral areas of the metropolis where most blacks reside. Then, when Eskom began installing individual pre-paid metering points in an effort to break the payment boycotts, these also cost more than ordinary hook-ups and the interest on the pre-paid funds went to Eskom. While some progress was made in equalising the unit rate of electricity in Johannesburg by 1996, this was not true in most other areas, and even Johannesburg never seriously cross-subsidised from rich to poor consumers as was called for in the *RDP*. Only in late 1998 was a change in the retail pricing structure to allow much greater cross-subsidisation finally promised by the National Electricity Regulator, (*Mail and Guardian*, 25 September 1998). But this change, disconnected from Department of Constitutional Development (World Bank-designed cost-recovery) policy, led to the full replacement of the latter agency's lead management.

28. The two reasons for the ANC's LGTA compromises were a) to bring the Conservative Party (KP) on board the transition process through huge concessions, so that the April 1994 elections would not be sabotaged in platteland dorpies under KP control; and b) to 'build trust' between local elites (as a key negotiator, Andrew Boraine, described it to

Mzwanele Mayekiso, as reported in the latter's 'From the Trenches to the Table', *Work in Progress*, February–March 1994).

It was debatable, to say the least, whether these two rationales vindicated such deep violations of basic democratic principles. To illustrate, the attempt to soothe the KP was self-evidently flawed, given both the KP's rejection of the concessions and of the entire process, and – contrary to the negotiating team's prediction – the very peaceful character of the April 1994 elections even in KP dorpies. For more detail on the process see Jennifer Robinson's *The Power of Apartheid*, London: Heinemann, 1996.

29. *Business Day*, 1 December 1993.
30. As *Business Day* editorialists (28 February 1996) cynically but accurately described the *National Growth and Development Strategy*, 'The correct marketing strategy is a difficult one, as government has to please the markets, the unemployed, foreign investors and organised labour – all at the same time. That makes for vague language and wish lists that no one will attack.'
31. Chris Heymans and Nick Vink of the Development Bank of Southern Africa, and Robin Bloch of the recently closed Urban Foundation.
32. Ministry of Reconstruction and Development, *Draft Urban Development Strategy*, Pretoria, 1995, p. 1.
33. *Business Day*, 28 February 1996.
34. Patrick Bond, Mzwanele Mayekiso, Darlene Miller and Mark Swilling, 'Response to Government's Draft *Urban Development Strategy*', *Urban Forum*, 7, 1, 1996.
35. Cited in my and Greg Ruiters 'The Development Bottleneck', *Southern Africa Report*, April–May 1996.
36. Ministry of Reconstruction and Development, *Draft Rural Development Strategy*, Pretoria, 1995.
37. Appointed by Mandela after the 1994 election to lead a formal commission on rural finance, Strauss subsequently came under attack by trade unionists who were furious not only about his membership in the 'Brenthurst Group' (the select half-dozen white corporate leaders whose companies control nearly the entire stock market and whose personal economic advice Mandela apparently solicited prior to – and even instead of – his own ANC National Executive Committee colleagues during the mid-1990s). Standard Bank had also led the bank interest rate increase in May 1996, which obliged Cosatu to file a criminal charge of collusion with the police. Apparently empowered by the total absence of formal anti-trust prosecution by the Department of Trade and Industry, Strauss and the rural finance commission called for the end of direct state credit provision (i.e. the demise of one of Standard Bank's competitors). He also refused to consider state subsidisation of interest

rates. Fortunately, the main dissident member of his commission, Helena Dolny, took a contrary view and was appointed Land Bank chief executive, where in 1998 she resisted neoliberal policy advice and implemented a (very mild) subsidy on loans to small black farmers.

38. Gavin Williams, 'Setting the Agenda: A Critique of the World Bank's Rural Restructuring Programme for South Africa', *Journal of Southern African Studies*, 22, 1, 1996.
39. For details see my and Meshack Khosa (eds), *An RDP Policy Audit*, Pretoria, Human Sciences Research Council, 1999.
40. Thabo Mbeki, 'Speech to the South African Communist Party Congress', Johannesburg, 2 July 1998, p. 2.
41. *Ibid*, p. 4.
42. African National Congress, 'Election Manifesto', Johannesburg, 1999.
43. *Business Day*, 23 December 1997.
44. Mbeki, 'Speech', p. 4.
45. Adrian Hadland and Jovial Rantao, *The Life and Times of Thabo Mbeki*, Johannesburg: Zebra Press, 1999, p. 73.
46. *Ibid.* p. 110.

4 THE HOUSING QUESTION

1. I have discussed aspects of the housing question at more length in several academic articles reprinted in my *Cities of Gold, Townships of Coal*, Chapters 6–10.
2. On this, see in particular the pathbreaking analysis of Rod Burgess, 'Petty Commodity Housing or Dweller Control? A Critique of John Turner's Views on Housing Policy', *World Development*, 6, 9–10, 1978; and 'The Limits of State Self-Help Housing Programmes', *Development and Change*, 16, 1985.
3. The postwar shift in neighbouring Zimbabwe from factory-based housing supply to township development is discussed in my *Uneven Zimbabwe*, Chapter 9.
4. Paul Hendler, 'Capital Accumulation, the State and the Housing Question: The Private Allocation of Residences in African Townships on the Witwatersrand, 1980 to 1985', Master's dissertation, University of the Witwatersrand, 1986; and 'Capital Accumulation and Conurbation: Rethinking the Social Geography of the "Black" Townships', *South African Geographical Journal*, 69, 1, 1987.
5. Rural housing was virtually ignored in apartheid and post-apartheid policy.
6. The burst of township housing construction and financing was characterised by extremely poor-quality construction practices (with no

consumer recourse), poor or non-existent consumer education, terrible location of housing (on the far sides of segregated townships), no protections against interest rate increases or against the emergence of negative equity (a condition in which, due to various factors, the value of most township bonds rose to levels higher than the value of the houses which served as their collateral), and an inability to sustain the building pace beyond mid-1990.

7. This was conceded, for example, in a report by a UF successor, the National Business Initiative, 'Evaluation of Informal Settlement Upgrading and Consolidation Projects', Johannesburg, 1995, p. 21.

8. Zach de Beer, 'Address to CSIR Conference: Finance – The Pathway to Housing', Council for Scientific and Industrial Research, Pretoria, 2 June 1998.

9. Jeff McCarthy, 'The Apartheid City and the Problem of Commercial and Industrial Location', Unpublished paper prepared for the Private Sector Council on Urbanization, Johannesburg, 1987.

10. Dan Smit, 'The Urban Foundation: Transformation Possibilities', *Transformation*, 18/19, 1992, p. 40. Smit 'welcomed' the UF delivery subsidiaries' shift towards an 'almost exclusive focus on site-and-service schemes' (subsidised by the IDT) in the wake of its market-oriented disaster.

11. These included Phil Bonner, Mike de Klerk, Bill Freund, Dave Kaplan, Alan Mabin, Mike Morris and several others. Though their work was initially secretive, it cannot be said that all of it was explicitly intended to serve capital's agenda.

12. In the case of two sociologists once considered among the country's diehard Marxists (Kaplan and Morris), this must have been frustrating. For their fairly progressive advocacy paper on the clear dangers of increasing centralisation in South Africa's primate Johannesburg metropolitan area – the 'winner region' in UF-speak – was consciously distorted and repressed when it emerged as a citation in an *Urban Futures* booklet which attacked geographical decentralisation policies (see Chapter 3).

    In the case of two Johannesburg-based scholars (Mabin and Bonner), the questionable research task of tracing land invasions internationally and historically would have been useful to a UF which was the owner of vast tracts of vacant land, some of which were already witnessing organised land invasions by the homeless.

13. Smit went so far in 1992 as to argue in the leftish journal *Transformation* that 'The possibility of utilising the UF to manage certain democratic alliance initiatives should be considered' (though to his credit he also conceded, without specifying, that 'Some of the senior executives within the UF are libertarians in the Thatcherite mould and have often been

responsible for the "meanness" of some of the UF's policy directions and proposals'). For Smit, the niggardly market orientation of the UF was perhaps offset by a different, feel-good experience: 'Reading through the list of contributors to the UF's research effort is not dissimilar from scanning a listing of "who's who" on the Left.' Black people and women, who were nearly completely absent from UF patronage, must not have ranked terribly high on Smit's who's who ('The Urban Foundation', p. 39).

14. Jeff McCarthy and Michele Friedman, 'On the Social Construction of Urban Problems: The Press and Black Housing, 1925–1979', in K. Tomaselli, R. Tomaselli and J. Muller (eds), *Narrating the Crisis: Hegemony and the South African Press*, Johannesburg: Richard Lyon, 1987.

15. Cohen, M. (1992), 'Comment', in N. Harris (ed.), *Cities in the 1990s*, London: University College London Press.

16. Republic of South Africa (1992), 'Report of the Task Group on National Housing Policy and Strategy', Department of Housing, Pretoria.

17. Moreover, in both analysis and recommendations, De Loor completely ignored women's housing concerns such as widespread discrimination in legal tenure arrangements, access to credit and inappropriate community and housing design. He acknowledged that there were 'maleless' households in rural areas, and claimed to take these into account in analysing housing for urban migrant labour. (However, this was doubtful since hostels were not considered in calculations of housing backlog.) In general, 'No information on rural areas was available and the backlogs in these areas could therefore not be quantified.' As a result, the rural housing crisis, especially pertaining to farmworkers, was simply dismissed. The many environmental issues raised by housing and urban development did not get even a token mention.

   Similarly, De Loor downplayed the thorny issue of market saturation of the top sliver of the black population (yet to his credit he did cite the role of skyrocketing interest rates and the depressed economy in limiting borrower affordability). And there was only passing mention of other structural barriers to housing, such as access to land and the building materials oligopolies, and even less in the way of solutions to such problems.

18. At least, to De Loor's credit, this involved the recognition that low-income people 'need and prefer (loan) instruments with a fixed repayment and therefore fixed interest rates' (a heretic notion in neoliberal terms).

19. Though erratic, these criticisms are worth a quick review to illustrate the establishment's fragmentation during the transition. For example, De Loor gave credence to attacks that the Independent Development Trust was 'politically partial' (true), but endorsed World Bank critiques

of the IDT that its R7,500 subsidy was 'unrealistically high' (false). (De Loor completely ignored progressive criticisms of the IDT's emphasis on site-and-service, on individual ownership requirements, and on rigid capital grants instead of more flexible loan subsidies.) While mention was made of the Urban Foundation's 'financial problems', De Loor missed noting the obvious implications, namely that UF policy directions – such as embracing the (vastly overvalued) township land market and 'fixing' the housing finance market with group credit scheme and a Home Loan Guarantee Company (both of which fizzled) – may have been to blame, and that the IDT bail-out loan to the UF's Land Investment Trust should have been directed at a developer with a worthier track-record.

Instead, De Loor supported IDT and UF group credit and home loan guarantee programmes, in the process neglecting to mention that notwithstanding extraordinary publicity and raised expectations, such schemes were already performing well below their projected output. De Loor even cited poor Khayelethu Home Loans (the SAHT loan subsidiary which was victim of most bond boycotts) as a model for a state housing agency. The notorious Department of Development Aid was given a few paragraphs, but mismanagement manifested in hundreds of millions of rands worth of DDA corruption apparently were not deemed worthy of comment. Unspecified 'data integrity problems' were cited in other state agencies' accounts, but De Loor could not manage even insubstantial commentary on these agencies.

The DBSA, in contrast, was not cited as 'politically partial' – in spite of its extremely close ties to apartheid puppets – nor as facing enormous though hidden financial problems (repayment of DBSA loans by most homelands and BLAs came in the form of central government bail-outs, not the project cost-recovery which loan documents anticipated). Indeed the DBSA illustrated, in De Loor's distorted view, a 'comprehensive and integrated approach to urban development and housing' – although the DBSA had a miserable record in integrating the viewpoints of community-based organisations and still shied away from offering direct housing support to community-driven projects. So while De Loor recommended replacement of SAHT, IDT and UF fundraising with 'a single corporate body to promote the issue of housing stock', no surprise, this was to be the DBSA.

De Loor also claimed that lotteries were 'achieving increasing acceptability', thereby ignoring their regressive effects on the distribution of personal income. And De Loor further posited that foreign loans for housing would be available 'often at concessionary rates', although there was in fact no evidence that this would be the case on a sustainable basis in view of SA's status as an upper middle-income developing country. Much of De Loor's incompetence in the field of development finance – particularly his servitude to the DBSA and to the virtues of foreign loans for housing – can be traced to the influence of top DBSA staffer and Task Force member Johan Kruger (who was later to run a major private sector financing agency for desperate municipalities).

20.   To illustrate the balance of forces and the limited range of NHF discourse, in October 1993 consultant Dan Smit was commissioned to investigate the basis for a new National Housing Bank (for which even sub-consultant Bob Tucker provided an extremely enthusiastic endorsement). But none of the arguments in favour of the idea were cited in a final report by Smit which, not surprisingly, rejected a new bank conclusively. Thus it came as a shock to conservative NHF participants when a National Housing Bank was strongly promoted not only in the *RDP* in early 1994, but by Slovo and Cobbett immediately following the election.

21.   Shill agreed to take a year off from running the Sage group of financial companies, and raised expectations that a rational, no-nonsense approach would replace the racially constituted collection of dozens of housing agencies and programmes. Things had degenerated so badly in the Department of National Housing that only half the budget was spent during the NP's last term in office, with each new 'low-income' house costing more than R70,000 to construct as a result of the bureaucratic waste.

   But prior to becoming Housing Minister Shill had represented the interests of the Life Offices Association at the NHF, and a good working relationship was widely anticipated. Some of Shill's business boosters initially overlooked the fact that his experience in property management included a massive gamble and loss on New York real estate investments, a controversy of such high profile that Shill persuaded a judge to clamp down on the publication of details obtained from wiretaps that were about to go to press in the *Financial Mail*. Shill's New York adventure badly damaged Sage, forcing it to merge with other sickly financial institutions in the ABSA bank group under conditions of a massive Reserve Bank bail-out. (Sage ultimately pulled out of the ABSA family after it had some time to recover.)

22.   For more details of the controversy, see my 'Housing Crisis Reveals Transitional Tension' and 'When Housing Pressures Boil Over', *Financial Gazette*, 11 November 1993.

23.   For more on bond boycotts, see my 'Money, Power and Social Movements: The Contested Geography of Finance in Southern Africa', in S. Corbridge, R. Martin and N. Thrift (eds), *Money, Power and Space*, Oxford: Basil Blackwell, 1994.

24. The maximum subsidy was raised to R15,000 by Slovo in 1994 and to just R16,000 by his replacement Mthembi-Mahanyele in 1998.
25. See my '"Housing for All" in South Africa', *Cross Sections*, Spring 1994.
26. *Ibid.*
27. South African National Civic Organisation, *Making People-Driven Development Work*.
28. It was tragically comic that Slovo fought a major battle to install Cobbett as his director-general via a consultancy arrangement, which entailed booting out Shill's man with a golden parachute. For this and this alone, Slovo was rewarded the distinction of being recognised as the most successful cabinet member after 100 days by *Weekly Mail and Guardian* editor Anton Harbor, who neglected to remind readers that Slovo was the only minister brazenly to violate Slovo-the-negotiator's rule that existing bureaucrats retain their jobs and status.
29. Ironically, Cobbett had come to the ANC from Planact, and initially remained on its board. Planact nearly went bankrupt in 1996, surviving only because it switched from supporting civic associations on a no-fee basis to becoming a garden-variety consultancy to local governments.
30. There were more formal bond boycotts against Khayalethu than all the others combined, and de Ridder did practically nothing to resolve these.
31. Indeed apartheid era bureaucrats and neoliberal consultants were not the only ones responsible for the degeneration of housing policy. An enormous power to decide and amend policy was quickly vested to capital, either implicitly or explicitly. This included the dominance of the National Housing Board, which – before being phased out – effectively over-represented the private sector; the secondment of key private sector personnel to government to assist in policy formulation; and growing ties between business lobbies and government (e.g., the National Business Initiative Task Team on 'unblocking delivery').
32. There was no more surprising a case of retreat than Moses Mayekiso, by then a backbench ANC Member of Parliament receiving technical advice from a bureaucrat of the Council for Scientific and Industrial Research, Tobie de Vos. De Vos and Mayekiso issued an error-filled document in October 1994 that estimated 'government has the financial and other resources to provide 5.16 million [*sic*] houses in the next five years. The programme would cost about R25.6 billion' (i.e. an unbelievably low R5,000 per house).
33. Another reflection of the void of strong political leadership was the initial attempt, immediately after the election, to launch a Community Reinvestment Act. Following the lead of radical community groups in the United States, Sanco intended that such a law would not only prohibit bank red-lining, but would do so in a manner aimed at empowering grassroots groups (who would have enforcement power)

in true 'non-reformist reform' style. But ANC banking official Neil Morrison, apparently anxious to curry favour in the banking world, insisted that in its draft form there be no provisions for punishing banks found guilty of discrimination; the law would be toothless in the spirit of national reconciliation. Morrison was not offered a Reserve Bank job as anticipated (he confided to several people), and promptly left the ANC to take a position with Rand Merchant Bank. Saboteurs were not only from the Afrikaans bureaucracies.

34. Cited in my 'The *RDP* of the Left'.
35. Patrick Bulger, 'Housing Summit', SA Press Association report, 27 October 1994.
36. Private correspondence with Pressage Nyoni, Seven Buildings, Johannesburg.
37. Private correspondence with employee of housing agency.
38. Botshabelo Conference, *Housing Accord: Housing the Nation*, Botshabelo, Free State, 27 October 1994, p. 2.
39. Department of Housing, *Housing White Paper*, Pretoria, 1994.
40. If we assume that, at that point, a minimally decent house cost approximately R30,000, and that – using National Housing Forum calculations – the country's income distribution required an average of 50 per cent subsidy for urban housing, there was no fiscal constraint to Housing for All. The actual cost to the budget of meeting the *RDP* goal of 1 million new low-income houses built over five years (an average of 200,000 per year), at an average cost to the state of R15,000 per unit – not including the other R15,000 per unit, which would come from private sector resources via the national housing bank, to be repaid at the market rate of interest – would be just R3 billion per year.

   Even if income distributions were more skewed than the National Housing Forum originally estimated, there remained sufficient funds budgeted for the state to afford the required subsidies to achieve Affordable Housing for All. Indeed, the 1995–96 budget alone contained more than R4 billion for housing (although more than R2 billion of this was rolled over, which again suggests that existing subsidy amounts have been excessively stringent). The 1996–97 budget was (including past rollovers) R4.6 billion. Simple mathematics shows the inaccuracy of the fiscal constraint argument.
41. The figure derived from Sanco, which adapted World Bank recommendations concerning the per cent of GDP (translated, reasonably, to the government budget) that should be devoted to housing.
42. See *Mail and Guardian* coverage in 1994–95.
43. *Business Day*, 21 July 1995.
44. The key policy documents were the Department of Housing's 'Record of Understanding' with commercial banks in October 1994, the

December 1994 *Housing White Paper*, a Housing Bill drafted in mid-1996 but brought to parliament only in 1997, and two reports (December 1995 and October 1996) by the Department of Housing's 'Task Team on Short Term Housing Delivery' (also known as the Ministerial Task Team). Together these represented an uneven but sustained official commitment to the market.

45. See my 'Do Blacks Like Shacks?: A Critique of *Evaluation of Informal Settlement Upgrading and Consolidation Projects*' (Report to the National Business Initiative by Jeff McCarthy, Doug Hindson and Mike Oelofse), National Institute for Economic Policy report, January, reprinted in revised form in *debate*, 3, 1996.

46. This was technically incorrect, since private capital could still be attracted into non-market housing, via state housing bank securities.

47. The bank would provide borrowers with low-interest loans by blending subsidies with private financial resources such as pensions that could be attracted out of stock market and luxury real estate portfolios by virtue of market-returns plus government guarantees.

48. Such subsidies would be repaid upon leaving or passed through into the stock owned by housing co-operatives.

49. These are documented at length in my and Angela Tait's 'The Failure of Housing Policy in Post-Apartheid South Africa', *Urban Forum*, 8, 1, 1997.

50. Given the costs of administering a large portfolio of small loans, it should not be surprising that banks do not favour low-income bonds. As profit-oriented companies, their rate of return is much higher when they service fewer, larger loans. In light of this, either mechanisms such as a Community Reinvestment Act were needed to compel banks to make available loans (and savings products) to low-income customers – along with providing (presently nearly non-existent) township and rural branch, agency or automatic teller facilities for payments and savings – and/or this function should have been outside the retail commercial banking system (such as through a national housing bank or transformed Post Office Savings Bank system).

51. *Housing Facts*, 20 September 1996; the figure did not notably improve in subsequent years.

52. *Sunday Times*, 22 September 1996.

53. There were approximately 14,000 houses in technical default within Servcon's portfolio, of which half were, by late 1996, settled upon with existing residents.

54. *SA Housing Scenario*, August 1996. Aside from a R25 million state grant, much of the agency's funding was sourced internationally, by development foundations (e.g. Open Society) and governments (e.g. Swedish) which would otherwise be better directed into funding actual housing.

55. Department of Housing, 'Report of the Ministerial Task Team on Short-Term Delivery', Pretoria, December 1995.
56. Relating to the latter point, the *HWP* had explained that declining rates of personal savings 'reduced the availability of savings for investment in housing'. This was highly questionable, given the massive increases in credit granted by the banks during the late 1980s (when savings rates were falling at their fastest levels). Indeed, as pointed out in Chapter 1, the SA financial system showed an impressive ability to disregard savings and instead create housing credit (mainly for the white market) based on factors such as the property market cycle, the unusually high spread on interest rates (the difference between what banks pay savers and lend to borrowers) and inter-bank competition. The failure of the *HWP* drafters to recognise this reflected a monetarist economic bias, boding ill for future interventions in housing finance markets.
57. Sankie Mthembi-Mahanyele, 'Speech to the Parliamentary Media Briefing Week', Cape Town, 6 August 1998.
58. A dramatic decline in the construction industry's contribution to GDP and employment was one reflection of this destroyed capacity. The sector as a whole contributed 6 per cent of GDP and 35 per cent of gross domestic fixed investment at its low point in late 1995; during the previous decade construction had reached a high of 49 per cent of gross domestic fixed investment (South African Reserve Bank, *Quarterly Bulletin*, Various issues). And according to Statistics SA and the National Productivity Institute, during the recession of 1975–78, the number of construction jobs declined from 485,000 to 346,000 (29 per cent), as real output dropped by 17 per cent. With real construction output up 12 per cent during the gold boom of 1978–82, the number of jobs rose by 42 per cent, to 493,000. It has steadily declined since, though a small upturn in employment occurred during the last major building wave, 1986–89, before falling dramatically from 468,000 in 1990 to 320,000 by mid-1996 and to fewer than 300,000 by mid-1998.
59. Cited in Bond and Tait, 'The Failure of Housing Policy in Post-Apartheid South Africa'.
60. Friedrich Engels, *The Housing Question*, Moscow, International Publishers, 1935 edn, pp. 71, 73, 74.

5 THE WORLD BANK AS 'KNOWLEDGE BANK' (*SIC*)

1. *Business Day*, 25 September 1992.
2. World Bank, *South Africa: Country Assistance Strategy*, Washington DC, 2 March 1999.

As a reflection of her commitment to knowledge banking, it might be noted that in 1996 the then Bank resident representative in Pretoria, Judith Edstrom, absurdly claimed (orally and on the Bank's web page) that the discontinuation of lending was because the Bank was opposed to apartheid.

3. Critics charged that the Bank also lent $8 million at concessionary rates through its International Development Association in order to arrange financing that would disguise the sanctions-busting. According to Korinna Horta of the Environmental Defence Fund, 'It had to be designed in such a way that it could not easily be linked to the apartheid regime ... World Bank documents show that the Bank was concerned about "the project being perceived as being in the Republic of South Africa's interest" and about other possible co-financiers' "political sensitivities" about aiding the apartheid regime. To assuage the other lenders' "sensitivities," the World Bank helped set up a trust fund in Britain through which South Africa could service its debt.' As even an official of the Development Bank of Southern Africa confirmed, 'Given the limited access to foreign funds by the South African government and the limitations on contractors' funding proposals – export credit was not available to South Africa – a very complex treaty was negotiated to bypass the sanctions. In Lesotho the credibility of the treaty was also questioned because the military government ruling Lesotho at the time did not permit open debate on the treaty.' This activity came to be described as 'sanctions busting' by even the first ANC Water Minister, Kader Asmal, himself a close ally of the Bank. For documentation, see my and David Letsie's 'Social, Ecological and Economic Characteristics of Bulk Water Infrastructure: Debating the Financial and Service Delivery Implications of the Lesotho Highlands Water Project', in M. Khosa and Y. Muthien (eds), *Infrastructure for Reconstruction in South Africa*, Pretoria, Human Sciences Research Council and London: Asgate Press, 1999.

4. For details, see my 'IMF Report: Shoddy and Thoroughly Predictable', *Work in Progress*, 81, March 1992.

5. Geoff Lamb, 'Managing Economic Policy Change: Institutional Dimensions', Washington DC: World Bank, 1987, p. 10.

6. Manuel Hinds, *Outwards vs. Inwards Development Strategy: Implications for the Financial Sector*, Washington DC: World Bank, 1990, pp. 15–17.

7. The memo is reprinted and discussed in David Harvey, *Justice, Nature and the Geography of Difference*, Oxford: Basil Blackwell, 1996, Chapter 13.

8. *Financial Gazette*, 27 May 1993.

9. Kevin Danaher, *50 Years is Enough: The Case against the IMF and World Bank*, Boston: South End Press, 1994.

10. Covered in *BankCheck*, Summer 1992.
11. The most fervent praise from colleagues, ironically, was bestowed upon his fundraising work on behalf of the American elite's two main cultural forums (Washington's near-bankrupt Kennedy Center and New York's Carnegie Hall). Indeed, Wolfensohn excelled in making his way onto boards of leading institutions: the CBS media empire, Rockefeller University and Princeton University's Institute for Advanced Study, the Brookings Institute think-tank (a centre-right Clinton Administration brain trust) and the Council on Foreign Relations (an elite group which often set US foreign policy directions). But later, in 1999, when Wolfensohn had problems selling lead Bank colleagues on a development strategy, international financiers criticised him publicly (see, e.g., *Mail and Guardian*, 26 June 1999).
12. Ministry of Reconstruction and Development, *Urban Infrastructure Investment Framework*, Pretoria, 23 March 1995. For critiques, see my *Cities of Gold, Townships of Coal*, Chapters 3–5.
13. This was also the case for the rural poor, for whom a vast majority of water supply projects broke down because of the assumption that they would pay full cost recovery. This, in turn, was the outcome of a decision by a few World Bank allies in government (as well as a former Bank official, Piers Cross, who in the mid-1990s ran the Mvula Trust water project implementing agency before returning to the Bank) to redefine 'lifeline' as entailing the 'operating and maintenance costs' of running projects, instead of the logical definition as 'free'. Having excessive expectations of rural people's ability to pay for water, the Department of Water Affairs had less than a 1 per cent cost recovery success rate, and in turn both allowed projects simply to crash (taps ran dry, diesel for generators ran out and unpaid maintenance workers simply stopped working) or to fail because residents desired better than a communal standpipe and tapped the water themselves. Somewhere between 50 and 90 per cent of government projects were thought to be inoperative, leading one Sunday newspaper to headline a May 1999 exposé 'Asmal's Disaster' (*Sunday World*, 9 May 1999; see also Asmal's paranoid rebuttal and further debate in *Sunday World*, 16 May 1999 and *Sunday Independent Reconstruct*, 16 May 1999). Perhaps the most telling point was that no one *knew* whether projects still worked, because no one bothered to do systematic, comprehensive monitoring.

    More generally, at least 10 million people were still without access to safe drinking water by 1999. Emblematic of the rural water fiasco was this December 1998 report on the plight of an ordinary Transkei resident, Ma Mofokeng, who 'complains once more about the lack of piped water in the Idutywa district. Thabo's rise to president of the ANC has so far resulted in few material changes in this part of the Transkei and this is beginning to annoy the village elders – as well as Ma Mofokeng' (who is Thabo Mbeki's mother) (Hadland and Rantao, *The Life and Times of Thabo Mbeki*, p. 2).

14. The political acceptability of such low standards for such a large proportion of the population was very much in doubt, and therefore the Bank's report and other documentation associated with the low standards had extremely low visibility, only coming to the attention of consumer and community groups in the National Economic Development and Labour Council in early 1996. The substantial social benefits associated with increased access to services were estimated by a team of progressive researchers, and arguments were advanced about the need for universal access to water and electricity on grounds that small businesses could prosper and the macroeconomy required a public infrastructure investment boost. See, e.g., *Mail and Guardian*, 16 November 1996.

15. *Mail and Guardian*, 13 December 1996 (letter) and 16 November 1996. Like Olver (who clearly regretted the Bank's drafting of infrastructure policy), another extremely important neoliberal bureaucrat, Ketso Gordhan (formerly the director-general of the Department of Transport in its most deregulatory phase, then chief executive of Johannesburg), invited trouble from Left critics such as the SA Municipal Workers Union when in 1999 he asked the Bank to do a R1 million economic analysis of Johannesburg. More rumours swirled of a large Bank loan to 'assist' the process of municipal restructuring.

16. See my and Mark Swilling's 'World Bank Report Ignores Complexities', *Work in Progress*, April 1993.

17. See, e.g., Franz Schuurman and Tom van Naerssen (eds), *Urban Social Movements in the Third World*, London: Routledge, 1989; John Walton and David Seddon, *Free Markets and Food Riots*, Oxford: Basil Blackwell, 1994; and James Petras and Morris Morley, *U.S. Hegemony under Siege*, London: Verso, 1990, Chapter 6.

18. Shlomo Angel, 'The Future Lies in a Global System of Competitive Cities', *Countdown to Instanbul*, 1, 1995, p. 4.

19. World Bank, *Urban Policy and Economic Development: An Agenda for the 1990s*, Washington DC, 1991. For practical critiques of this approach, see Gareth Jones and Peter Ward, 'The World Bank's "New" Urban Management Programme: Paradigm Shift or Policy Continuity?', *Habitat International*, 18, 3, 1994; and Rod Burgess, Marisa Carmona and Theo Kolstee (eds), *The Challenge of Sustainable Cities: Neoliberalism and Urban Strategies in Developing Countries*, London: Zed Press, 1996.

20. Urban Institute, *Urban Economies and National Development*, Report prepared for the US Agency for International Development, Washington DC, 1990.

21. World Bank, *Options for Land Reform and Rural Restructuring in South Africa*, Johannesburg: Land and Agricultural Policy Centre, 1993. For critiques, see Charles Murray and Gavin Williams, 'Land and Freedom in South Africa', *Review of African Political Economy*, 61, 1994; and Alistair McIntosh and Anne Vaughan, 'Enhancing Rural Livelihoods in South Africa: Myths and Realities', in M. Lipton, F. Ellis and M. Lipton (eds), *Land, Labour and Livelihoods in South Africa*, Durban: Indicator Press, 1996, Volume 2.

22. World Bank, *Country Assistance Strategy*, Annex C, p.5; John Roome, 'Water Pricing and Management: World Bank Presentation to the SA Water Conservation Conference', unpublished Power-Point presentation, South Africa, 2 October 1995.

Roome's Lesotho work – as the central organiser and intellectual motivator of the largest infrastructure project in Africa, damming water and tunnelling it through mountains to the Johannesburg region – was just as pernicious. Roome was challenged on the quality of his work by three Alexandra residents who formally opposed Bank board approval for a second huge Lesotho dam, on grounds that too much water leaked from Alexandra and other township pipes – the repair of which should be the first priority for investment – and that too much incoming Lesotho water would be consumed by rich Johannesburg households and industries but at a higher unit cost for all consumers, including poor township residents. As they complained to the *Mail and Guardian* (30 April 1998),

> World Bank staff have responded inadequately to our concerns. Last month they filed a report advising against a delay, making the assumption of at least a 3.3 per cent annual water demand increase in Gauteng. In contrast, an official of Rand Water has been quoted saying that 40 per cent reductions are possible, leading to a long delay in the Mohale dam – perhaps 20 years – with a savings of R800 million per year.
>
> With such great sums at stake, calculations must be scientific. In the mid-1980s, when the LHWP got off the ground, the Bank estimated 40 per cent higher water demand than actually occurred, its new report admits.
>
> The Bank's report still downplays the urgent need to rectify the existing maldistribution of water resources. By consuming less than 2 per cent of all South Africa's water, black township residents together drink up less than a third of the amount used in middle- and upper-income swimming pools and gardens, not to mention the massive waste by farmers who have had enormous irrigation

subsidies over the years and who use 50 per cent of South Africa's water.

As the Bank task manager himself admitted in an internal memo last October, 'All of this shows that if demand management had been on the table in 1986 at the time of the treaty negotiation, and if the commitment to [Phase] 1B had not been made on the terms that it was – then the whole story would be different. Lesson: push the demand management stuff.'

But now, just before a major lending decision is made, and without further studies on demand management, the same Bank staffer says the opposite: push the loan.

What is most disturbing is that the Bank did its initial calculations hand-in-hand with apartheid-era bureaucrats. The bureaucrats and Bank experts never thought to look into how much water is needlessly wasted, through no fault of ours, in Alex and other Gauteng townships ...

So to the Bank, we residents of Alexandra – and many other Gauteng consumers – say, thanks for the advice and the offer of loans, but no thanks!

23. Williams recounted that when Bank economists ran into strong opposition from progressive local researchers in 1992, a variety of positions once held dear dropped quickly away:

> In 1993 the World Bank projected a more radical profile on the land issues. [Bank economists] Binswanger and Deininger revised their paper and altered their conclusions to take on board a number of issues raised by South Africans with first-hand knowledge of land issues. Rather than emphasising individuals purchasing land, they now envisaged resettled communities adopting a range of possible arrangements which could include 'collectives on which plots are not tradeable to cooperatives with inalienable individual rights and condominiums with largely unrestricted individual rights to rent and sell land to other members of the community.' Rather than selecting tenants by their ability to pay for part of the land, vouchers to buy land 'would be targeted to the poor, via some form of means testing, in order to avoid having the scheme benefit the middle class, bureaucrats and tribal chiefs.'

This, concluded Williams, 'reveal[ed] the continuing tensions and ambiguities in the World Bank's vision of land reform in South Africa'. Perhaps it indicated, as well, that Bank economists could also think ahead to the possibility of a loan (successful lending was ultimately the basis for salaries and career success). Flexibility in their ideology – up to a point (note that expanded state ownership of land was still off the agenda) – was just a means toward a more awful end.

24. Robert Christiansen and David Cooper, Presentation to 14th Symposium on Agriculture in Liberalizing Economies, Washington DC, 1994.

25. *Business Day*, 19 October 1993.

26. See my *Uneven Zimbabwe*, Chapter 10.

27. Abie Ditlhake, 'Land and Agrarian Reform in South Africa: Prospects and Challenges', *Southern African Political and Economic Monthly*, October–November 1998, pp. 10–11. For critiques along much the same lines, see Henry Bernstein (ed.), *The Agrarian Question in South Africa*, London, Frank Cass, 1996; Richard Levin and Dan Weiner (eds), *No More Tears ... Struggles for Land in Mpumalanga, South Africa*, Trenton, Africa World Press, 1997; Fana Sihlongonyane, 'What Has Gone Wrong with Land Reform?', *debate*, 3, 1997; and Steve Greenberg, 'Agrarian Reform in Perspective', *debate*, 4, 1998.

28. *New Nation*, 9 February 1992.

29. African National Congress, *The Reconstruction and Development Programme*, s.6.5.16. For discussion of commentators' reaction (in the next two paragraphs), see my 'International Financial Follies', *Financial Gazette*, 21 October 1993, and 'Bank held at Bay in the New SA?', *BankCheck*, Summer 1994, as well as *Business Day*, 24 March 1998.

30. See my *Uneven Zimbabwe*, pp. 399–406.

31. *New Nation*, 15 July 1993.

32. World Bank, *Paths to Economic Growth: South Africa*, Washington DC, November 1993.

33. Again, an incorrect Bank assumption. Having spent a great deal of time from December 1993 to March 1994 with Alec Erwin, who was directing the *RDP* project, my most ingrained and painful memory was sharing copies of the November 1993 Bank report with the editing committee, so that anyone accusing the *RDP* of fiscal populism could be rebutted from a reliable source. The look on Erwin's face made it clear that my bringing *Paths to Economic Growth* to his attention was not in the least welcome.

34. One, the Independent Development Trust, was badly burned in October 1992 when with vague approval from Mandela, a $100 million bond was launched with JP Morgan at the helm. Extensive protest followed, Morgan was persuaded to pull out, and the IDT furiously agreed to retract the issue. Another was Eskom, which raised R700 million from foreign sources in 1993, in spite of going through a rationalisation process which cut back generating capacity by 13 per cent. Eskom was South Africa's largest foreign borrower, but in early 1993 had trouble selling a major Deutschmark bond and Commerzbank had to repurchase

DM80 million out of the DM300 million issue. Third, the most visible foreign funding effort was undertaken by the Development Bank of Southern Africa, known for maintaining bantustans and corrupt black local councils, but winding its way into respectability. The DBSA gained such a positive response for a Eurobond issue in 1992 that they raised the offering by 33 per cent, to DM200 million.

For details see my 'Tough Time ahead for World Bank President', *Financial Gazette*, 15 February 1992; and Brian Ashley, 'Challenging Apartheid Debt', *debate*, 3, 1997.

35. See my article, 'International Financial Follies'.

36. *Business Day*, 4 November 1993, 24 January 1994, 24 March 1994.

37. *Business Day*, 30 May 1994.

38. Peter Fallon and Robert Lucas, 'South Africa: Labor Markets Adjustment and Inequalities', World Bank Southern Africa Department, Washington DC, 1998, pp. ii, iii.

39. *Business Day*, 18 November 1997.

40. *Business Day*, 7 April 1998.

41. *Business Day News Service*, 3 October 1995.

42. World Bank, 'South Africa: Industrial Competitiveness and Job Creation Project', Africa Regional Office, Washington DC, 8 May 1997.

It must be conceded, however, that two far lower-profile Bank subsidiaries – the International Finance Corporation investment-ownership arm and the Multilateral Investment Guarantee Agency – did more business. The former claimed to have invested $98 million from 1996 to 1999 in financial services, the pulp and paper sector, and cement/construction sector activities, but its strategic investments in Domino's Pizza, the privatisation of municipal infrastructure – approved at $50 million via the Standard Bank Infrastructure Fund, though not immediately disbursed – and a private health clinic belied the IFC's developmental philosophy. The latter provided $53 million in investment guarantees from 1996 to 1998, as well as supporting SA corporate investment in the controversial Mozal aluminum smelter in Maputo. The Global Environmental Facility also granted $12 million to the Cape Peninsula Biodiversity Conservation Project (World Bank, *Country Assistance Strategy*, pp. 19, 35, 43).

43. When I asked Eskom's treasurer about this in 1992, he answered, in essence, 'The Reserve Bank told us to.' The Reserve Bank wanted the foreign currency from the Eskom loans, at even a usurious cost, in order to repay the apartheid debt to foreign banks and to cover an import bill bloated with luxury goods for mainly white consumers and inappropriate capital-intensive machinery. In a more democratic transition, such would surely have been questioned as social priorities.

44. As one reflection, new Mozambique loans *and* debt relief in 1998 were conditioned (through the Bank's insistence) upon quintupling the cost recovery on primary health care services, and on privatising municipal water systems in the major cities (imposing what the Bank termed 'dramatic' tariff increases).

    This point became a matter of debate in *Sunday Independent Reconstruct* in early 1999, until internal Bank/IMF concessions in April 1999 that the Highly-Indebted Poor Countries debt relief initiative was simply not working. See my 'Mozambican Parliament Questions Debt Management', 21 December 1998; rebuttal letters from the Bank's Mozambique officer Phyllis Pomerantz on 24 January 1999, and from myself and Joe Hanlon on 7 February 1999; and the debate's initial resolution in Charlotte Denny and Larry Elliott, 'Fund Admits Debt Plans Will Fail Poor', *Guardian*, 19 April 1999 (see also *Sunday Independent Reconstruct*, 10 July 1999).

45. World Bank, *Country Assistance Strategy*, p. 18.
46. *Mail and Guardian*, 18 October 1996.
47. *Mail and Guardian*, 15 November 1996.
48. *Mail and Guardian*, 8 November 1996.
49. *debate*, 2, 1996.
50. *Ibid*.
51. Goodman, *Fault Lines*, p. 354.
52. Fine and Rustomjee, *The Political Economy of South Africa*, p. 252.

6 BEYOND NEOLIBERALISM? SOUTH AFRICA AND GLOBAL ECONOMIC CRISIS

1. The statistics are partly drawn from the National Institute for Economic Policy's *NGQO!: An Economic Bulletin*, 1, 1, pp. 1–3; and from the Department of Finance, *Gear*. Were the *Gear* economists who drew up the mid-1996 projections – already so far out of touch with reality by mid-year – lying, or were they incompetent?

    But underlying the surface-level variables was the continuation of South Africa's 1970s–1990s overaccumulation problem. In mid-1999, evidence included the fall in manufacturing capacity utilisation from an already low peak of 83 per cent in 1995 to 79 per cent (of which more than 75 per cent of the idle manufacturing capacity was due to insufficient demand, up from levels below 60 per cent during the mid-1990s business cycle upswing). The most overaccumulated industries, where 1999 capacity was dramatically (between 9 and 22 per cent) lower than 1995, included clothing and textiles, leather, footwear, wood, iron and steel and motor vehicles. (Data drawn from the *Financial Mail*, 4 June 1999.)

2. Thabo Mbeki, *Africa: The Time Has Come*, Cape Town: Tafelberg and Mafube, 1998; see also Hadland and Rantao, *The Life and Times of Thabo Mbeki*, and the superb mid-1999 biographical sketches of Mbeki in the *Sunday Times* (and a forthcoming book) by Mark Gevisser.

3. *Business Day*, 20 February 1997.

4. Mandela's televised comment is cited in my 'Global Financial Crisis: Why We Should Care, What We Should Do', *Indicator SA*, 15, 3, 1998. But this was not atypical. Jonathan Michie and Vishnu Padayachee are right to conclude that 'In the South African context, globalization has become a synonym for inaction, even paralysis, in domestic economic policy formulation and implementation' (Jonathan Michie and Vishnu Padayachee, 'The South African Policy Debate Resumes', in J. Michie and V. Padayachee (eds), *The Political Economy of South Africa's Transition*, London: The Dryden Press, 1997, p. 229).

5. Karl Marx and Friedrich Engels, *The Manifesto of the Communist Party*, London: Verso, 1998 edn.

6. Originally cited from *Barron's*, 20 February 1995.

7. Peter Galli, 'Investors Wary of ANC Two-Thirds', *Johannesburg Star Business Report*, 5 June 1999. Corporate pressure on the ANC at the time South Africa's interim and final Constitutions were being drafted included not just property rights but a variety of other fundamental Bill of Rights protections (equivalent to those of natural persons, such as freedom of speech which made it impossible to regulate tobacco company advertising), protection from being taxed at provincial level and an independent Reserve Bank. None of these was in question in the 1999 campaign (although the Reserve Bank issue had been raised as worth revisiting the previous year, during the height of Chris Stals's irresponsibility and unaccountability).

Indeed, the short-term prescience of the markets was witnessed in the subsequent days' events. As recounted by Alan Fine of *Business Day* ('SA Electorate Repeats 1994's "Perfect Fluke"', 9 June 1999), the somewhat fishy story (harking back to an initial democratic election sometimes described by insiders as 'fixed') is worth quoting at length:

> The new SA's electorate is truly wise beyond its (five) years. The almost unbelievably precise results it delivered in the past two general elections is proof of this ... In 1994, the critical issue was KwaZulu-Natal. Then, the electorate contrived to give the Inkatha Freedom Party (IFP) a 50.3 per cent provincial majority. The 0.3 per cent gave the IFP the single seat required to govern – and exceeded even the most optimistic opinion poll scenario for the party.

This outcome arguably rescued the province and the country from, at worst, civil war or at the very least, continuing instability due to the feeling of marginalisation the IFP was then feeling. And, funnily enough, it all came right after the hiatus of several days in the counting process ...

The 'worst' that could have happened in the second democratic election would have been a two-thirds majority for the ANC. No matter that all manner of august commentators and newspaper editorial writers had repeatedly explained that the two-thirds majority fears were a shoal of red herrings. The international markets were unconvinced, and most of the opposition parties continued to try mobilising their supporters on the basis of those fears.

All the polls from March onwards suggested that those fears would be realised. And so did the initial slew of results from late Wednesday night up to lunchtime on Thursday. The psephologists were at that stage unanimous – patterns shown by the first 10,000,000 or so votes counted indicated a fairly comfortable two-thirds majority for the ANC. The newspaper, radio and television headlines screamed out the news.

Then, not unlike 1994, came the hiatus in the transmission of results. From early afternoon on Thursday to around midday on Friday, the total number of votes counted remained stuck just above 10 million, or about two-thirds of the final total of 15,977,026 votes cast ... Friday afternoon and the weekend saw a significant shift in the pattern of results. It gradually began to dawn on those monitoring the results that the expected ANC two-thirds majority was evaporating. And the final result on Monday evening confirmed it. The ANC, with 66.36 per cent of the vote, had failed by a single seat – and, coincidentally, by precisely the same 0.3 per cent of the vote by which the IFP succeeded in 1994 – to win the two-thirds ... Markets are thrilled. On Friday, as the pattern changed, the rand swung from a worst of close to R6.25 to the dollar to a best of below R6.08 ...

The outcome could not have been more suitable, all round, if it had been devised through old fashioned horse trading.

8. In an important overview of the debate over global financial reform, Walden Bello, Kamal Malhotra, Nicola Bullard and Marco Mezzera ('Notes on the Ascendancy and Regulation of Speculative Capital', Paper presented to the Conference on 'Economic Sovereignty in a Globalised World', Bangkok, 24 March 1999) argue that there are three of global financial reform: 'It's the wiring, not the architecture' (Washington Consensus plus Group of 22), 'Back to Bretton Woods' (a strong version

of Post-Washington Consensus), and 'It's the development model, stupid!' (New Social Movements) – ignoring the far right critique and collapsing nationalists and Post-Washington-Consensus economists into the second category.

The term 'Washington Consensus' comes from John Williamson, 'The Progress of Policy Reform in Latin America', *Policy Analyses in International Economics*, Washington DC, Institute for International Economics, 1990. As one minor personal indication of the awesome power invested in Washington Consensus leaders, *Time* magazine (15 February 1999) anointed Rubin, Summers and Greenspan the 'Three Marketeers' who could save the world from depression.

The arrogance of Consensus-think was evident in Camdessus's description of the Asian crisis as a 'blessing in disguise' (*Wall Street Journal*, 24 September 1998). Illustrative of crisis era justifications are articles and speeches by Robert Rubin, 'Strengthening the Architecture of the International Financial System', Remarks to the Brookings Institution, Washington DC, 14 April 1998; by Laurence Summers, 'The Global Economic Situation and What it Means for the United States', Remarks to the National Governors' Association, Milwaukee, Wisconsin, 4 August 1998; by Stanley Fischer, 'IMF – The Right Stuff', *Financial Times*, 17 December 1997, 'In Defence of the IMF: Specialized Tools for a Specialized Task', *Foreign Affairs*, July–August 1998, and 'On the Need for an International Lender of Last Resort', IMF Mimeo, Washington DC, 3 January 1999; and by Michel Camdessus, 'The IMF and its Programs in Asia', Remarks to the Council on Foreign Relations, New York, 6 February 1998, and 'Capital Flows, Crises and the Private Sector', Remarks to the Institute of International Bankers, Washington DC, 1 March 1999. In the latter paper, confirming the ability of the IMF – no matter how weakened by the 1997–99 disasters – to recover power when acting in the broader class interests of financiers, Camdessus carefully spelt out the need for 'creditor councils' (organised by the IMF) which discipline those 'individual "dissident" creditors' who catalyse 'panic-stricken asset-destructive episodes' through too-zealous foreclosure actions. (See also Organisation for Economic Cooperation and Development, *Report of the Working Group on International Financial Crises*, Paris, 1998.)

9. See Jagdish Bhagwati, 'The Capital Myth: The Difference between Trade in Widgets and Trade in Dollars', *Foreign Affairs*, 77m, 3, May/June 1998. Dornbush cited in Doug Henwood, 'Marxing up the Millennium', Paper presented to the 'Marx at the Millennium' Conference, University of Florida, 19 March 1999.

10. For a good description, see Richard Leaver, 'Moral (and Other) Hazards: The IMF and the Systematic Asian Crisis', Paper presented to Conference

on 'Economic Sovereignty in a Globalising World', Bangkok, 24 March 1999. For their own words, see Cato Institute, http://www.cato.org/research/glob-st.html; Henry Kissinger, 'IMF no Longer Able to Deal with Economic Crises', *Los Angeles Times*, 4 October 1998; George Shultz, William Simon and Walter Wriston, 'Who Needs the IMF?', *Wall Street Journal*, 3 February 1998.

11. G. Franke-Ruta, 'The IMF Gets a Left and a Right', *The National Journal*, 30, 3, 1998.

12. Joseph Stiglitz, 'More Instruments and Broader Goals: Moving Toward a Post-Washington Consensus', WIDER Annual Lecture, Helsinki, 7 January 1998. See also his 'Towards a New Paradigm for Development: Strategies, Policies, and Processes', Prebisch Lecture, UN Conference on Trade and Development, Geneva, 19 October 1998. Illustrative of Stiglitz's attack on conventional wisdom – including self-corrective financial markets (for which his two decades work will no doubt soon be rewarded with a Nobel Prize) – are the following lines from the Helsinki paper: 'the policies advanced by the Washington Consensus are hardly complete and sometimes misguided ... the advocates of privatization overestimated the benefits of privatization and underestimated the costs ... [below 40 per cent per year] there is no evidence that inflation is costly ... The focus on freeing up markets, in the case of financial market liberalisation, may actually have had a perverse effect, contributing to macro-instability through weakening of the financial sector.'

13. In *The Crisis of Global Capitalism: The Open Society Endangered* (New York: Public Affairs, 1998), Soros asserts, 'To put the matter simply, market forces, if they are given complete authority even in the purely economic and financial arena, produce chaos and could ultimately lead to the downfall of the global capitalist system.' In another article – 'Avoiding a Global Breakdown', *Financial Times*, 31 December 1997 – he specifies what is wrong with financial market forces: 'The private sector is ill-suited to allocate international credit. It provides either too little or too much. It does not have the information with which to form a balanced judgment. Moreover, it is not concerned with maintaining macroeconomic balance in the borrowing countries. Its goals are to maximize profit and minimize risk. This makes it move in a herd-like fashion in both directions. The excess always begins with overexpansion, and the correction is always associated with pain.'

14. In a perceptive review of the 1998 book, Doug Henwood ('Let George Do It', *Left Business Observer* 88, February 1999) argues that Soros has lifted from post-Keynesian economist Paul Davidson unattributed arguments about financial market disequilibrium ('nonergodicity'), and that his analysis is far less convincing in these matters than Keynes,

Joan Robinson, Karl Polanyi and Hyman Minsky – who pioneered theories of imperfect financial markets long before Stiglitz. (Stiglitz told me personally that he did not take terribly seriously the ideas of Soros, whom he saw mainly as a practitioner with insufficient intellectual distance; interview, 1 October 1998, Ottawa.)

Most tellingly, Soros's solutions wilt when it comes to national exchange controls, and at a time when honest economists were reviewing this once widely practised technique as part of the solution to financial market turbulence – and at a time Stiglitz, who initially worried that the September 1998 Malaysian exchange controls represented 'too much of a backlash' (preferable, he told me three weeks later, were dual currency controls like South Africa's 1985–95 finrand), prepared to endorse Malaysia's controls. After all, Stiglitz conceded in mid-1999, 'There was no adverse effect on direct foreign investment ... there may even have been a slight upsurge at some point' (Agence France Press, 23 June 1999). Soros, whose famous tiff with an evidently anti-Semitic Mohamad Mahathir in 1997–98 may have influenced matters (*The Economist*, 27 September 1997), shied well away from exchange controls, for if widespread, these would end his speculating days. And as Henwood concludes of Soros's insurance proposal, 'Making creditors bear the risk of lending beyond sanctioned limits might not do all that much' to cool down hot money flows in any event.

15. Paul Krugman, 'Saving Asia: It's Time to get RADICAL', *Fortune*, 7 September 1998.

16. Jeffrey Sachs, 'The IMF is a Power unto Itself', *Financial Times*, 11 December 1997; 'The IMF and the Asian Flu', *The American Prospect*, March–April 1998.

17. *Sunday Independent*, 16 May 1999.

18. See especially the work of UNCTAD economist (and post-Keynesian) Yilmaz Akyuz, 'Taming International Finance', in J. Michie and J.G. Smith (eds), *Managing the Global Economy*, Oxford, Oxford University Press, 1995 and 'The East Asian Financial Crisis: Back to the Future,' in Jomo K.S. (ed.), *Tigers in Trouble*, London, Zed Press, 1998.

19. James Wolfensohn, 'A Proposal for a Comprehensive Development Framework (A Discussion Draft)', Washington DC, World Bank, 29 January 1999. David Moore, 'Neo-liberalism, Globalisation and the Governance of Africa', Unpublished paper.

20. Hirakawa Hitoshi, 'The Asian Monetary Fund and the Miyazawa Initiative', Paper presented to Conference on 'Economic Sovereignty in a Globalising World', Bangkok, 24 March 1999; Oskar Lafontaine and Christa Mueller, *Keine Angst vor der Globalisierung: Worhlstand und Arbeit für Alle*, Bonn: Dietz Verlag, 1998.

21. Mohamad Mahathir, 'The Future of Asia in a Globalised and Deregulated World', Speech to the conference 'The Future of Asia', Tokyo, 4 June 1998. In a spirit mirroring Mahathir's, other rulers of two formerly free market Asian countries defended themselves from speculators in September 1998; the Hong Kong state prohibited the short selling of local stock market shares and also bought $14 billion in shares to prop up the Hang Seng index, and Taiwan outlawed what were described as illegal funds-trades by Soros hedge funds.

   For background to Mugabe's hate–love–hate relations with the IMF and World Bank, see my *Uneven Zimbabwe*, Chapters 11–12, and 'Zimbabwe's Political Reawakening', *Monthly Review*, 50, 11, May 1999. The IMF's Zimbabwe objectives were straightforward: Mugabe must reverse the only two progressive things he had done in a long time, namely the imposition of a luxury import tax in 1997 and of price controls on staple foods in mid-1998 in the wake of IMF riots. According to a blunt Michael Nowak, IMF assistant director for Africa, 'There are two issues outstanding and these have stopped the IMF from making the [$53 million] standby credit available to the country. These issues are, one, we want the government to reduce the tariffs slapped on luxury goods last September, and secondly, we also want the government to give us a clear timetable as to when and how they will remove the price controls they have imposed on some goods' (see Abel Mutsakani, 'IMF says Tariffs, Price Controls Last Hurdles to Aid', *Financial Gazette*, 12 March 1999). Later in 1999, the IMF agreed to increase the loan amount to $200 million, but according to an IMF official, yet more conditions emerged, namely, access to classified Congo war information and a commitment to a fiscally-responsible source for any new war expenditure: 'The Zimbabweans felt offended, shocked, but they all the same agreed to give us the information, we got all the clarification we wanted. They had no choice ... We have had assurances [that] if there is budgetary overspending, there will be cuts in other budget sectors' (Agence France Press, 'IMF Agrees to Lend Zimbabwe 200 Million US Dollars: IMF Source', 20 July 1999).

   The jury remains out on Chavez, who courageously challenged his internal foes on the grounds of good governance, but remained wary of alienating international financial interests.

22. It may be useful to list several of the critical English-language books – not to mention seminal articles and papers, for the list is vast – about global capitalism (and resistance) just prior to the turn of the century (here 1997 is an arbitrary cut-off because in 1996 important books were produced by Alexander, Berger and Dore, Boyer and Drache, Clarke, Helleiner, Hirst and Thompson, Hopkins and Wallerstein, Mander and Goldsmith, Michie and Grieve Smith, Robinson, and others and in 1995,

etc.): Samir Amin, *Capitalism in the Age of Globalization*, London: Zed Press, 1997; Robert Blecker, *Taming Global Finance*, Washington, DC: Economic Policy Institute, 1999; Robert Brenner, *Turbulence in the World Economy*, London: Verso, 1999; Catherine Caufield, *Masters of Illusion*, London: Macmillan, 1997; Michel Chossudovsky, *The Globalisation of Poverty*, London: Zed Press, 1997; William Greider, *One World Ready or Not*, London: Penguin, 1998; Robin Hahnel, *Panic Rules!*, Boston: South End, 1999; Doug Henwood, *Wall Street*, London: Verso, 1997; Ankie Hoogvelt, *Globalisation and the Postcolonial World*, London: Macmillan, 1997; Joshua Karliner, *The Corporate Planet*, San Francisco: Sierra Club, 1997; Jomo K.S., *Tigers in Trouble*; Hans-Peter Martin and Harald Schumann, *The Global Trap*, London: Zed Press, 1997; Kim Moody, *Workers in a Lean World*, London: Verso, 1997; Harry Shutt, *The Trouble with Capitalism*, London: Zed Press, 1999; Mrinalini Sinha, Donna Guy and Angela Woollacott (eds), *Feminisms and Internationalism*, Oxford: Blackwell, 1999; Robert Wade, *The Gift of Capital*, London: Verso, 1999; Peter Waterman, *Globalisation, Social Movements and the New Internationalisms*, London: Cassell, 1998; and Linda Weiss, *The Myth of the Powerless State*, Cambridge: Polity, 1998.

23. James Tobin, 'A Proposal for International Monetary Reform', *The Eastern Economic Journal*, July/October 1978; John Eatwell and Lance Taylor, 'International Capital Markets and the Future of Economic Policy', CEPA Working Paper Series III, Working Paper 9, New School for Social Research, New York, September 1998; Hazel Henderson, *Building a Win–Win World*, San Francisco: Berrett-Koehler, 1996 and 'The Global Financial Casino: A View Beyond Textbook Economics', Paper presented to Conference on 'Economic Sovereignty in a Globalising World', Bangkok, 24 March 1999; Paul Davidson, 'Are Grains of Sand in the Wheels of International Finance Sufficient to do the Job when Boulders are often Required?', *The Economic Journal*, 107, 1997, and 'The Case for Regulating International Capital Flows', Paper presented at the Social Market Foundation Seminar on Regulation of Capital Movements, 17 November 1998.

Interestingly, a few Washington Consensus and Post-Washington Consensus economists once engaged these issues with a degree of intellectual rigour that is surprising in retrospect, given their present reluctance to offend financial markets in substantive ways. Most notably, Lawrence Summers co-authored an article the practical implications of which he would distance himself from in later years: 'When Financial Markets Work Too Well: A Cautious Case for a Securities Transactions Tax', *Journal of Financial Services* 3, 1989. Likewise, one of the most fanatical mid- and late 1990s financial liberalisers, Stanley Fischer, argued as recently as 1991 that 'domestic firms should not be given unrestricted access to foreign borrowing, particularly non-equity financing' (in his book *Issues in International Economic Integration*, Bangkok, 1991, p. 20). And although Stiglitz confided to me that he would not support a Tobin Tax in today's environment, because the emergence of large-scale derivative trading made it unworkable (interview, 1 October 1998), he did once offer a tax-based approach in the article, 'Using Tax Policy to Curb Speculative Short-Term Trading', *Journal of Financial Services*, 3, 1989 (which Davidson has ridiculed as a 'noise-trader-as-fool argument').

24. For a description of CoNGOism from a pro-IMF angle, see Jan Scholte, 'The IMF Meets Civil Society', *Finance and Development*, 35, 3, 1998, and 'Civil Society and a Democratisation of the International Monetary Fund', in P. Yeros and S. Owen (eds), *Poverty in World Politics: Whose Global Era?*, London: Macmillan, 1999. More generally, see Alan Fowler, 'Capacity Building and NGOs: A Case of Strengthening Ladies for the Global Soup Kitchen?', *Institutional Development*, 1, 1, 1994.

25. ANC, 'The State, Property Relations and Social Transformation', ANC Discussion Document (mimeo) reprinted in the *African Communist*, fourth quarter 1998, p. 13.

26. ANC Alliance, 'The Global Economic Crisis and its Implications for South Africa', Discussion Document, Alliance Summit, Johannesburg, 24 October 1998, pp. 2, 3.

27. It is worth noting that at roughly the same time, Finance Minister Trevor Manuel gave a speech at the Commonwealth Finance Ministers' meeting in Ottawa in September 1998 (which went unreported, except in my 'Time again for the Finrand', *Mail and Guardian*, 16 October 1998), containing the following heresy:

> It is interesting that at times like this Mr Keynes is again resurrected. There is a recognition that the standard prescription for macroeconomic stability and growth has not worked for everyone ... As we attempt to find solutions a number of common themes are emerging: the need for capital regulation, improved supervision, greater transparency, reform of the Bretton Woods institutions, the need to shift away from the 'Washington Consensus', to name a few.

28. ANC Alliance, 'The Global Economic Crisis', p. 5.

29. Notwithstanding the Marxist phraseology, the most specific international economic proposal in the conclusion to 'The State, Property Relations and Social Transformation' was that the ANC should link with the Socialist International – by 1998 a thoroughly discredited informal network, given the dominance of neoliberal, centre-right Blair, Schroeder, Gonzales and likeminded Social Democrats (the

subsequent departure of Lafontaine cemented the Socialist International's neoliberalism):

> The bankruptcy of some of the precepts of world financial institutions is generating honest soul-searching among economists, politicians and others, including within the World Bank, the IMF and Unctad, as well as associations of developing countries. We should encourage, and become an active part of, this discourse ... The forces searching for a better world include, to varying degrees, parties and movements that enjoy significant power in the developed countries. These forces, including in particular members of the Socialist International, share most of our views regarding the nature of globalisation and how it can be tamed to serve the interest of development and poverty alleviation ... It is critical that the ANC and its allies elaborate a programme to address, among others, the following issues: ... particularly, should the ANC join the Socialist International!

30. See my 'South Africa, the Non-Aligned Movement and the Bretton Woods Institutions', in *Conference Proceedings*, Foundation for Global Dialogue, Department of Foreign Affairs and Department of Trade and Industry conference on 'Preparing for the Non-Aligned Movement', Pretoria, 29 April 1998.

31. For instance, the document endorsed a key *Gear* shibboleth, 'the need for fiscal discipline'. On this score, while the Alliance recorded that 'Whatever resources are released as a result of macro-economic relaxation, these must be directed strategically to growth, development and sustainable transformation', in reality the following week's *Gear* revisions simply amounted to an extra 0.5 per cent latitude on the budget deficit/GDP ratio (from the 3 per cent goal to 3.5 per cent), of which most went to servicing a higher state debt than had originally been expected prior to Stals's meteoric June–August interest rate increases. And on the extent to which state pension funds were to be 'fully funded' as opposed to 'pay-as-you-go' – NGOs and churches had begged Manuel to choose the latter to free up resources for current development investments (at the risk of alienating old guard civil servants who want a fully funded, hence gold-plated guaranteed pension) – the document actually took the debate in a more conservative direction by innocently enquiring, 'can we sustain the funding at its present partially funded levels?' (of 70 per cent). Other minor tinkering included suggestions for 'a more nuanced understanding of the key challenges in terms of Tax policy', more flexibility when it came to cutting protective tariffs, 'less rigidity on inflation, and less anxiety about defending the value of the rand – and therefore the prospect of easing

pressure on interest rates'. None of these represented any hint of a challenge to the logic of macroeconomic policy, merely a set of concessions that operated within the existing framework of *Gear*.

32.   Koh Young-joo, 'Alternatives to the "Corporate State"?', Paper presented to Conference on 'Economic Sovereignty in a Globalising World', Bangkok, 24 March 1999. In my discussion with Young-joo in Bangkok, I discovered that the South Korean workers' movement had, after a great deal of soul-searching, firmly committed itself to opposing narrow corporatist solutions associated with Dae Jung's neoliberal turn and the IMF's 1998 imposition of structural adjustment, instead promoting the principle of 'globalisation of people, *not* of capital'. As Young-joo put it in the paper:

> The effort to build global alternatives must be informed by a conscious endeavour to create a different discourse for solidarity and ideas for a common future delinked from the agenda of capital. We must consciously build up a new internationalism and solidarity different from 'statism', 'patriotism' and 'competitiveness'. The effort to build alternatives is especially difficult for those people in countries which are subject to increasing imperialist pressure. We must build a capacity – not only for solidarity, but – for cross-border unity and joint or common struggle.

33.   ANC, 'The State, Property Relations and Social Transformation', p. 14.
34.   *Ibid*, p. 12.
35.   Far more insightful than the various hagiographies – by Meer, Meridith, Sampson or Mandela himself – on this point is an article by Andrew Nash, 'Mandela's Democracy', *Monthly Review*, 50, 11, May 1999. But see Martin Meredith's *Nelson Mandela: A Biography* (London, Penguin, 1997, pp. 525–6) for details on how Mandela 'assiduously courted' conservatives – politicians and big business alike.
36.   As Deputy Minister of Arts, Culture, Science and Technology, for example, Madikizela-Mandela accused government 'elites' of selling out the masses. After her tumultuous dismissal, in a March 1996 speech to the ANC Women's League, she charged, 'Nothing has changed. In fact, your struggle seems much worse than before, when the fight was against the Boers' (cited in Meredith, *Nelson Mandela*, p. 536).

Mahlangu's remark to a televised press conference (*Business Day*, 23 June 1999) was generally considered to be a naively honest reflection on the character of leadership in South Africa's banana republic province. Mahlangu was then gagged by ANC Luthuli House bureaucrats. His new media adviser, Sefako Nyaka, refused journalists a chance to ask Mahlangu questions after the opening of the provincial parliament on 6 July: 'He cannot comment on the content of the speech because he did not write it, and you may therefore ask him something he does not know' (*Star*, 7 July 1999). Mbeki stuck by the appointment (and Mahlangu's cabinet) in the interests of provincial 'stability'.

37. *Sunday Independent Reconstruct*, 11 July 1999.
38. See my articles 'Zimbabwe's Political Reawakening' and 'Zimbabwe Workers Go Political: Too Soon, Too Late, To What End?', *Southern Africa Report*, 13, 4, 1999.
39. Cited in my 'Ethiopian Scholar Unnerves Regional Strategists', *Financial Gazette*, 23 April 1992.
40. For details see my 'Regional Resource Flows: Integration or Disintegration for Southern Africa?', *Development Update*, 2, September 1997.
41. ANC, *Reconstruction and Development Programme*, s.4.9.1.
42. Citations in next sentences are from *ibid.*, s.4.9.
43. Stiglitz interview, 1 October 1998. See, works of Ben Fine on this issue, including 'Industrial Policy Revisited', *Indicator SA*, 15, 4, 1998; a forthcoming edited collection drawing upon the School for Oriental and African Studies 1998–99 economics seminar; and 'The Developmental State is Dead – Long Live Social Capital?', *Development and Change*, 30, 1, 1999. See also a discussion of implications for South Africa in my 'Moving Toward – or Beyond? – a "Post-Washington Consensus" on Development', *Indicator SA*, 15, 4, 1998.
44. *Mail and Guardian*, 8 January 1999.
45. Gemini News Service, 29 April 1998.
46. Stiglitz, 'More Instruments and Broader Goals: Moving Toward a Post-Washington Consensus'.
47. After Interpress Service reported in early 1998 that a Bank official joked of locking up Stiglitz in the basement to shut him up after Helsinki (and indeed it was several months before he made headlines again), I asked him in private discussion whether he'd won the battle of hearts and minds amongst his lead staff. The main student of Bank culture, Wade, doubted the answer I received: 'I would be surprised if the figure is anywhere close to 80 per cent. What Stiglitz is saying is contrary to what so many have built their career espousing. I'm not quite so cynical to think that people can change their "pre-analytic visions" as quickly as Stiglitz's figure implies – although the may change the tenor of what they say *when they know it might get back to Stiglitz*' (personal correspondence, 15 October 1998). See Robert Wade, 'The Gathering World Slump and the Battle over Capital Controls', *New Left Review*, 231, September–October 1998, and 'From "Miracle" to "Cronyism": Explaining the Great Asian Slump', *Cambridge Journal of Economics*, 22, 6, November 1998.

48. *Sunday Times*, 17 January 1999.
49. *International Viewpoint*, 310, April 1999; for an official Sangoco report on the meeting, see also *NGO Matters*, January 1999.
50. Moody, *Workers in a Lean World*, p. 304.
51. The residues of several Trotskyist groups are far smaller and dispirited at the turn of the century than they were a decade earlier (under the repression of apartheid). The main electoral parties conventionally understood to line up to the 'left' of the ANC are extremely marginal, judging by the 1999 election. The Pan Africanist Congress won half the 2 per cent of the vote they received in 1994, under the leadership of Methodist Bishop Stanley Mogoba (whose barbaric call for criminals to be punished through amputation gained his party publicity, but also ridicule). Two other more explicitly left-wing parties which registered for the first time in the 1999 election – the Azanian People's Organisation (based on the Black Consciousness legacy of Steve Biko), the Socialist Party of Azania (led by Lybon Mabasa, who broke from Azapo to form the leftist splinter group in 1998) – together could not muster even 1 per cent.
52. Cited in my 'The African National Congress Landslide', *GreenLeft Weekly*, 8 June 1999.
53. Cited in Norm Dixon, 'ANC Reassures Big Business after Win', *GreenLeft Weekly*, 6 July 1999.
54. *Washington Post*, 6 June 1999.
55. Moody, *Workers in a Lean World*, p. 21.
56. Waterman, *Globalisation, Social Movements and the New Internationalisms*, Chapter 1.
57. Sonia Alvarez, 'Latin American Feminists "Go Global": Trends of the 1990s and Challenges for the New Millennium', in S. Alvarez, E. Dagnino and A. Escobar (eds), *Cultures of Politics: Politics of Cultures – Revisioning Latin American Social Movements*. Boulder: Westview, 1998, p. 317.
58. Leila Rupp, 'Forum', in Sinha, Guy and Woollacott, *Feminisms and Internationalism*, p. 194.
59. Giovanni Arrighi, Terence Hopkins and Immanuel Wallerstein, *Anti-Systemic Movements*, London: Verso, 1989, p. 74.
60. See Samir Amin, *Delinking*, London: Zed Press, 1990. For Amin, 'The response to the challenge of our time imposes what I have suggested naming "delinking" ... Delinking is not synonymous with autarky, but rather with the subordination of external relations to the logic of internal development ... Delinking implies a "popular" content, anti-capitalist in the sense of being in conflict with the dominant capitalism, but permeated with the multiplicity of divergent interests' (Amin, 'Preface',

in A. Mahjoub (ed.), *Adjustment or Delinking? The African Experience*, London: Zed Press, 1990, pp. xii–xiii).

61. To relate the earlier (1970–1980s) progressive objective of Third World nationalist delinking to subsequent global, regional and national struggles, we turn to Dot Keet, a Zimbabwe-born scholar-activist (based at the University of the Western Cape during the 1990s) ('Globalisation and Regionalisation: Contradictory Tendencies? Counteractive tactics? Or Strategic Possibilities?', *Institute for Global Dialogue* Working Paper, June 1999). Keet's experience across national, class and gender struggles, and across Southern African borders, provides a sense of how an internally-oriented regionalism can 'challenge and effect changes in what is perceived to be a dangerously polarising and divisive global system':

> In Africa, this approach is promoted by the veteran African economist and strategic analyst Samir Amin, and is a development upon/from his earlier proposals for the relative de-linking of African and other Third World economies from the international capitalist system. This was envisaged as a means of partial/tactical withdrawal from a hostile international system, to enable weaker 'peripheral' economies to escape the effects of exploitative 'core' capitalism. In the era of a so-called 'single integrated global economy' ...
>
> ... the strategic aims in this proactive approach, through regionalisation, to the current mode(s) of globalisation are: the defence of economic, social and cultural pluralism, the (re)creation of economic diversity and revived independence with/in fundamental interdependence, and South–South and South–North co-operation based on common interests ...

62. Sam Ginden, 'Rising from the Ashes: Labour in the Age of Global Capitalism', *Monthly Review*, 49, 3, July–August 1997, p. 156, cited in Moody, *Workers in a Lean World*, p. 308.

63. Such books as these often end with a slogan, a sometimes hackish call to action. But when 'A Luta Continua!' (the banner of revolutionary nationalism) confronts 'There Is No Alternative' (the siren of neoliberalism) and is retranslated by local cynics as 'May the Looting Continue', then there must, surely, be an alternative.

Index

Index by Sue Carlton